Y0-CDA-976

THE
RELIGIOUS
IMAGINATION

To Jerry Agel

with the greatest

appreciation

from

Patrick L. Robertson

November 27, 1985

BROWN CLASSICS IN JUDAICA

Editorial Board

Jacob Neusner
Chairman

Dagmar Barnouw

Wendell S. Dietrich

Ernest S. Frerichs

Calvin Goldscheider

Sidney Goldstein

David Hirsch

Alan Zuckerman

Robert Warnock

BROWN CLASSICS IN
J · U · D · A · I · C · A

THE RELIGIOUS IMAGINATION

A STUDY IN PSYCHOANALYSIS AND JEWISH THEOLOGY

RICHARD L. RUBENSTEIN

University Press of America, Inc.

Series Introduction, Introduction Copyright © 1985 by

University Press of America,® Inc.

4720 Boston Way
Lanham, MD 20706

All rights reserved

Printed in the United States of America

Copyright © 1968 by Richard L. Rubenstein

This edition reprinted in 1985 by
University Press of America, Inc.
by arrangement with The Bobbs-Merrill Company, Inc.
New York, New York

Library of Congress Cataloging in Publication Data

Rubenstein, Richard L.
   The religious imagination.

   (Brown classics in Judaica)
   Reprint. Originally published: Indianapolis :
Bobbs-Merrill, c1968. With new introd.
   Bibliography: p.
   Includes index.
   1. Judaism—History—Talmudic period, 10-425.
2. Judaism—History of doctrines. 3. Judaism and
psychoanalysis.   I. Title.   II. Series.
BM177.R82   1985   296.3   85-15825
ISBN 0-8191-4539-4 (pbk. : alk. paper)

To Betty

Prefatory Note

I wish to acknowledge my special indebtedness to the work of the late Professor Louis Ginzberg of the Jewish Theological Seminary of America, my former teacher. Without the aid of his monumental scholarship, it would have been impossible for me to have carried through the research which led to the present book. The vast majority of the legends I discuss were suggested by Ginzberg's amazingly comprehensive work, *The Legends of the Jews* (Philadelphia: Jewish Publication Society, 1909-1913), Vols. I-VII. After more than half a century, Ginzberg's legends remain one of the greatest works of scholarship in the history of religion of our times. I am particularly indebted to Volumes V and VI which contain the footnotes describing the primary sources from which the legends have been taken. In almost all instances, Ginzberg's scholarship is presupposed and serves as a foundation for my work. Nevertheless, all sources suggested by Ginzberg have been examined. Significant textual variants have been noted. Where the footnotes contain a reference to Ginzberg in addition to the sources cited, this usually indicates that his notes contain important information not directly cited in my footnotes.

R. L. R.

Contents

BROWN CLASSICS IN JUDAICA

Classics of scholarly exposition of important problems and themes in Judaism gain renewed life in the series at hand. The criterion for selection for reprint explains the purpose of the editors. We seek to place into the hands of a new generation the enduring intellectual achievements of an earlier time in our own century and in the one before. The issues of Judaism and the life of the Jewish people, analyzed in a rigorous and responsible way, retain perennial relevance. For what being a Jew meant in times past derived from the on-going imperatives of Judaism, on the one side, and the condition of eternal Israel, the Jewish people, on the other. The editors therefore maintain that scholars speaking to a broad audience in one age continue to address the lasting realities of ages to come. For scholars to begin with ask not what is current but what is true, not what presses today but what is urgent everyday, for all times.

The records of the past teach diverse lessons. The one we wish to impart is how first-rate minds confront the record of the past as an on-going encounter with an enduring condition and an on-going human reality. So we promise that the books of this series exemplified in this one, will speak to today's readers as much as it did to the ones who first received the works we now reprint. The series highlights modes of address we find exemplary. When scholars speak, they demand a hearing because they ask the tough questions

and trouble to discover rigorous answers to them. Scholars
are not always right. Time alone will sort things out. But
scholars always take responsibility for knowing the require-
ments of truth and attempting in good faith to meet them.
They do not make things up as they go along and declare
new truth morning by morning.

This series proposes to renew the life of classics of Judaic
learning because the editors deem an important task the on-
going renewal of sustained learning in the realm of Judaic
discourse. So this book is in this series because it shows, in
one way or in another, how, when it comes to the study of
Judaism and of the life of the Jewish people, we think people
should carry on the labor of learning.

Jacob Neusner

In behalf of the board of
editors

Introduction to the Brown Classics in Judaica Series Edition

Richard Rubenstein presents the world of Judaic Studies with a rich and remarkably broad perspective. In his wide-ranging intellectual adventure in Judaism, over the past three decades, he has made original and important contributions to the study of the Hebrew Scriptures, the interpretation of the mind and the system of the Talmudic rabbis, the study of the development of Christianity out of Judaism, with particular interest in Paul, and to the analysis and theological response to the situation of the Jews and Judaism in modern times. His reflections on the meaning for the theology of Judaism of the destruction of European Jewry in World War II represent the single most influential statement of his side of the argument ever to appear. His counterparts without exception concede the cogency and challenge of both his views and his mode of expressing them, even while presenting different conclusions. His analysis of the place of the destruction of European Jewry in the history of the West, his theory of the disposal of surplus populations, have won for him a place among the more thoughtful and incisive analysts of Western civilization today. So Richard Rubenstein takes his place among the formidable and consequential thinkers of modern and contemporary Judaism.

Less well known, however, is the fact that Rubenstein has made a major contribution to the theological and psycho-logical interpretation of the formative writings of Judaism, that is, the Talmud and related works. In the work at hand, now returned to print for a new generation of readers, Rubenstein confronts those writings that, beyond the Hebrew Bible, constitute the authoritative canon of Judaism. Since the theology of Judaism always draws its ideas and its principal justification upon the Torah, meaning both the Hebrew Scriptures and the writings of the rabbis of late antiquity, Rubenstein has followed the path of all substantial figures in the theology of Judaism. He has given us his reading of the classical writings. It is original, fresh, utterly idiosyncratic, and therefore important in its own right. What we learn is how a first rate theological mind reads a familiar corpus of writings, not the sense or meaning of the writings in particular. For that, we turn elsewhere. For new perspectives, we listen to the author of this book.

What are these writings? They are, first, the Mishnah, completed at ca. A.D. 200, then the Talmud of the Land of Israel, of ca. A.D. 400, and the Talmud of Babylonia, of c.a. A.D. 600. The two Talmuds serve as sustained exposi-tions of the ideas of the Mishnah, which itself is a philo-sophical law code meant to define the life of Israel, the Jewish people. In addition these same rabbis produced a sizable body of exegesis of the Hebrew Bible, in such works as the Mekhilta to Exodus, Sifra to Leviticus, Sifre to Numbers, and another Sifre to Deuteronomy, as well as Genesis Rabbah, to the book of Genesis, and Leviticus Rabbah, serving the book of Leviticus. There are some other compositions, on books important in synagogue liturgy, for example, the books of Jonah, Ruth, Lamen-tations, Song of Songs, and Qohelet (Ecclesiastes). All of these books contain important comments on biblical verses and themes, and Rubenstein's work responds to the way in which the ancient rabbis understand biblical stories and heroes. Rubenstein draws broadly and freely upon all these works both in the original and in the anthology of Louis Ginzberg, *The Legends of the Jews,* to which Rubenstein gives ample credit. In treating the literature as essentially homogeneous, as he does in this book, Rubenstein writes fully in accord with the scholarly canon of the period in which he worked. If today we should do matters differently, we cannot criticize him from pursuing his studies in accord with the best theories of the time at which he did his work.

His question, however, is not a historical one, rather, a problem of theological and psychological interpretation. Rubenstein brings a question to these ancient rabbis' pictures of the biblical heroes. He wants to know how, in light of Freud's theories of human development, particularly human sexuality, we are to read the ancient rabbis' imaginative life, hence "the religious imagination." Rubenstein brings a psychological question to the law, lore, and theology of Judaism. He asks Freud to help us understand how Judaism as we know it, that is, the Judaism of the canon just now spelled out, took shape, not historically, but psychologically. Why does it stress the things it stresses, and how are we to understand, as a psychological reality, the faith of Judaism? Rubenstein's enterprise, then, is, as he says, to examine rabbinic legends concerning sinners and their fate, so as "to compare the unconscious motives of the rabbinic community, made manifest in legend and myth, with those suggested by Freud as prototypical of both Judaism and Christianity."

No one can imagine that Rubenstein wishes to present a scholarly treatise. The question of how the Talmud testifies to Freud's issues is not a matter of scholarship but of intellect and interpretation, to which systematic learning merely contributes information. What we have in the book at hand forms part of an on-going intellectual adventure, a single and cogent inquiry, pursued over a number of books and researchers. This book flows out of Rubenstein's *After Auschwitz* and directs attention to his *My Brother, Paul,* which appeared in sequence later on.

We have to read this book as an essay in historical theology. What do I mean by that? A historian of theology expounds the ideas of giants of an earlier age and frames his or her own system in response to those classic and formidable constructions. So here Rubenstein approaches the classical writings of Judaism and, through his studies of them, says what is on his rich mind. That is why what we learn in this book is not about the religious imagination of Talmudic Judaism in its formative writings. It is, as Rubenstein says, "a study in psychoanalysis and Jewish theology," and Rubenstein *is* the theologian. What he says about his predecessors and antecedents forms part of a systematic expression of his own quite cogent system and viewpoint. That is what makes the book so creative, the interplay between sustained learning in someone else's writings and original thought on one's own account. So this work presents an essay in Jewish religious thought and should be read as such: an argument, not merely a set of analyses. What Rubenstein sets out here constitutes doctrine, not mere description.

Rubenstein reads the lore of Judaism, its theology in the form of stories, with deep respect. He sees its merit in helping "the Jew to formulate a conception of his place in the cosmos, his obligation to his peers and to his God, the meaning of his precarious historical situation, the irrational psychic conflicts which threatened his personal and social order, and the nature of things hoped for in a broken and tragic world." That is a considerable statement. Rubenstein's conclusion in this book points to directions in which he would move only later on. That is especially apparent in the closing lines. He calls the lore at hand, that is to say, the theology of Judaism, "an irreparably lost haven of human truth." For Rubenstein perhaps, but for the generality of believing Jews, not lost, but still a haven, and assuredly true.

But what is important is that Rubenstein enjoy a fresh hearing for his challenging and important reading of

Judaism in its definitive writings. There is no book like this one, none before, none afterward. That fact by itself demands that the work gain a lasting hearing. No one can read the writings at hand in such a way as to pretend that what we have learned about humankind, its psychology and imaginative life, for example, since the time of the ancient rabbis can be ignored when we wish to make sense of the faith of Judaism. To state matters affirmatively, we can understand Judaism, especially in its classical and canonical literature, only when the best of knowledge of our own day teaches us how to read those writings out of another age. Rubenstein provides a splendid example of what it means to learn in new ways about old and classic writings.

Jacob Neusner
For the editors

Introduction

No systematic attempt has ever been made to determine whether Freud's interpretation of religion can be validated by an examination of rabbinic lore and legend. The classical literature known as Midrash and Aggadah is a crucial source for such an inquiry.[1] This literature consists of the records of countless rabbinic sermons, legends, myths, and homilies on biblical themes. Much of the material consists of projections of the aspirations, yearnings, and anxieties of the rabbis within the sacred precincts of synagogue and school. A great deal is said about sinners and their ways. The rabbis repeat and sharpen the Bible's tales of the punishment of the wicked. Frequently they also added from their own fantasies details of great interest concerning the reasons why sinners offended and how they met their demise. Since these embellishments are not found in Scripture, they can tell us a great deal about the rabbinic unconscious.

Freud's tale of the bloody origins of mankind's religious institutions is rooted in a vision of men incapable of escaping or accepting their own violence.[2] By examining the rabbinic legends concerning sinners and their fate, it is possible to compare the unconscious motives of the rabbinic community, made manifest in legend and myth, with those suggested by Freud as proto-typical of both Judaism and Christianity.[3] These rabbinic legends exist in great abundance. They offer an important body of data with which the Freudian interpretation of religion can be evaluated.

In the present work I have examined the rabbinic legends concerning the sinful behavior of approximately forty personalities of significance in the Bible.[4] In the course of studying these legends, I explored a very large portion of the literature known as the Aggadah. Nevertheless, the limitations of time and human energy required that some restriction be placed upon the scope of the study. Additional biblical personalities could have been studied with profit. Perhaps some figures could have been eliminated. However, given the scope of the survey, I am convinced that the sampling was sufficiently representative to yield a number of valid conclusions.

In pursuing this study I was especially interested in several religious and psychological problems. I have attempted to deal with them in the course of this book. The following problems suggest the areas of fundamental concern:

Does Freud's "primal crime" hypothesis have any merit in the light of rabbinic legend? This was by far the most important question at the outset; but as the answer became apparent, it receded as a dominant problem. Nevertheless, the awesome image of the guilt-ridden parricides, caught between their Promethean feelings of triumph and their inexpressible and largely unconscious sense of guilt, hovers over this work as the prototype of *homo religiosus*. I do not believe that an original divine-human parricide ever occurred as a historical or proto-historical event. I do believe that Freud has offered us a powerful and definitive myth that expresses some of the most significant and inescapable conflicts to which all men are forever condemned and which they unconsciously express in their religious life.

Parricide and infanticide are inseparable themes. They reflect the inevitable instabilities of the most intimate and indispensable of human institutions, the family. I was concerned with the extent to which rabbinic legend reflects the stresses of the human family; and interested in the question of whether there was a characteristically Jewish way of coping with these stresses. I have concluded that the differences between Judaism and early Christianity were deeper than matters of conscious creedal debate. Sublimation is the characteristic Jewish way of handling the stresses of the family situation as they are projected in religious belief and practice.[5] Early Christianity handled many of the same dilemmas by permitting unconscious feelings to surface under strictly controlled circumstances in a rigidly defined sacred precinct.

I have been fascinated by the career of Paul of Tarsus. In the light of rabbinic literature, I regard Paul's break with Judaism as largely resulting from his failure to handle the dilemmas of the unconscious by means of sublimation. I hope to elaborate on Paul's break with Judaism in a forthcoming volume.

I see Christianity and Judaism as psychologically preoccupied with the very same problems. Nevertheless, I see Jew and Christian using vastly different psychic instrumentalities to cope with these common areas of fundamental human concern.

I reject any attempt to interpret religious belief or practice as unrelated to the basic needs of the human body as it is nurtured within the family and the larger society. I view with the greatest skepticism any suggestion that any aspect of religious doctrine and ritual is independent of the vicissitudes of human biology. I would hasten to add that human biology is not animal biology. The conflicting needs of human beings exhibit an order of complexity and sophistication without parallel elsewhere in nature.

I was interested in the problem of anxiety. The fear of the loss of love and the fear of death have always had an extraordinary power to move men of all ages and conditions. Were men without a measure of anxiety, religious institutions would never have developed as they did. Because I was convinced that the family situation was the soil out of which religion has grown, I sought to determine whether fear of father or mother was more decisive in rabbinic legend. Freud was convinced that fear of the father and castration anxiety were decisive. His conviction was consistent with his primal crime theory. I was unable to concur. My conclusions are, however, largely Freudian, but they envisage the origins of religious and personal anxiety as rooted in the child's oldest encounters with its maternal environment. Much anxiety was evident in rabbinic legend. There was fear of the father, but it was not primary. An older, more archaic terror of the Great Mother goddess was consciously suppressed in rabbinic Judaism. It did not thereby lose any of its overwhelming power.

I also sought to determine the ultimate goal of the sinner in the light of rabbinic legend. I concluded that the terminal yearning of the sinner was to displace and become God. This resembles aspects of Freud's primal crime theory. It even more closely resembles Jean-Paul Sartre's description of man's futile quest to become a nonexistent God.[6] I found Sartre's insight strangely applicable to the world of ancient rabbinic myth.

In *After Auschwitz* my central concern was the theological significance of the most drastic catastrophe in almost four thousand years of Jewish history.[7] I was sadly and even bitterly compelled to reject belief in God as the Lord of history. I could find no remainder of meaning in the Jewish tragedy of my own times. I am convinced that a disaster of such magnitude must decisively affect Jewish religious sensibility. I concluded that Jewish paganism represents the most viable religious option available to the contemporary Jew. In spite of its vulgar caricatures, paganism is an honorable and a responsible religious path. It is the religion of most Americans, Christian and Jewish, lay and clergy, though they are seldom aware of it.

I study the legends of the rabbis in this work. They were largely formed under the impact of the most decisive Jewish catastrophe before Auschwitz—the defeat of the Jews by the Romans in 70 C.E. and 135 C.E. The ancient and the modern catastrophes are inextricably connected. In the first two centuries of the Christian era, normative Judaism lost two of the most decisive struggles it has ever engaged in. By the year 200 C.E., the Jewish community was overwhelmingly defeated both politically and religiously. The religious and the political defeats were not unrelated. The more obvious one was that inflicted by the Romans. As a result, the Jewish community was violently deprived of effective political control over its own destiny. A process of estrangement from its ancestral homeland resulted in the two-thousand-year night of Jewish existence as a rejected and despised minority in the homeland of others. The terrible events leading up to Auschwitz began in 70 C.E.

One of the most important psychological consequences of the Roman wars was the destruction of the sanctuary at Jerusalem. Most contemporary expressions of Jewish theology still see a measure of progress in this terrible event.[8] They regard it as having forced the Jewish community to turn from sacrificial violence to prayer and study as the characteristic mode of encountering the sacred. I cannot concur. While the Jerusalem temple stood, Jewish religious life was not predominantly abstract, verbal, and alienated from direct sensuous contact with life and death in the religious act. Once the sanctuary was destroyed and verbal prayer and study became the predominant modes of Jewish religious experience, scholars and their disciples studied and debated the laws of a defunct sacrificial order. Instead of offering real sacrifice, Jews prayed that their ritual recitations of the laws of sacrifice be accepted as a surrogate. A book—the Torah—became the center of Jewish life. Sensuous involvement in the religious act largely disappeared from synagogue and school, although it continued to be operative within the home, especially at the sacred meals of the Sabbath and festivals. An enormous shift in the media of religious expression from the concrete and the sensuous to the linear, the verbal, and the abstract took place.

The results of that two-thousand-year-old shift are still visible in the occupational distribution of contemporary Jews outside of Israel. The media shift reflected a fundamental alteration in the personality of the Jew.[9] Incidentally, there is much work to be done on the full meaning of the transformation of the media of religious expression on the inner life of the Jew.

As terrible as was the military defeat, it was overshadowed by an even greater disaster, religious defeat. There is no other way to interpret the effect of the triumph of Christianity on normative Judaism. Christianity began as a movement of messianic fulfillment among a small group of Jews. The reaction of normative Judaism was emphatic—it rejected the claims of the new movement. Nevertheless, within a very short time, the Christian movement won the allegiance of the Mediterranean world. For almost two thousand years, it proclaimed the defeat of Judaism in art, religion, literature, music, and philosophy. The Romans claimed a human defeat over the Jews. The Christian claim was total. For almost two thousand years, the Jewish community was largely compelled to live among people who were convinced that Jewish defeat and degradation had far deeper significance than mere human rejection. Wherever Jews went in the Christian world, they were met by peoples convinced that they were the rejected of God. No matter how faithful Jews were to their own traditions, it was impossible for them not to be influenced by the Christian conviction in some measure.

In studying the legends of the rabbis, I have been constantly aware of the fact that the community which created these legends was both defeated and powerless. I have marveled, not without a measure of genuine pride, at the extraordinary capacity of the Jewish community to keep itself morally, religiously, and psychologically intact under the most difficult circumstances for so long a time.

Nevertheless, in the face of the disasters of the twentieth century I find it impossible today to share the religious and ideological response of the rabbinic community to the misfortunes of ancient times. I believe that the ancient response was adaptive in its time. One of the dominant concerns of this book is to elaborate on why the normative religious reaction of the rabbis to Roman victory was functional then although it has ceased to be useful today.

I am profoundly convinced that the interpretation of Jewish misfortune as the punitive visitation of the Lord of history is dysfunctional as a response to Auschwitz. The rabbinic community of ancient times endured bitter defeat at the hands of an overwhelmingly powerful army. Nevertheless, the enemy did not seek the total extermination of the Jews. Defeat was not genocide. One of the greatest tragedies of modern Jewish history was the fact that European Jews reacted to Hitler as if they were once again confronted by an enemy who sought to defeat and degrade them. Two millennia of Jewish history had taught the community what were the optimal adaptations to the challenge of the powerful against the powerless. The Jews submitted. They reluctantly cooperated with the foe. They mistakenly waited for the oppressor's fury to diminish, as it had so often before. The Jewish reaction to the Nazis was one of the most disastrous misreadings of the character of an opponent by any community in all of human history.[10] In the face of the Nazi threat, the Jewish community trusted its ancient adaptive instincts and failed totally. That failure was understandable. Jews had never been confronted by genocide before.

The Germans succeeded in the one war that really counted for them, their war against the Jews. Furthermore, the Germans taught the world that human technology can make genocide psychologically, morally, and physically practical. The Germans experienced few serious after-effects. A few jailers received insignificant prison sentences for the slaughter of hundreds of thousands of human beings. That was the total cost. Neither God nor man proved to be adequate deterrents to genocide, given the extraordinary capacities of contemporary technology not only to destroy life efficiently but so to sterilize the moral impact of mass murder that the latter ceases to be anything more than a problem-solving exercise.[11]

Genocide has radically changed the situation of the Jewish community. It has also changed that of the rest of the human community. Before the Nazis, genocide was the pathological wish of a few chronically disturbed fanatics. The Nazis proved that technology is capable of turning even this demonic wish into reality with little or no disturbance of conscience.

Any action, once carried out, invites repetition. The threat of genocide will never again depart. Any time a prankster inscribes a swastika on a wall he uses an extraordinarily effective and economical symbol to express his dark yearning for a repetition of mass murder. With a few strokes, he proclaims his fascination with mankind's technology of death. Furthermore, the Jews are by no means the only people so threatened. Wherever the need is felt to "dispose of" a troublesome but powerless minority, the German success will invite imitation.

Paradoxically, there is both greater safety as well as a greater risk in the Jewish situation as a result of the proven success of genocide.[12] Because the anti-Semite no longer desires merely to "put the Jew in his place," there is bound to be greater hesitation before such drastic proposals are acted upon. It would be unwise were Jewish communal and rabbinic leaders to continue to believe, as many of them do, that Auschwitz was simply the latest misfortune experienced by Jews and that it was qualitatively no different from the earlier defeats. Genocide is radically novel. The Jewish situation *has* changed radically.

It is also a very serious mistake to believe that Job can serve as a model for the Jewish religious response to Auschwitz. Most contemporary Jewish theologians insist that the post-Auschwitz Jew is a contemporary exemplar of Job.[13] It is argued that we have been sorely tried. We are urged to maintain a Job-like faith in God's ultimate beneficence, in spite of Auschwitz. I cannot concur. There can be a question for Job only when there is a Job. Hideously afflicted, Job sat on his dung heap. No matter how terrible his condition became, he was at all times recognized as a person by both God and man. At Auschwitz, the Jew did not sit upon the dung heap. He became less than the dung heap. At least the dung heap has the ability to expand earth's life-giving capacity. No "Thou" was addressed to the Auschwitz Jew by either God or man. The Jew became a nonperson in the deepest sense. Neither his life nor his death mattered. There was no question because there was no Job. Job went up in smoke. His question went with him.

This book is a continuation of the quest which permeates *After Auschwitz*. In both works I have attempted to understand the meaning of Jewish existence in our times. I believe this to be the appropriate content of contemporary Jewish theology. In *After Auschwitz*, I addressed myself to the theological issues of contemporary Judaism. I attempted to be a religious witness to the final destruction of European Judaism. My quest for theological self-understanding drew my attention from the catastrophe with which European Judaism was exterminated to the catastrophe with which it was begun. No genuine self-understanding is possible without the perspective of historical and psychological depth. We cannot understand the contemporary religious situation if we avert our gaze from the classical period of two thousand years ago in which the characteristic institutions of both Judaism and Christianity were formed.

Nor can there be any measure of self-understanding if we investigate what men say and do and fail to understand *why* they so act. The twentieth century has witnessed the gross magnification of personal, political, and pseudoreligious irrationality combined with the power of contemporary technology. No contemporary theology will speak with any degree of relevance or accuracy to the human condition if it fails realistically to assess the profound capacity of the irrational darkly to move men. I have not turned to psychoanalysis out of any faddist desire to exhibit an impressive sophistication. In the first instance I turned to psychoanalysis quite simply out of bitter and desperate need —my own.

David Bakan has commented that both psychoanalysis

and religion have a common concern. He tells us that both agree "that the manifest is but the barest hint of reality, that beyond the manifest there exist the major portions of reality . . ."[14] From earliest times far too much has happened to the Jewish people that defies simplistic explanation for anyone to rest content with a vision of Judaism which takes its practitioners at the manifest meaning of their words. I have attempted to penetrate beneath the surface in a few crucial areas of concern to Jew and Christian alike. Without the aid of psychoanalysis, this project would have been impossible.

Perhaps no Jewish religious insight possesses the abiding relevance of Judaism's perennial rejection of every temptation to idolatry. Idolatry consists in ascribing to a segment of reality the significance which properly belongs to the Source of the whole. In the perspective of Judaism nothing human is without flaw. My utilization of psychoanalytic insight for the understanding of Judaism could very easily become an idolatry. Psychoanalysts have uncovered much that was hidden beneath the human surface, but psychoanalysts remain, as do all men, the products of their time and their culture. In the course of my attempt at theological self-understanding, it became apparent that rabbinic tradition and legend are also relevant to the psychoanalytic understanding of religion and culture. Psychoanalysts have frequently offered premature conclusions concerning Judaism while ignoring the most important single repository of the unconscious in Judaism—the legends of the rabbis. As I have been enabled to come to a heightened measure of self-understanding through psychoanalysis, it is my hope that this book may suggest insights of some relevance for the psychoanalytic understanding of religion and culture.

The Religious Imagination

1 / Freud and the Origins of Judaism

THE PSYCHOLOGY OF RELIGION has been one of the oldest and most abiding interests of psychoanalysis. This concern had its practical side. Almost all of the early psychoanalysts in Freud's circle were Jewish. They were subject to the painful vicissitudes of Jewish life in Central Europe during the first part of the twentieth century. The religion they knew best was the religion of their family inheritance. In large measure, their attempt to understand religion analytically reflected their attempt to achieve a heightened measure of self-understanding.[1] Clinical practice also made psychoanalysts aware of personal rituals and delusional systems in many of the patients. There was a striking analogy between these private systems and the official beliefs and practices of Judaism and Christianity.[2] The "scandal" of religion, its apparent opacity to the categories of common sense, acted as another impetus to psychoanalytic research. Just as irrationalities of personal life such as dreams, slips of the tongue, cleansing rituals, jokes, eating and evacuatory anxieties had proved to be keys to the unconscious strivings of the individual, the irrationalities and superstitions of religion were understood to play an analogous role in the life of the group.[3]

The most comprehensive and influential attempt to formulate a psychoanalytic interpretation of religion was made by the great master, Sigmund Freud. Freud was interested in the psychology of religion throughout his career. In addition to treating religion directly or obliquely in a large number of papers, Freud wrote about religion in great detail in at least four books, *Totem and Taboo* (1913), *The Future of an Illusion* (1928), *Civilization and Its Discontents* (1930), *and Moses and Monotheism* (1939). While other analysts have made important contributions to the psychoanalytic understanding of religion, Freud's contributions have proved to be the most influential. Psychoanalytic writers on religion have tended to take issue with Freud over details rather than overall conception.

Freud's interpretation of religion was dominated by a single perspective. That perspective infused such a later work as *Moses and Monotheism* with the same force as an early work, *Totem and Taboo*. His theory of the origin of religion rested on an extension of his use of the Oedipal metaphor in personality theory. Freud maintained that the Oedipal project, the son's ambivalent yearning to become like the father by violently displacing him in the affections of the mother, was the nuclear component in all neurotic strivings.[4] Out of the son's feelings of identification and rivalry with the father for the possession of the mother, the earliest and most precious love-object, Freud drew the elements of his picture of the origins of religion. He interpreted religion as a group expression of an easily identifiable neurosis. The Oedipal conflict remained the hub of the psychoanalytic wheel in matters religious. From the beginning to the end of Freud's career, he used the father-son conflict as the explanatory metaphor for the dilemmas of human religious behavior.[5]

In *Totem and Taboo,* Freud first suggested that civilization, religion, and morality had their origins in a primal crime which has continued deeply and darkly to affect human beings. According to Freud, mankind originally dwelt in primal hordes dominated by tyrannical patriarchs. The primal father possessed exclusive right of sexual access to the females of his horde. Categories such as mother, sister, and daughter had yet to be formulated.[6] There was as yet no incest taboo. As soon as the young males became a potential threat to the father's dominance, they were murdered, castrated, or exiled. Normally the young males were driven off and forced to find sexual partners elsewhere.

The first-born male was, according to Freud, regarded by the father as especially threatening. In consequence, he was in greatest danger of becoming the victim of murderous paternal hostility.[7] Castration was the principal threat used to deter the sons' sexual rivalry with the father. Freud maintained that all too frequently the threat was carried out. The unconscious racial memory of the tendency of the primitive fathers to castrate their sons was so anxiety-laden that it became part of the phylogenetic inheritance of mankind. This memory helps to account for the supposedly overwhelming castration anxiety Freud saw as besetting males in Europe and America.[8] Freud also related the archaic phallic violence to current Jewish ritual. The initiatory rite of circumcision was regarded as a ritual compromise in which both the human and divine fathers rest content with the foreskin as a *pars pro toto* surrogate for the entire organ.[9]

According to Freud's "scientific myth," the exiled sons' enforced sexual deprivation was destined not to last.[10] Driven by intense sexual need, the deprived brothers finally banded together to achieve as a group what they had failed to achieve singly, the violent displacement of the primal father. The brothers admired the father and wanted to be like him. They desired to possess the females of the horde as he did. To accomplish this, it was necessary to be rid of him.

The contradictory aims could be brought about only by cannibalistically consuming the father. Freud maintained that the sons simultaneously identified with the victim and destroyed him by eating him. Cannibalistic parricide was, according to

Freud, the terrible deed with which human social and religious institutions had their beginnings.[11] Every man is tempted to repeat the crime. Though the deed is hardly ever committed in actuality, the existence of mankind in family units condemns every man to commit the deed in fantasy and to suffer intense feelings of guilt for the terrible wishes.

Freud's story does not end with parricide. It was less the deed than the brothers' guilty reaction to the deed which accounted for the peculiarities of human religious and social organization. For eons nature had indifferently witnessed countless instances of the young devouring their progenitors. Man differed from all other animal species. He had reached a level of verbal competence which allowed him to objectify his deeds and feel intense regret for them. The origins of the sons' remorse lay in their conflicting feelings of love and hate toward the father. The peculiarities of human personality are in large measure due to the fact that man is a symbol-making animal.[12] Freud pictured the brothers as afflicted with intense regret after the deed. Man was cursed with memory.

What were the women doing during the commotion? Freud has nothing to say about them save that they were the objects of the brothers' desire. His picture is masculine. He has been criticized—with much justice—for his failure to enlarge his perspective.[13]

The events following the murder can be described as a Sartrean tragedy. The sons lacked the courage to accept responsibility for their homicidal act. The deed was *denied;* and there followed the apotheosis of the victim as the vengeful, omnipotent Divinity.[14] The sons' earthly progenitor became the progenitor and lawgiver of heaven and earth. As in Sartre's works, the sons' *mauvaise foi,* their incapacity to accept responsibility for their acts, contained an irony. By denying that they had murdered the father, the sons removed any realistic impediment to the unlimited expansion of his imagined power or to the terror that power inspired in their fantasy.[15]

In contrast to Freud's repentant parricides, Orestes, the

protagonist of Sartre's play *The Flies,* is an unrepentant matricide. He is redeemed, after a fashion, in spite of the horror of his crime, because he accepts full responsibility for it.[16] Freud's parricides hopelessly condemn themselves and their progeny to lives infused with anxiety, guilt, and the futile effort to appease a nonexistent God, because of their denial of the crime. Mankind is incarcerated in a prison of guilt of its own making. Men repent and do penance through religion because of the "unconscious memory" of a primal parricide which pervades their psyche. The terrible deed can never be exorcised.

The murdered father was infinitely more potent dead than alive. The sons had removed him from all rational measurement and calculation. They had not removed him as an actor in their own psychic lives. The unconscious memory of the murder and the feelings of guilt it engendered acted to increase the depth of their retaliatory anxiety. The sons felt the terror of the father's presence after he died as they had never felt it while he lived. Their feelings of guilt and their desire to appease his anger through fulfilling the norms thought to be his became the dominating motives of the ironically victorious sons. The origin of mankind's belief in an all-powerful, all-knowing God lay in the murdered father now projected into the cosmic sphere. God, according to Freud, is none other than the first object of human criminality. The fear of God and the desire to obey him were motivated by the unconscious memory of the first crime against his person.[17]

This may seem an odd and paradoxical conception of God. It is paradoxical. It ceases to be odd when we keep in mind, as did Freud, that Christianity celebrates at its most sacred moments the memory of the death and resurrection of the Christ as God. Furthermore, the decisive symbol of that faith is the instrument of his execution. Freud was keenly aware of the paradoxical nature of much of Jewish and Christian belief. He was unconvinced of the literal truth of both religions. He was, however, impressed by their psychological truth.[18]

Religious ritual had its beginnings in mankind's ambiva-

lent feelings toward the suppressed but unconsciously remembered crime. At least two forces prevented complete suppression
of the memory of the deed: (a) the feelings of guilt on the part
of the brothers demanded the catharsis of confession; (b) their
Promethean feelings of triumph over the father's manifold authority demanded the repeated celebration of the victory. The
totem sacrifice, in which first an animal and later a human victim
were offered at a communion meal, made possible the intersection
of the contradictory motives of regret and triumph in a single
deed, the sacrificial ritual of confession and re-enactment of the
original parricide.[19]

Freud interpreted the archaic totem sacrifice as a recapitu-
lation of the primal crime. He argued that the sacrificial victim
was sacred and normally unavailable for consumption. The victim could be consumed only on very special occasions, during
which the group was permitted a normally prohibited license.
The group was regarded as sharing a common descent with the
victim. This provided Freud with a link to the primal father.
He regarded the act of consuming the sacrificial victim as an unconscious repetition of the original parricide. The animal victim
was regarded as a surrogate for an earlier human offering in the
traditions of many peoples.[20]

Freud also argued that the distinction between human
and animal life is relatively recent. If anything, primitive man
stood in far greater awe of animals than of his own kind.[21] The
consumption of animal flesh was a very serious matter among
the ancients. In Judaism it remains so to this day. Among religiously compliant Jews the consumption of meat is permitted only
under the highly regulated conditions of the laws of Kashruth.

With the origin of totemism, men began the paradoxical
mixture of Promethean self-assertion and guilt-ridden submis-
siveness which Freud saw as perennially characteristic of religion.
The totem sacrifice was also an effective means of enforcing the
prohibitions with which civilization began. No man was permitted to participate in the sacerdotal life of the community who

had violated its interdict against incest and its other customary norms.[22] Sacrifice became, and remains in the Roman Catholic Church, an effective means of moral and social control.

The point made by Freud is illustrated by Graham Greene in his novel, *The Heart of the Matter*. An adulterous police inspector knows that by refraining from Holy Communion, he will betray himself to his already suspicious wife. He is faced with the choice of alleviating his wife's suspicions by taking the wafer in a state of unpardoned sin, thereby estranging himself from God, or, by refraining from the wafer, of maintaining his peace with God but betraying his adultery. He very humanly chooses to deceive his wife and in this act finds his spiritual downfall.[23]

The use of the sacrifice as an instrument of social control was pertinent to the predicament of the brothers after the death of the father. In time they came to understand that the primal crime could not be repeated. Yet, until some satisfactory social arrangement was made whereby group solidarity was not threatened by sexual competitiveness, a repetition of the crime threatened every male who possessed a female. The brothers solved the problem through the renunciation of incest and the law of exogamy.[24] This was difficult because of the especially strong attraction close relatives of the opposite sex feel for each other. The power of the incest taboo is an index of the power of what it prohibits. This indispensable renunciation creates a continuing instability in all human institutions. One returns to one's first love, at least in fantasy. For the immortal infant within us, realistically available sexual partners are to a degree surrogates.[25]

There came a time when the totem sacrifice was re-enacted with an actual human being or when a crime explicitly akin to the primal crime was repeated. In *Moses and Monotheism* Freud applied his conception of the origins of religion to a theory of the origins of Judaism. There are in actuality two hypotheses in *Moses and Monotheism*. The first stated that Moses was an Egyptian follower of the monotheistic pharaoh Ikhnaton and sought to create a monotheistic people of the Hebrew slaves after the

Egyptians had rejected Ikhnaton's religion. The second hypothesis was not necessarily consequent upon the first. Freud maintained that the religion of Moses was not received by the Hebrews as an unmixed blessing. They bitterly resented the instinctual renunciation demanded of them. They finally murdered their religious leader. Like the primal father, Moses-dead proved infinitely more potent than Moses-alive. Only after murdering their leader did the Jewish people feel themselves guiltily compelled to obey his teachings.[26] According to Freud, the birth of Judaism recapitulates the earliest acting out of the Oedipal conflict, the primal crime.

The powerful hold of the Torah over the Jews was due to their inability consciously to admit the primal crime against God the Father and their later violence against Moses. Freud's interpretation of Judaism stresses the unconscious sense of guilt active in every Jew, the retaliatory anxieties Jews feel lest they further offend the God they unconsciously recognize as the murdered father, and their attempts to appease His wrath by an infinitude of observances ascribed to Him. Freud regarded Judaism as an almost undiluted example of "superego" religion.[27]

Freud also interpreted Christianity in the light of the primal crime. He regarded the crucifixion as a dramatic repetition of the first parricide as well as mankind's attempt to alleviate its feelings of guilt and its punitive anxieties over the original deed. The dual role of Jesus as the "Son" and Incarnate Deity permitted both the reparation and the repetition of the primal crime.[28]

Freud also used the Oedipal metaphor to interpret religious ritual. This was evident in his interpretation of the Roman Catholic Mass. Freud regarded the Mass as a symbolic act of ritual cannibalism in which the divine-human victim is consumed in a manner reminiscent of the primal crime.[29] The priest offers the believer the host. It is substantially transformed into the true body and blood of the Christ. The believer is physically united with the divine-human victim through oral incorporation. During the Middle Ages, Jews were often accused of desecrating the host or of doing violence to it until it bled.[30] Psychoanalysts who have counseled priests or ministers have reported on the depth of involvement of their clients in the Communion ritual. Fantasies of union with God, destructively consuming God, and even turning God into feces have been reported. [31] Such phenomena would be interpreted by Freud as evidence of the abiding power of the memory of the crime in the religious life of mankind.

Psychoanalysts have also interpreted ritual circumcision in the light of the Oedipal project. In circumcision there is a double renunciation.[32] The father renounces castration as a punitive deterrent and the son renounces his incestuous strivings for the mother. The son's gift and the father's acceptance of the foreskin as a surrogate for the entire organ is a symbol of mutual renunciation. The necessities of the social process triumph over anarchic impulse.

This double renunciation is also implicit in Jewish infant circumcision although it takes place on the eighth day after birth. When the child becomes aware of what was done to him as a helpless infant, his castration anxiety is inevitably magnified.[33] This anxiety is heightened by frequent overt and implied castration threats directed by parents or parent surrogates toward the child, especially during masturbatory activity.[34] The anxiety may be further intensified when boys first see the female genital organs. They may mistakenly assume that the female has been punitively deprived of her male organs.[35] Castration anxiety and neurotic repression of Oedipal longings may reinforce each other. They lose none of their potency thereby.

According to Freud, man's deepest yearning is to displace the father that the mother might be incestuously possessed. The father is thus the pivotal figure but not the final object of desire. This remains the mother. Compliance with social norms, from the time of the earliest totem group until the present, has been possible only through renunciation of incestuous yearnings. This submission is extremely difficult. It can be accomplished only through the process of identification in which the son makes the will of the father his own.

In religion, this is accomplished by submission to the will of God, the father projected into the cosmic sphere. Freud believed that every individual recapitulates the experience of the race, that ontogeny follows phylogeny. The individual's image of God is compounded of the unconscious memory of the murdered father and of the individual's feelings concerning his actual parents or parental surrogates. The very same inordinate feelings of guilt and the desire to appease which afflicted the earliest sons after the primal crime afflict each individual with regard to his actual father. Every individual commits parricide in fantasy. The superego, the harsh, punitive, censoring faculty of the psyche, makes no distinction between deeds actually committed and deeds committed in unconscious fantasy. It punishes both with comparable severity. The superego invokes a never-ending need to appease those elements of the father image which are projected as God.[36]

The other mode of identification with the will of the father arises in normal social development. At about the age of five, the child renounces the quest for the mother. He seeks identification with the father by introjecting his image. The introjected father is not the real father. The child is unconsciously aware of his own hostile feelings toward the parent. He is beset by abnormally harsh retaliatory anxieties. The father-within-himself is far more rigid and unforgiving than all but the harshest of real fathers.[37]

This is well illustrated in Freud's famous paper on the case of "Little Hans." Hans was afraid to go out into the street because horses might bite him. Upon analysis, Hans's fear of horses turned out to be his unconscious fear that his father might castrate him in retaliation for his incestuous yearnings. This case was especially significant because of Hans's use of the horse as a symbolic disguise for his real father.[38] Such examples tended to confirm Freud's belief that both present-day neurotics and primitive men utilized animals as symbolic substitutes for significant persons, especially the father.

Later in his career, Freud became increasingly aware of the role of the mother and the fear of loss of her love as a source of social compliance. This was never stressed with the same force as fear of the father in his interpretation of religion.[39] The father's role remained crucial in both religion and social life. He was seen by Freud as the source of all norms. The fear of his retaliation was regarded as the decisive deterrent against behavioral deviance. This was expressed by Freud:

> The rest of our inquiry is made easy because this God-Creator is openly called Father. Psychoanalysis concludes that he really is the father, clothed in the grandeur in which he once appeared to the small child. The religious man's picture of the creation of the universe is the same as his picture of his own creation.[40]

"The fear of the Lord is the beginning of wisdom." No psalmist, prophet, or ancient religious teacher ever spelled out as explicitly or as gruesomely the content of that fear as did Freud. In the Freudian scheme the Oedipal project is the decisive human project, at least for men. The male organ would offend against the will of the father; the male organ is to be punished for transgression. Primitive man saw punitive retaliation as directed against the offending organ in accordance with the "measure for measure" principle. The "fear of the Lord" is ultimately the unconscious anxiety lest He castrate those who fail to obey Him.[41]

If Freud's analysis is correct, the binding deterrent in religious life is the explicit or the disguised threat of castration. It is easy to understand why Freud and his followers have stressed the significance of circumcision in Judaism and have interpreted it, I think a mite too hastily, as a form of symbolic castration. This would seem, at first glance, to corroborate the hypothesis that the religious Jews are primarily bound to their Lord by fear of punitive castration.

At every turn in Freud's interpretation of religion, the son's ambivalent feelings toward the father are dominant. Hardly any mention is made of the mother, save as the distant object of yearning. Freud confessed himself at a loss within his scheme to make much sense out of the maternal deity religions.[42] This has led Bruno Bettelheim and some other analysts to divide religions into matriarchal and patriarchal groupings. Bettelheim limits the relevance of Freud's insights to patriarchal religions. Some analytic thinkers regard Freud's interpretation of religion as peculiarly appropriate to Judaism. Judaism remains for many analysts an example of a rigidly compulsive system compounded of elements of guilt, subservience, anxiety, and unconscious resentment toward a nonexistent God.[43]

Freud's theory attempted to explain religious origins. Bettelheim contends that Freud may have offered insight into the origins of patriarchal religion but not religion *per se*. Furthermore, if religion is largely a projection of the family situation, as Freud maintained, the child's relations with the mother are at least as emotionally significant as those with the father.

An examination of Jewish legend offers considerable evidence which suggests that the dilemmas of the child's earliest encounters with the mother are a decisively important part of the psychological and cultural context out of which Jewish religion was formed. This is especially significant because of the tendency to regard Judaism as the most patriarchal of religions.

Freud's imaginative reconstruction of the origins of religion and its special application to the origins of Judaism was based on little first-hand knowledge of the sources of Jewish traditions. This lack of first-hand knowledge has frequently characterized his followers as well.[44] There has been very little sustained effort by psychoanalysts to apply the insights of their special competence to the examination of significant sources in the psychology of religion.[45] The history of religion is replete with personalities and movements which beg for psychoanalytic interpretation. The careers of Paul, Augustine, Calvin, Wesley, and the Baal Shem Tov are among those that await disciplined psychoanalytic comment. To date, Erik Erikson's effort on the young Luther has stood out as one of the few comprehensive and disciplined efforts in the direction of a psychoanalytic interpretation of religious phenomena and religious personalities.[46] Instead, psychoanalysts have exhibited a tendency to pick and choose religious and anthropological theories that seem most congenial to their own hypotheses, no matter what status these theories have been accorded by specialists. Freud, for example, acknowledged that he had resorted to Robertson Smith's theory of totemism because it was in accord with his own theories, even though he knew that later anthropologists rejected many of Robertson Smith's findings.[47]

Freud's reason for rejecting inhospitable hypotheses had some merit. His reconstruction of religious origins was based upon the assumption of an analogy between the behavior of individuals and of groups. He had, as we have seen, concluded on the evidence of his clinical findings that the Oedipal project was decisive for the individual. He was convinced that the group must exhibit similar tendencies. Since Robertson Smith's theories seemed congenial to his hypothesis, he preferred them to other theories. He reasoned that only a science which illuminated the role of the unconscious could properly evaluate the dynamics of human behavior. Freud and his colleagues expected their discipline to assume a measuring and a critical function with regard to the other social sciences. Theories at variance with psychoanalytic findings were thought of as inaccurate or as dealing with social and psychological problems at restricted levels of insight.[48] Nor was this claim without some justification. Psychoanalysis has enormously enhanced our understanding of the dynamic factors at work in human action and fantasy. There is hardly a discipline within the social sciences that has not been strongly influenced by it.

In the long run, Freud's interpretation of religion was to prove at variance, not only with research in anthropology and the history of religion, but with his own theories about the development of personality. This was a far greater problem from the point of view of valid systematization. One could reject the findings of other behavioral sciences as long as psychoanalysis offered a coherent theory of the wellsprings of religious action and belief. Freud's interpretation of religion, outlined in 1913 in *Totem and Taboo,* became increasingly less tenable, as he continued to develop his theory of personality.

Freud's later findings in personality theory reduced the importance of the Oedipal conflict in the development of the individual. That conflict was seen in a broadly developmental context.[49] The decisive personality for the child in the earliest years was increasingly understood to be the mother. The vicissitudes of the child's ambivalent relations with the mother culminate in the resolution of the Oedipal conflict and the formation of the superego at about the fifth or sixth year. In the earliest and most decisive years, the child's most important psychic projects center about the mother. The child in earliest infancy is far more dependent upon the mother than upon the father. The child's yearnings and anxieties with regard to her are modified to a far lesser degree by experience than its feelings toward the father. If one seeks for the roots of religious belief in the bio- and sociogenesis of human personality, the mother's relationship to the child is far more "god-like," for good and evil, than the father's.

The importance of the mother was noted by Freud as he worked out the problems of girls. His interpretation of female sexuality was at first largely appended to the hypotheses which stressed the centrality of the father-son conflict. Freud came to realize that one of the girl's earliest projects is to get the mother with child. She later develops the equivalent of the castration complex when she realizes that she lacks the appropriate organ. Her later preferences for masculinity originate in her desire to impregnate the mother and its attendant disappointments. The role of the father is quite secondary and derivative at the time.[50]

From the time of the writing of *The Ego and the Id* (1923), Freud also recognized that ambivalent feelings toward the father, which were thought to be responsible for superego formation, can also develop toward the mother. This insight has been deepened by later psychoanalysts who have stressed the fear of loss of the pre-Oedipal mother's love as decisive in creating the rudiments of the superego before the phallic stage.[51] It was no longer necessary to derive the institutions of society from the acting out of the son's murderous hostility to the father. The very same institutions could develop without any reference to the male parent.[52]

Later psychoanalytic writers have enlarged and enhanced our understanding of the child's earliest relationship to the mother as well as the special importance of his archaic mode of relating to the world through the mouth.[53] Since the basic drive of psychoanalytic theory is to trace mental developments to their earliest origins, there was good reason to press back beyond the Oedipal stage. The principle that the child is father to the man did not permit psychoanalysis to rest content with locating the origin of neurotic conflicts in the relatively late Oedipal conflict.

The turning from the father to the mother as the pivot around whom the dilemmas of the individual originally developed should have led Freud to a heightened emphasis on the importance of the mother in the development of religion and society. Unfortunately, it did not. The Jungians were the first to stress the importance of the Great Mother in the psychology of religion.[54] Freud's inability to see beyond the paternal element in religion was seized upon, not without a measure of malice, by some Jungians. They tended to regard Freud's system as Jewish both in origin and relevance. It was, they claimed, inapplicable to Christianity and to paganism. The non-Jewish religions were depicted as more atuned to the needs of free autonomous spirits than "legalistic," "unspontaneous," "unloving" Judaism.[55] Though the Jungians employed the language of "scientific" psychology, they tended to restate an old theological polemic in which Christians contrasted their faith as a religion of freedom and love with Judaism, the religion of servitude to the law.[56]

This tendency transformed a psychological debate into a theological conflict. It is evident in the work of Peter J. R. Dempsey, a Catholic scholar. He rejected Freud's characterization of religion *per se* as obsessional and limited the relevance of Freud's observations to Judaism. As we have seen, Bruno Bettelheim suggested a similar limitation of the relevance of Freud for other, less polemical reasons. Dempsey contended that Freud erred because of his background. He denied that his perspectives were in any sense applicable to Catholicism.[57]

A similar tendency infused the work of C. G. Jung. He often made a point of contrasting his Aryan perspectives with the Mosaic bias of his rival. He regarded the entire Freudian image of man as derivative of "legalistic" Judaism and, as such, without special relevance for Aryan (!) religion. He dismissed the Freudian superego as dependent upon Jewish imagery rather than clinical investigation. Jung wrote: "As for Freud's idea of the 'superego,' it is a furtive attempt to smuggle in his time-honored image of Jehovah in the dress of psychological theory."[58] Apparently, Jung regarded his own "Aryan" formulations as scientific in character but saw Freud's as disguised theology. Victor White, an English Dominican of strong Jungian sympathies, has heartily concurred with Jung's evaluation in his oddly interesting book, *God and the Unconscious*.[59]

The Jungians had a point, which even their ill-will could not conceal. By Freud's own admission, his theory of religion could not account for the religions of the Great Mother. It made little sense to talk of the *origins* of religion in an act of cannibalistic parricide, when almost no mention was made of the overwhelming body of religious and historical data in which the Divine Mothers and their Sons predominated. Jung was not the only depth psychologist to stress the importance of the maternal element in religion. A similar emphasis appeared in the writings of Otto Rank and Erich Fromm. Furthermore, the

Jungians were not entirely unfair when they suggested that Freud's incapacity to deal with the maternal element in religion had something to do with his own makeup. There is a peculiar opacity in Freud's thinking about the origins of religion. Long after he had realized the decisive importance of the earliest years of the child with the mother, he continued to underscore his preference for the paternal in his writings on religion and society. It can be found in *Group Psychology and the Analysis of the Ego* (1921) and in *Moses and Monotheism* (1937). Writing in the first person in *Civilization and Its Discontents* (1930), Freud said: "I could not point to *any need* in childhood so strong as that for a father's protection."[60] Apparently, Freud was never able to see a maternal element at the root of deity, even when his research pointed that way. In psychoanalytic terminology, this may have been one of the unanalyzed residues of his personality.[61]

For some, the question of the priority of the maternal element in religion became a test of Freudian theory. Many orthodox Freudians continued to reiterate Freud's assertion of the paternal character of deity in the face of Jungian and neo-Freudian criticism. There were those who felt—I think mistakenly—that the validity of the psychoanalytic interpretation of religion stood or fell with the primal crime myth. They were understandably reluctant to deviate from the master's conclusions. Nevertheless, by ignoring an important body of empirical evidence to save Freud's theory, they were doing something Freud rarely did in his own clinical work. In addition to reassessing the importance of the mother in the pre-Oedipal period, Freud made other great revisions in his theory as new and more detailed empirical evidence became available. In *The Problem of Anxiety* (1927), Freud revised his earlier theory of the nature of anxiety. At first, he had regarded the damming up of repressed libido as the cause of anxiety. In his revised theory, he maintained that anxiety was more likely to bring about repression than vice versa.[62] In *Beyond the Pleasure Principle* (1920), he revised his earlier hypothesis that dreams primarily served the pleasure principle. Instead of interpreting dreams in terms of wish fulfillments, functioning to prevent the disturbance of sleep, he postulated that a conservative tendency, common to all instinctual life, was operative. In dreams the organism returns to earlier states or occurrences, even when these occurrences are radically traumatic, as in the experience of shell-shocked soldier patients after World War I. These men recapitulated their battlefield agony in nightly fantasy long after the cessation of hostilities.[63]

In *The Ego and the Id* (1922), Freud revised his earlier and somewhat crude division of the mind into conscious and unconscious functioning. He postulated a tripartite topography of the psyche, seeing mental functioning as the result of interaction of the ego, id, and superego, and thus refining his earlier models of the relationship between consciousness and the unconscious.[64]

None of these revisions was a rejection of fundamental psychoanalytic theory. All served to clarify and give greater precision to psychoanalytic research. In all instances, the Oedipal conflict was regarded as part of a broader genetic pattern, though it retained a real measure of importance. The area of religion was the principal realm in which no revision was ever forthcoming. One gets the impression of little originality in reading the work of most of Freud's disciples on religion. They tend to repeat the master with a minimum of critical acumen. This lack of originality has been noted by psychoanalysts themselves. In successive issues of *The Annual Survey of Psychoanalysis,* Almansi, Tarachow, and Arlow have concluded their surveys of current research in the field of religion and mythology with comments on the continued stress on the Oedipal conflict in this domain. Arlow even refers to a "lag" between psychoanalytic studies of religion and other branches of psychoanalytic research.[65]

The failure of the Freudians to extend their insights beyond the image of God as the murdered patriarch was regarded by some as corroboration of the contention that psychoanalysis is a "Jewish science." From the very inception of the movement, Freud was deeply fearful lest his work be rejected because of the preponderance of Jews among his professional disciples. The selection of Jung, a non-Jew, as the first president of the International Psycho-Analytic Association was very largely dictated by these fears.[66] Ironically, Jung was later to do as much as any man to exploit anti-Semitism as a tool in fostering a rejection of the psychoanalytic movement. This was by no means merely a propagandistic device, though Jung's record with regard to Nazism and anti-Semitism has been, at the very least, highly dubious.[67] Jung postulated that conscious feeling and opinion was determined by racial memory and the collective unconscious. This implied that "racial" groups, such as Aryans and Semites (or Jungians and Freudians, by and large), patterned their worlds in accordance with their differing backgrounds. This was, in turn, a polite way of psychologizing a vicious racialism which was to turn millions of people into smoke in the twentieth century.

There have been times when an inherited mythology has played an important role in the formation of "scientific" theory. Nowhere has the formative role of myth in creating "science" been more in evidence than in the psychology of religion. The old theological image of the Jew as a fearful servant of a tyrannical law-giving Master stands behind the psychological image of God as the commanding, tyrannical patriarch (the projected superego). This view of Judaism and its God has been a perennially important element in Christian theology. It is related to the image of the Pharisees (read rabbis) as overly meticulous conformists who stressed formal compliance with the Law while inwardly doing violence to its spirit. It is hardly surprising that the psychoanalytic interpretation of Judaism has followed the lines of the general cultural estimation. Happily, one of the fruits of modern critical research in religion has been the acknowledgment of the distorted character of this polemic by such authoritative Christian scholars as George Foote Moore and R. Travers Herford.[68]

Although Freud's theory of religion was not subject to the

same degree of theoretic revision or refinement as his other work, his abiding contribution to the scientific study of religion must be acknowledged. The very terms "matriarchal" and "patriarchal" betray a Freudian bias. These terms tell us whether the mother or the father is the central personality about whom fundamental dilemmas are projected in a given religious system. Few contemporary researchers would question Freud's basic contention that the psychological roots of religious belief are to be found to a significant degree in the complexities of the human family situation. To argue that the role of the mother is more decisive than the father's in the formation of religion is to refine Freudian theory, not to negate it. The situation in the psychology of religion is not unlike that in anthropology. Anthropologists may question Freud's theory of religious origins, but they do not fail to take careful note of child-rearing practices such as infant feeding and toilet training in their studies of other cultures.[69]

For all of its shortcomings, *Totem and Taboo* remains a classic in the psychology of religion. It may not tell the whole story, but it tells a great deal. It lays the foundation for all subsequent work in the field. Frequently, criticism of Freud's primal crime hypothesis tends to ignore the imposing tragic grandeur of Freud's theoretical edifice.

Obviously, no one could with certainty reconstruct the facts of an unavailable archaic past. To the extent that Freud believed that he had succeeded in so doing, if indeed he did, it is difficult to take him seriously. Yet, if Freud has given us problematic history, he certainly has given us one of the most potent etiological myths of the twentieth century. Furthermore, out of this myth, he created the haunting, prophetic image of the leader in *Group Psychology and the Analysis of the Ego*. Writing before Hitler was to become the absolute conscience and will of his people, Freud drew a picture of the way in which groups under stress tend to identify their ideals and their moral standards with those of their chosen leaders. There is an awesomely prophetic quality in Freud's analysis of the God-like power available to the leader as well as his description of the fickle desertion of the leader by his community once he has failed. It is sometimes difficult to remember that Freud wrote this work before the career of Adolf Hitler as Führer of the German Reich.

Nor ought the scientist be held in little repute because he exhibits a strange and almost haunting power as a myth-maker. The myth of primal origins may tell us more about the contemporary status of religion than it does about its beginnings. One of the most significant insights suggested by Freud is that religion is an inescapable balancing of Promethean arrogance and abject humility. If Freud is fundamentally correct about religion, and I am convinced he is, there is a tragic and ironic inevitability which destines men to celebrate their asocial and demonic natures in the very institution to which they come seeking an (impossible) ending to guilt and evil.

Finally, Freud's myth is extremely helpful for the understanding of opaque and irrational religious rituals. Before Freud, no explanation of such rituals as Jewish circumcision and the Catholic Mass were available that were heuristically compatible with contemporary psychodynamic insights. Freud has demonstrated that religious rite is more than gross and deceived superstition, and that it is, in fact, rooted in the deepest ironies of the human condition. He has demonstrated that inescapable dilemmas such as the conflicts of parent and child are reflected in and engender many of the disciplines and institutions of the Judaic religions. After Freud, one may reject religion as a pathetic attempt to perpetuate and endow with cosmic significance the dilemmas of childhood beyond their period of relevance. One may also find heightened meaning in religion as a decisive and fundamental expression of the human predicament. Freud thought that he had found the intellectual key to the psychological understanding of the origins of religion. Contemporary scholarship can only partially concur in his claim. Nevertheless, it is difficult to proceed in the psychology of religion without standing on his shoulders.

2/Dreams, Psychoanalysis, and Jewish Legend

T HE AGGADAH is that part of Jewish literature which consists of legends, myths, and folklore of the rabbis of the Talmudic period. At an early date the Aggadah came to comprise the non-legal part of Jewish religious study, exegesis, and speculation. Midrash Aggadah embraced the interpretive illustration or expansion of the nonlegal portions of the Bible.[1] It was handed down orally for centuries. The beginnings of this activity can be traced at least as far back as Ezra, ca. 400 B.C.E.[2] However, as late as the middle of the third century C.E., Rabbi Joshua ben Levi, an eminent Palestinian Aggadist, had misgivings about the use of written "Aggadah books," although they were consulted by other authorities.[3] This material was finally put down in writing because of the fear that it would otherwise be forgotten.

The Aggadah has been the subject of much controversy throughout the history of Judaism. Some Jewish religious authorities have praised this literature unreservedly. Others have found much of its content acutely embarrassing. One of the best known commendations of the Aggadah counsels: "If thou wishest to know Him at whose word the world came into being, learn the

Aggadah, for through it thou shalt know the Holy One, praised be He, and follow his ways."[4]

As with all myth and legend, many of the Aggadah's tales run counter to the canons of common sense. Hyperbole abounds. Some traditions have offended puritan sensibilities. Others are primitive and archaic. Jewish thinkers who regard Judaism as a religion of reason have tended to devalue this literature. Even as balanced a critic as Solomon Schechter exhibited an uneasiness with the Aggadah characteristic of many of his learned contemporaries. In a review of I. H. Weiss's history of Jewish tradition, *Dor Dor weDorshaw,* Schechter wrote:

> Much space is given to the Aggadah and so called "Teachers of Aggadah." Weiss makes no attempt at apology for that which seems to us strange or even repugnant in this part of Rabbinic literature. The greatest fault to be found with those who wrote down such passages as appear objectionable to us is, perhaps, that they did not observe the wise rule of Johnson, who said to Boswell on a certain occasion, "Let us get serious, for there comes a fool." And fools unfortunately did come in the shape of Jewish commentators and Christian controversialists, who took as serious things which were only *the expression of a momentary impulse,* or represented the opinion of some isolated individual, or were meant simply as *a piece of humorous by-play* calculated to enliven the interest of a languid audience. But on the other hand, as Weiss proves, the Aggadah contains also many elements of real edification and eternal truths as well as abundant material for building up the edifice of dogmatic Judaism.[5] (italics mine)

Schechter valued those traditions which possessed "eternal truth" and offered "real edification." He was obviously uncomfortable with the more bizarre legends. Since Freud, we tend to see far greater significance in "humorous by-play" and "momentary impulse" than Schechter did. A very real shift in cultural sentiment has taken place. Many traditions which were most difficult for Schechter are among those we would regard as possessing the

greatest importance for the psychological understanding of
Judaism.

There was another reason for downgrading the Aggadah.
It was regarded by the rabbis as less authoritative and less representative of Jewish religious sentiment than the Halakah, the
corpus of religious and legal norms binding upon the Jew. One
of the foremost contemporary Jewish historians, Salo Baron, has
offered an important admonition concerning the relative merits
of Aggadah and Halakah for the study of Judaism:

> The Talmud is primarily law. This truism needs special em-
> phasis, in view of tendencies in recent generations to elevate
> the aggadic or legendary part of it to a position of prominence
> which it certainly does not deserve in the perspective of Tal-
> mudic doctrine. To the Talmudist, law really mattered, while
> the *Aggadah represented an accession of often irresponsible,*
> *private and uncontrolled tales* which, even if incorporated in
> the Talmud or Midrash, did not by any means become repre-
> sentative of the whole of Judaism. Even the reiterated saying,
> "One must not question an Aggadah" was merely intended
> to convey the idea of the latter's irrationality, not its indis-
> putable authority.
>
> Not that the interest in the Aggadah of modern
> scholars and laymen is without profound historic justifica-
> tion. Certainly, the historian of ancient Judaism and of its
> linguistic, literary, or social manifestations will often find in
> the Aggadah more vital information than in the more re-
> stricted field of law. . . . Viewed from the inside, however,
> of what really mattered to the compilers of these tomes
> themselves and their more serious students, the Aggadah was
> but the handmaid of the Halakah—an important, even in-
> dispensable handmaid, but no more.[6] (italics mine)

Baron's view can be regarded as authoritative. If one
wishes to understand what really mattered to the rabbis, one must
study Halakah. However, if one wishes to investigate how the
rabbis felt about what really mattered to them, the Aggadah may
very well provide the key.

Schechter flourished as a Jewish thinker at the beginning of the twentieth century. At the time, there was little appreciation in Jewish circles of the importance of myth and legend for the understanding of religious and social movements. Their significance became apparent partly as a result of Freud's work on the interpretation of dreams. Freud's scientific predecessors were unable to comprehend the psychological significance of dreams. They tended to regard them as an irrational degeneration of mental life. Freud was impressed with dreams as a key to the unconscious motivations of his patients. He also recognized that myths and legends function in the life of the group as do dreams in the individual.[7] In the light of Freud's insights, it has been possible to take a wholly new look at the exaggerated fantasies of the Aggadah which so disturbed Schechter.

In order to comprehend the functional similarity of dreams, legends, and myths, it is necessary to understand some of Freud's insights into the psychological significance of dreams. The most important is the principle of "psychological determinism."[8] This principle has often been misinterpreted by Freud's critics as a denial of human freedom. In reality, it reflects the conviction that no aspect of human behavior is accidental, that slips of the tongue, memory lapses, seemingly innocent witticisms, dreams, and other fantasy productions are purposeful expressions of human needs and goals.

The second insight concerns the "role of the unconscious."[9] Freud realized the impossibility of explaining human behavior in terms of its overt manifestations. By searching for unconscious motivations, he was able to discern coherent, purposeful patterns in the bizarre material presented by his patients during therapy.

Freud distinguished two levels of mental functioning, the "primary process" and the "secondary process."[10] The secondary process is in the service of the "reality principle." It is realistic, logical, and guided by common sense. The secondary process is absolutely necessary for the survival of the organism.

Without it, the individual would be driven to gratify his impulses regardless of the realistic impediments which so often thwart him. The primary process is the older mode of mental functioning. It is in the service of the "pleasure principle." It is indifferent to the realistic consequences of the actions of the organism. It is the mode of mental functioning characteristic of the unconscious. In terms of Freud's revised model of the structure of the psyche, the secondary process is the ego's normal mode of mental functioning; the primary process is the id's. Much of the content of dreams, myths, legends, and religious ritual is primary process thinking.

Normally the unconscious does not reveal itself through direct inspection. Freud sought to comprehend its aims through the methods of free association and dream interpretation. The technique of free association consists in encouraging the patient to reveal everything that comes to mind during the analytic encounter. Freud discovered that in free association his patients often referred to their dreams, usually of the previous night. Though the manifest content of these dreams usually was meaningless, the latent content was discovered to be associated with the patients' dominant psychological concerns.

In sleep, Freud maintained, the conscious mind is relatively inactive. It is released from its reality-testing functions and its responsibility for the execution of the organism's decisions. The inward intellective and affective processes have free rein. While the secondary process continues to function in a highly restricted way, the mental processes of dreams are fundamentally primary process. Ordinary laws of time and space are frequently violated in dreams. Dreams are part of the world of wish rather than the world of reality. However, socially unacceptable desires cannot normally be expressed in undisguised form even in dreams. Dream contents are frequently expressed symbolically. According to Freud, symbolic disguise is necessary because dreams function to preserve sleep. Were unacceptable desires openly expressed in dreams, we might awaken as we do in the course of nightmares. The psyche utilizes an elaborate symbolization process to prevent the disturbing character of those wishes from becoming manifest.

Freud distinguished the "latent" and "manifest" content of dreams. The manifest content is frequently without meaning or purpose. The latent content reflects the subject's underlying goals. A major concern of dream interpretation is to pierce the distortions of the manifest content in order to discover the latent content.

The resemblance between dreams, legends, and myths was noted by Freud in *The Interpretation of Dreams*.[11] These similarities especially interested C. G. Jung. Jung contended that many of the symbols in his patients' dreams were also to be found in the "collective unconscious" of mankind. Freud saw the interpretation of dreams as the royal road to understanding the individual unconscious. Jung regarded the universal symbols and myths of religion and dreams as keys to the understanding of the collective unconscious of the race.[12]

It is not necessary to agree with Jung about the existence of a collective unconscious to recognize the parallels between dreams and myths. The parallels were obvious to both Freudians and Jungians. The alogical quality of mankind's perennial myths no longer impeded their appreciation. Even the "childlike" quality which Schechter found in rabbinic legend took on new significance. The "childlike" legends were regarded as worthy of serious attention. Freud concluded that dreaming was in part a "regression" to the dominant concerns of the dreamer's earliest childhood.[13] He anticipated Jung in suggesting that the analysis of dreams might lead to a knowledge of "man's archaic heritage."[14] Similar regressive tendencies are evident in myth and legend, which are the repositories of mankind's archaic heritage. In the light of psychoanalytic insight, the very elements Schechter valued least in the Aggadah offered the greatest promise of providing a key to understanding the underlying motivations operative in Jewish religious sentiment.

Many of the same unconscious thought processes that Freud found in dreams can also be found in myth and legend. In dreams there is a tendency toward the concretization of abstract problems.[15] A similar tendency is evident in rabbinic legend. Normative Judaism does not have an explicit theology. There are no abstract summations of rabbinic belief in philosophic categories.[16] One can discern definitive trends in Jewish theology, but only by examining the concrete stories about interpersonal and divine-human encounters that abound in the Bible and rabbinic literature. There was a rabbinic consensus on most theological issues. The legends which illustrate this consensus deal with biblical heroes in concrete situations. It is, for example, impossible to speak of an explicit doctrine of original sin in Judaism. Rabbinic thought lacks abstract theological formulation. Nevertheless, the elaboration of the biblical tales about Adam, Eve, and the serpent indicate a consensus concerning the inevitability of sinful conduct in all men. Although normative Jewish religious sentiment can be reduced to abstract conceptions, its real life was expressed in highly concrete images.

Freud observed a certain lack of logic operative in dreams and other forms of primary process thinking. In dreams, for example, the normal rules of time and space are disregarded. This fact is related to another aspect of dreams which is also present in the Aggadah, the tendency toward "condensation." By condensation is meant that complex ideas are telescoped into a word, a phrase, a brief scene or story. In rabbinic legend, Hiram, prince of Tyre, is properly identified as the prince who assisted Solomon in the building of the Jerusalem temple about 950 B.C.E. He is also regarded by the rabbis as the object of Ezekiel's condemnation in the verse "Son of man, say unto the prince of Tyre . . . because thine heart is lifted up, and thou hast said, I am a god . . ."[17] Hiram is also anachronistically identified with Hirah the Adullamite, who figures as a friend of Judah the son of Jacob before the Egyptian sojourn. Hiram would have to have lived over eleven hundred years to have been all three men condensed by rabbinic legend into a single person.

A similar tendency toward condensation is present in the legends concerning Dathan and Abiram. According to the rabbis, Dathan and Abiram were rebels par excellence against the authority of Moses. They are identified by the rabbis with a number of unnamed opponents of Moses, such as the fighting Israelites whom Moses sought to pacify after he had slain the oppressive Egyptian overseer,[18] the informers who reported to Pharaoh that Moses had slain the overseer,[19] the Israelite elders who opposed Israel's departure from Egypt,[20] and the leader of the rebels who collected manna on the Sabbath.[21] Dathan is also identified by the rabbis as the unnamed leader the people proposed to set in Moses' place after the spies returned with an evil report of the land of Canaan.[22] The rabbis condensed a number of situations involving rebels and identified them with the pair.

There is an inner logic at work in the condensation process. The rabbinic stories concerning the rebelliousness of Dathan and Abiram graphically suggest that lesser leaders in subsequent generations are not likely to fare any better in the exercise of authority than did Moses, the greatest of all Jewish leaders. The stories served as both a warning and a consolation to the rabbis as they sought to lead their precarious community. The traditions intuitively express insights which today require the technical vocabulary of the social sciences.

Instead of dismissing the tendency of dreams to violate common sense rules of ordinary experience, Freud saw them as data for psychological investigation. Similar distortions are to be found in the Aggadah. There is, for example, a tradition that before God gave Israel the Torah, He caused the wombs of all the pregnant women present at Sinai to become transparent as glass so that the embryos could see God and speak with Him. God gave Israel the Torah only after the embryos agreed that their lives would be forfeit were their fathers to disobey its commandments.[23] This tradition violates the canons of ordinary experience. It has, nevertheless, an inner logic. The rabbis used it graphically to assert that the Torah was equally binding on all generations, not on the Sinai generation alone. The legend thus reinforced the resolve of the community to maintain its religious traditions in the face of challenge by the pagan and Christian world.

There is a great deal of punning and word-play in dreams. The dreamer is an excellent punster. Formal associations of similar-sounding words are taken as identical in content. Words are distorted to conform to the pre-existent concerns of the subject. This also occurs frequently in the Aggadah. One well-known example is the play on the phrase *haruth al ha-luach,* which means that the letters of the ten commandments were "graven" on the tablets of stone. The rabbis taught that the phrase ought to be read *héruth al ha-luach,* which means that there was freedom on the tablets, from which they derived the teaching that "There is none free save he who is occupied with Torah."[24] The rabbinic conviction that observance of the Law offers true freedom was not derived from the biblical text through word-play. The rabbis' word-play illustrated a conviction deeply held apart from the verse. The rabbis assimilated the biblical text to their conviction.

"Substitution" is one of the most interesting dream processes, for which an analog can be found in Aggadah. By substitution is meant that a censorable idea or object is replaced by a seemingly neutral idea or object. A disturbing dream content is *devalued* by translation into a trivial circumstance or by being represented as its own opposite. This mechanism was especially important in Jewish thought. Like all men, the rabbis were beset by sore religious doubts, often against their deepest aspirations. These doubts had to find expression. Because of the perilous condition of the Jewish community after its defeat by Rome in 132-35, it was impossible for responsible leaders openly to express religious reservations in their own name. Nevertheless, they did question the fate meted out to the Jewish people, the truth of Scripture, and the justice of its laws. They expressed their doubts by placing them in the mouths of sinners such as Manasseh,

Korah, Dathan, and Abiram.[25] In this way they were able to give expression to censorable ideas, in a context which did not threaten to disrupt the Jewish community. According to Freud, substitution and devaluation are employed in dreams to prevent the dreamer's sleep from being disturbed. The rabbis used similar mechanisms to prevent the delicate balance of the community's well-being from being disturbed.

There are, however, significant differences between dreams and legends. Legends are transmitted verbally during waking hours in an intersubjective context. Dreams are private, isolated expressions of the inner life of an individual. Only on the rarest occasions are they communicated or even remembered. Most dreams are usually "forgotten" before the dreamer awakens. The world of the dreamer is very different from the world of myth and legend. Dreams occur only after normal ego-functions have receded. Legends are normally presented under conditions in which ego-functions are not significantly interfered with.[26]

Attainment of insight into the latent content of dreams is no easy task. Freud specifically warned against "wild analysis," by which he meant the attempt to comprehend dream symbols without reference to the private associations such symbols have for the dreamer.[27] Entering a house, in a dream, may mean entering a woman sexually, but it does not necessarily have that meaning under all circumstances. The interpretation of legend and myth is even more difficult than dream interpretation in a therapeutic transaction. The psychoanalyst usually possesses sufficient knowledge about the underlying preoccupations of his patient to be able to place the dream in a larger dynamic context. He also has the benefit of the patient's spontaneous associations concerning the meaning of the dream symbolism. Such information is normally unavailable in the interpretation of legend. Legends differ from dreams in at least two respects: (a) legends are the product of many minds transmitting traditions over a long period of time; (b) the original authors are unavailable for psychological examination. There are, however, a number of checks available in the

interpretation of dreams which can prove helpful in the interpretation of legend:

    1. The underlying trend of the latent contents must be
discernible through the repetition of themes in diverse contents.

    2. Latent contents must have internal consistency.

    3. The latent contents must be consistent with what is
already known about the subject.

    4. The interpretation must readily lead to a fruitful elabo-
ration of our understanding of the subject.[28]

One of the difficulties with psychoanalytic studies of religion is that they frequently make sense only to the initiated.
Some interpretations of religious symbols seem very farfetched
even to those sympathetic to psychoanalysis. One analyst has interpreted the menorah as a disguised idol signifying the sadistic,
castrating father.[29] Another has seen Jonah's deliverance from the
whale as the resolution of his conflict with the father "who had
created him."[30] These analysts may very well have had clients for
whom the menorah and the whale had these associations. Nevertheless, such associations have little value for the interpretations
of religion. There would have to be much corroborating evidence.
Failing such evidence, the danger of wild analysis is very great.

    Legends actually resemble rumor far more than they do
dreams. The problem of gaining insight into the latent content of
legends and myths, while not doing violence to the manifest content, was significantly advanced by the work of Gordon Allport
and Leo Postman on the psychology of rumor during World
War II.[31] Allport and Postman suggested that legend and rumor
conform to the same dynamic processes. They demonstrated that
ambiguous, verbally transmitted information of interest to the
listener has a tendency to become distorted in such a way that,
when retold, it conforms to the latent as well as the manifest
preoccupations of the teller. A rabbinic legend was normally a
verbally transmitted account of an originally ambiguous biblical
story. Since the subject matter of religious legend was usually of
permanent interest to those who communicated it, the same

dynamic processes at work in rumor were also at work in it.

The psychology of rumor can uncover the latent content of any legendary material, provided one can determine how the legend distorted the original source in retelling and embellishing it. Since the Aggadah normally interprets or embellishes a known biblical tradition, one need only compare the original account with the retelling in the Aggadah in order to determine the alteration.

One such instance occurs in the rabbis' interpretation of the story of Noah's planting a vineyard and his subsequent drunkenness.[32] In the Aggadah, Satan is regarded as Noah's partner in planting the vine. Together the pair offer illicit sacrifices of a sheep, a pig, a lion, and an ape on the spot where the vine was planted. The blood thus sprinkled enters the vine. Noah's guilt in becoming drunk is compounded. He committed one of the most thoroughly taboo acts in the catalog of Jewish sins, the illicit drinking of blood. Throughout the ages, men have intuitively associated the "blood of the grape" with real blood. Few symbolic associations have more deeply divided Judaism and Christianity than the meaning of the ritual drinking of wine when it is symbolically equivalent to blood.[33] It is not at all surprising that the mere mention of Noah's vinicultural activities elicited an emotionally overdetermined reaction on the part of the rabbinic interpreters of the Bible. Following Allport and Postman, we can say that the way in which the elaborative process was handled by the rabbis offers a key to some of their deepest feelings concerning the subject matter of the original source. Such instances abound throughout the Aggadah.

Allport and Postman's work on the psychology of rumor grew out of interest in the uncontrolled rumors generated during World War II. The two researchers sought to understand the phenomenon by creating their own rumor chains under laboratory conditions. Taking a group of students as a control, they exhibited an illustrated card to the first student and requested that he describe it to a second. The second student was then asked to trans-

mit the information to a third, and so on. The original stimulus—
the illustrated card—was at last compared with the final description, distorted through repeated retelling. On the basis of these
experiments, Allport and Postman defined rumor as "a specific
(or topical) proposition for belief, passed along from person to
person, usually by word of mouth, without standards of evidence
being present."[34] At least two conditions must be present if a
rumor is to be passed along: the theme must be of interest to the
speaker and to the listener, and the true facts must be shrouded in
some ambiguity.[35] Allport and Postman suggested the following
formula for measuring the intensity of a rumor:

$$R \sim i \times a$$

The amount of rumor in circulation varies with the importance
of the theme to the individuals concerned multiplied by the ambiguity of the evidence pertaining to the topic at issue.[36]

When these conditions are met, three main lines of distortion occur:

1. A leveling process takes place in which the account
tends to grow shorter, more concise, more easily grasped.[37]

2. Concurrently, sharpening occurs. Allport and Postman
defined sharpening as the "selective perception, retention, and
reporting of a limited number of details from a larger context."[38]
Time sequences tend to be obliterated, and events are described as
if they had occurred in the immediate present. Sharpening frequently exaggerates the size or the relative prominence of an
object of interest. Sharpening also occurs in relation to familiar
symbols that convey meaning to a subject.

The authors describe "closure" as an important form of
sharpening. This refers to the subject's urge to make his experience as complete, coherent, and meaningful as possible. Meaningless phrases such as "Lucky Rakes" were read as "Lucky
Strikes." Closure was also manifest in the tendency to introduce
explanations and rationalizations. Wartime shortages, setbacks,
and discomforts were "explained" through specious tales of

imagined setbacks or by ascribing blame to minority groups. Most people tend to give their experiences some sort of explanation, regardless of whether an explanation is in fact appropriate.[39]

A very strong tendency toward closure can also be discerned throughout the Aggadah. Disasters and defeats are invariably described as God's punishment for the victim's sins. The rabbis apparently preferred self-blame to the possibility of an irrational universe devoid of correlation between virtue and good fortune. Closure is of decisive importance for the understanding of the historic reactions of the Jewish community to disaster under conditions of stress.

3. Assimilation is another type of distortion evident in both rumor and legend. Allport and Postman described assimilation as a function of the "attractive force exerted upon rumor by the intellectual and emotional context existing in the listener's mind."[40] By assimilation is meant the fact that items become twisted and simplified to render the story more coherent. This is related to condensation, the tendency already discussed in connection with dreams. Previous experience is exploited to bring about a more coherent mental configuration. Frequently, what actually transpires is distorted in favor of what one expects to take place. Allport and Postman showed their students a picture of a white man holding a razor and standing next to a Negro. Usually the students reported the razor in the Negro's hand.[41]

The subject's special interests, sympathies, hatreds, loves, feelings of guilt, and other passions exercised a distorting influence on the stories they told. Women tended to manifest a strong interest in clothes and bargains, where the pictures lent themselves to such concerns. Many subjects reported that the Negro was wildly brandishing the white man's razor or threatening him with it![42]

Sexual interests are important in assimilation. Allport and Postman report that their subjects invented lurid rumors of rape and unwelcome approaches by Negroes toward white women. They suggested that these rumors frequently betray the sexual dilemmas of their authors. Guilt feelings, fear of loss of status, and violent and aggressive feelings were also introduced without warrant.

As assimilation proceeds, there is a tendency for nondynamic elements in the story to level out. There is concurrently a sharpening of and a concentration on pressing motivations within the subject. Frequently, the subject is only partially aware of his motivations. This corresponds to unconscious motivation in psychoanalysis. When rumors deal with matters involving strong desire and equally strong prohibition, both elements tend to be emphasized. Lurid descriptions of wickedness are frequently conveyed together with strong indications of religious or moral disapproval. In psychoanalytic terminology, the id and the superego sharpen their roles in assimilation, while the normal ego functions tend to level out.

Allport and Postman have suggested that the same psychological processes at work in rumor are also at work in legend. They regard a legend as a solidified rumor. They quote La Piere and Farnsworth's definition of a legend as "a rumor which has become part of the verbal heritage of a people."[43] Rumors may become legend, but only if the issues they convey are of importance and interest to successive generations. The same formula

$$R \sim i \times a$$

that Allport and Postman postulated to measure the spread of rumor can be applied to legend. Persistent interest is necessary before rumor becomes legend. Rumors about impending food or gasoline shortages swept through the United States immediately after Pearl Harbor. They pertained to matters of intense interest to most people. They have, at best, only limited historical interest today. At the time, they overrode in interest many legends of abiding human concern whose staying power has not diminished. Legends usually develop out of topics of universal concern. The crises of life, such as birth, marriage, sickness, sin, righteousness, and death, are excellent material for legends. So too are the dilemmas of interpersonal relationships. Guilt, hatred, aggression, sexuality, and love are among the themes which are of perennial concern to successive generations. They are the concerns out of which legends are formed.

Rabbinic legend conforms to the same mental processes that Allport and Postman have described in the transmission of rumor. The subject matter of the Aggadah reflects topics of abiding human interest. Aggadah was not the isolated activity of a small class of learned exegetes. Louis Ginzberg, the pre-eminent modern authority, stressed the popular character of much Aggadic material. He said it was popular in the double sense of appealing to the people and being in part produced by them.[44] In the Aggadah the stories and legends concerning the heroes and villains of Scripture and Jewish history were told, retold, amplified, and embellished for the self-edification of the rabbis and the moral and spiritual edification of the Jewish people. This body of tradition was communicated in the learned discussions of scholars, the sermons of religious leaders, and the folklore of the people. It comprised an extremely wide range of topics of perennial religious and psychological interest. The meaning of life, the sacred history of Israel, the defense of traditional values, the exaltation of the righteous as models to be imitated and the condemnation of the wicked as examples of temptations to be avoided, speculation about ultimate human destiny and God's relation to the world, theosophical speculations concerning the Beginning and the End, Messianic speculation, and a search after the meaning of Jewish existence with its peculiar dilemmas, are among the themes of this literature. Hardly any aspect of the Jew's search for a meaningful existence is absent from the Aggadah.[45]

Rabbinic legend resembled rumor in being verbally transmitted. It was communicated orally for generations before being reduced to written form. Strictly speaking, the Aggadah was that part of the rabbinic exegesis of Scripture known as Midrash, an interpretive activity which sought out the implications of Scrip-

ture for the life, law, and lore of the Jewish community. The
question of when the various Midrashic texts were redacted is one
of the thorniest problems confronting scholars. It is beyond the
scope of our present inquiry. What is important for our purposes
is that this material was orally transmitted for centuries.

Allport and Postman found that ambiguity is necessary for
the spread of rumor. Ambiguity is found throughout Scripture.
The growth of the Aggadah was possible only because of the
ambiguity of the original biblical text. The proliferation of
exegesis in both Judaism and Christianity was partly due to this
ambiguity. In a strange way, the rabbis unintentionally anticipated
the psychoanalytic conviction that all mental contents are meaningful and goal-directed. Both the rabbis and Freud, though for
very different reasons, rejected the notion that the character of the
thought contents with which they were preoccupied could be
accidental. The rabbis regarded every single letter and every asso-
ciative connection of the Torah as significant. Where the significance was not immediately apparent to the rabbis, they began a
diligent search after meaning. Admittedly, the rabbis did not regard the Torah as primarily ambiguous. They saw Scripture as
possessing a rich multiplicity of hidden meanings.[46] Nevertheless,
whether Scripture was regarded as ambiguous or possessed of
multiple meanings would make little practical difference. The
rabbinic exegesis of Scripture will prove to be of psychological
significance to the extent that we can discern how the rabbis interpreted or altered known biblical traditions.

Ambiguity was also a concomitant of the terseness of the
original biblical stories. The historical books of the Bible cover
the history of Israel from its beginnings until the Persian period.
Only a bare sketch could be included. The urge to understand
and to specify led the rabbis to add details of their own invention.
The reign of Manasseh lasted fifty-five years. It was covered in
the second book of Kings in eighteen verses.[47] The rabbis, of
necessity, described his career and the careers of other biblical
figures largely as they imagined them to have been.

Inevitably, the rabbis assimilated the terse accounts to their own meanings. Of the three fundamental processes at work in the psychology of rumor, the most important for the study of the Aggadah is probably assimilation. Italian Renaissance painters depicted biblical heroes as if they were contemporary Italians. Swedish folk art illustrates Moses as a Swedish prince in Swedish garb. These examples could be endlessly multiplied. This is the process of assimilation applied to artistic creation. Similarly, without violating the fundamental intent of Scripture, the rabbis represented biblical personalities in typical rabbinic settings. David the king, for example, is depicted as humbly consulting Mephibosheth, his teacher in matters of rabbinic lore. The setting of David's court was anachronistically interpreted as if David were a rabbinic scholar.[48]

Motivations were sometimes altered when the rabbis retold biblical stories. This is evident in the way the rabbis interpreted the story of David and Bathsheba. Since David was the founder of the legitimate royal house of Israel and the progenitor of the future Messiah, his conduct with Bathsheba and Uriah the Hittite demanded explanation. The rabbis tended to mitigate the seriousness of David's offense. Rabbi Simeon ben Yohai held that David was not the sort of man to act as he did. God predestined the incident in order to teach Israel the power of repentance and the extent to which it was operative.[49] Rabbi Samuel ben Nahman denied that David had sinned at all. He derived this from the verse "And the Lord was with him."[50] He also maintained that Uriah and all who went to war in those days wrote bills of divorcement for their wives. This practice was instituted lest the husband perish and evidence of his death be unavailable. In such a case, the wife would be unable to remarry according to Jewish law. Bathsheba, the rabbi held, was thus unmarried at the time David took her.[51] These examples of the assimilation of biblical episodes to rabbinic settings could be multiplied indefinitely. Such examples constitute a large part of the subject matter of this book.

Allport and Postman found that rumor could serve as an excellent personality test.[52] They pointed to the fundamental similarity between the processes at work in rumor and legend and those at work in the Rorschach and Thematic Apperception Tests.[53] In the Rorschach test, the subject is presented with an unstructured ink blot. He is asked to describe his feelings concerning the stimulus material. Some individuals report that they see male and/or female genital organs, figures fighting or copulating, witches, and animals.[54] The subjects level out a host of details in order to "see" such figures in haphazard ink blots. In this type of projective test the subject very often reveals his inner feelings and preoccupations without being conscious of his unintended self-revelation.

The Thematic Apperception Test is another projective test which has a similar result. The subject is presented with a series of pictures and is asked to tell whatever stories about them spontaneously come to mind. According to Bellak, the testee's responses give basic data on his relationship to "male and female authority figure, to contemporaries of both sexes . . ."[55] The responses also reveal the "heirarchy of needs and the structure of compromises between id, ego, and superego."[56] The underlying assumption of the T.A.T. is that the ascriptions of feelings, sentiments, needs, and drives elicited by the pictures are in reality reflections of the inner life of the testee. In the terminology of the psychology of rumor, the subject assimilates the ambiguous image in the source to his own pre-existing concerns.

The psychology of rumor, the Rorschach and the T.A.T. all point to the special value of homiletic and expository interpretations of Scripture, such as the Aggadah, for the psychology of religion. In rabbinic legend, the original biblical account functions as do the original stimulus materials in projective tests. The events recorded in the Bible elicited responses which can reveal the underlying preoccupations of its interpreters. Since we possess both the original biblical account and its rabbinic embellishments, we seldom have to resort to conjecture concerning the latent intent of this kind of mythic or legendary tradition. The elaborations and embellishments through which the biblical stories passed at the hands of the rabbis are visible to all. The ways in which the rabbis leveled, sharpened, and assimilated biblical tradition can provide an excellent "personality test" for the psychological understanding of normative Judaism. The legends of the rabbis offer the kind of information about the group which dreams offer concerning the individual. This will prove true, incidentally, of all religious myth and legend based on Scriptural elaboration. The same methods can fruitfully be employed in the psychological investigation of Christianity and Islam.

The basic presupposition of this method is that the way in which a subject or group of subjects alters an original source offers insight into their inner psychological concerns. This method has been in constant use in psychoanalytic practice. During the course of free association, religious symbols and traditions are frequently called forth by the client. Usually, the client utilizes this material in a highly personal way. Thus, Margaretta Bowers has reported that the ritual of Holy Communion has a wide variety of meanings to the members of the clergy who have been her psychotherapeutic patients. Some of her patients identified themselves with the Christ who is sacrificed. Others, with a somewhat more sadistic and aggressive bent, saw themselves as the perpetrators of violence against the Christ. Some saw the Christ in almost feminine terms. The Holy Communion ritual resembled a Rorschach ink blot or a T.A.T. card. It elicited very subjective responses according to the basic personality structures of the celebrant. Very frequently, the highly subjective interpretations offered by psychiatric patients concerning known religious traditions can serve as a key to the dynamic understanding of their unconscious motivations.[57]

While rabbinic Judaism was never a monolith, there was a powerful consensus binding the rabbis and their people. It was an unspoken consensus engrained in their deepest instincts. For all of the seeming surface variety, the Aggadah reveals a large measure

of agreement on the conduct of life, the meaning of Jewish existence, and the meaning of the divine-human encounter. It is possible to study the sayings, traditions, and reflections of individual
rabbis and arrive at a psychological image of the Jewish people as
a whole. No matter how wild or exaggerated some of the legends
may have been, the vast majority conform to a point of view which
could have arisen only out of the peculiar historical, religious,
and psychological conditions faced by the Jewish people in the
first three post-Christian centuries. Were it not for the fact that
the experiences of the rabbis and their community in the face of
Roman hostility and Christian rivalry were paradigmatic of the
Jewish situation in the Western world since that time, their
very special perspectives would have ceased to command the
authority they retain before the Jewish people. There were ex-
ceptions. Nevertheless, there was and is a Jewish religious, and
cultural, and psychological mainstream. It was first given expression in the classical literature of the rabbis of the period under
investigation in this work. Much valuable research remains to
be completed on the psychology of individual rabbis. Such studies
will add immeasurably to the precision with which the psychological understanding of rabbinic Judaism can be advanced. Nevertheless, there need be no delay in attaining a measure of insight
into some of the larger psychological configurations of normative
Judaism. The Aggadah is a veritable treasure of raw material out
of which such insight can be formulated.

3 / Adam, Eve, and the Primal Crime

THE LEGENDS concerning Adam, Eve, and the serpent form a special group within the Aggadah. They are concerned with primal origins and some of the continuing dilemmas of human civilization. Two themes predominate. The first was that a primal offense had been committed against God at the beginning of human history. The second was that, as a consequence, the natural limitations of human existence became punitive in character. Without mankind's first disobedience, none of life's ironies and limitations would have held sway. The rabbis, Paul of Tarsus, and Sigmund Freud have all dealt with the two themes, each in his own way.

In ancient times the careers of Adam, Eve, and the serpent were of crucial importance to the theology of both rabbinic Judaism and Paul of Tarsus. Paul and the rabbis differed on their views concerning the human condition. These were reflected in the way they interpreted the story. The rabbis believed that Adam's offense had alienated his progeny from God. It had brought in its train all the ills that flesh is heir to. The rabbis yearned for a reparation of the breach between man and God.

They did not believe that the time of healing had yet come in their days.

Paul agreed with the rabbis concerning the drastic effects of Adam's sin. His newly found faith led him to far greater hopefulness concerning the human condition. Paul was convinced that Jesus, the second Adam, had reconciled man and God by atoning for the original Adam's misdeed. For Paul existence was, in principle, no longer punitive. Death, brought into the world by Adam's sin, was no longer victorious.

In modern times, the Adam, Eve, and serpent legends have had a curious career. Naïve rationalists regarded them as primitive, unscientific attempts to understand human origins, attempts that had been discredited by Darwin. Few modern thinkers have been as impressed with these legends as Sigmund Freud. He regarded them as ancient parallels to his primal crime hypothesis in *Totem and Taboo*. Freud's speculations concerning a primal crime at the beginning of history were not spun out of thin air. The myths of primal origins in both Judaism and Christianity interpret history as beginning with an act of Promethean disobedience. There are tantalizing parallels between the Adam and Eve story and Freud's myth. In both the condition of man is guilt-ridden, incomplete, and unsatisfactory as the result of an original misdeed. In both the original sin involves a forbidden act of oral incorporation. In *Totem and Taboo* the victim is the primal father. In the Bible the Fall is brought about by the "forbidden fruit." Few ancient or modern commentators have interpreted this aspect of the story literally. Freud saw the biblical account as a distorted "remembrance" of the primal parricide. According to Freud, the forbidden fruit was the primal father.[1]

Freud's interpretation of Adam as the original parricide rests heavily on Paul's myth of the first and second Adam. Paul depicted Jesus as the second Adam who atones for the sins of the first. The apostle explained the broken condition of human finitude as a result of the original sin: "By one man sin entered the world, and death by sin . . ."[2] Paul linked the primal disobedience of Adam to the sacrificial obedience of the Christ. What Adam destroyed, Jesus would repair. As all men were alienated from God through Adam, all would be reconciled through Jesus, the second Adam:

> It follows, then, that as the issue of one misdeed was con-demnation for all men, so the issue of one just act is ac-quittal and life for all men. For as through the disobedience of the one man many were sinners, so through the obedience of the one man the many will be made righteous.[3]

Freud was deeply impressed with the psychological relevance of Paul's argument that the crucifixion offered reparation for Adam's sin. Freud argued that Paul did not specify the original crime for which mankind was condemned to death; that he was, however, moved by an unconscious racial memory of the real nature of Adam's offense. Freud argued that since Adam had brought death into the world by sinning, only a capital crime could warrant so dire a punishment. Adam's crime could only have been the orig-inal parricide. This was the reason for Paul's insistence on the atoning character of the crucifixion and the insufficiency of all other forms of penance. Adam was the generic prototype of the brothers who had murdered the primal father. Freud saw his own myth as making manifest what had remained unconscious in Paul.[4]

According to Freud, Paul's importance largely resided in his ability to formulate the unconscious guilts and anxieties of mankind concerning its original crime and to interpret the death of Jesus as its psychological resolution. Paul's genius lay in the degree to which he was intuitively aware of the unconscious di-lemmas of the race. This accounts for Paul's enormous ability decisively to influence the religious history of the world.

Freud's interpretation of Paul's myth of the second Adam is rich and suggestive. Nevertheless, it suffers from an obvious difficulty. In Scripture, Adam is not the first son but the primal father. Furthermore, Eve and the serpent are the principal vil-lains rather than Adam.

Rabbinic tradition had its own special perspectives on Adam's and mankind's original offense. The rabbis regarded Adam as the first historical personality. They interpreted his predicament as a paradigm of what was to beset his progeny. It is not surprising that Paul shared their views to a great extent. He was trained in their traditions. His thought processes were very similar to theirs. He differed with them primarily on the empirical question of whether Jesus was in fact the awaited Messiah of Israel.

In the rabbinic legends, Adam is primal father and prototype of all mankind. The rabbis express dismay that he was unable to obey even a single commandment.[5] In many traditions he is not regarded as fundamentally evil or rebellious. He is usually a lazy innocent who stumbles into sin. The rabbis followed Scripture and place greater blame on Eve and the serpent than on Adam. Adam sins at Eve's urging after she is persuaded by the real troublemaker. There are legends in which Adam is regarded as a frequent sinner. According to Rabbi Simeon ben Lakish, he was not banished from the garden until he had reviled God.[6] In other traditions, he is depicted as a *min* (heretic) and as an epipastic, one who removed the sign of circumcision.[7] Nevertheless, the rabbis did not stress the singular culpability of Adam, in contrast to Eve and the serpent, as much as did Paul.

Rabbinic literature elaborated greatly on Adam's punishments. It did not alter the biblical theme that Adam is condemned to live by the sweat of his brow because of his sin. Some rabbis referred to ten punishments. This is a schematic reference. It also occurs with Eve and the serpent. Adam lost his celestial clothing. He was forced to eat his bread in sorrow. His food turned bad. His children were destined to be wanderers and exiles. His body began to exude sweat. He was cursed with the *yetzer ha-ra,* the evil inclination. In death his body was prey to worms. Animals were destined to have power over him and to be capable of slaying him. His days were to be few and full of trouble. And, at the last, he was to render an account of all his doings.[8] There is a common thread running through the catalog of Adam's misfor-

tunes: the natural limitations of the human condition are a punitive degradation from a state of primordial grace.

The theme that existence is punitive is constantly reiterated. Adam is depicted as being punitively reduced in size because
of his sin. Before sinning his proportions were global. He extended from one end of the world to the other. Afterwards, he
became so small that he could hide "among the trees of the garden."[9] Rabbi Aibu, a Palestinian teacher, held that Adam's
stature shrank from huge primordial dimensions to one hundred
cubits.[10]

Paul's view that Adam brought death into the world by
sinning coincides with rabbinic teaching: "They asked Adam:
Who brought death to thee?" . . . He replied: "I myself have
caused my death. If I had given heed to what the Physician
[i.e., God] had enjoined me, I would not be dying."[11] Theoreti-
cally, the rabbis held, every man could live forever were he completely without sin.[12] Rabbi Ammi states the rabbinic view of sin
and death: "There is no death without sin, and there is no sin
without iniquity . . ."[13] Without sin, according to the rabbis,
human existence would have been a deathless paradise of effortless
gratification.

Eve is the prototype of her sex as Adam is of the race. Her
portrait is hardly flattering. The rabbis followed Scripture in regarding her as easily beguiled. In the Bible she offends by eating
the forbidden fruit.[14] In the Aggadah her sin is explicitly sexual.
Eve was infused with lust when she copulated with the serpent.[15]
She went from the serpent to promiscuous relationships with
night demons during the one hundred and thirty years that Adam
held aloof from her. She also bore the night demons many children.[16] Eve was the despair of God, according to the rabbis. He
tried His best, but failed to make her chaste and modest. God is
depicted as saying:

"I will not create her [Eve] from [Adam's] head, lest she be
lightheaded (frivolous); nor from the eye, lest she appear

to be a coquette; nor from the ear, lest she be an eavesdropper
. . . But, [I will create her] from the modest part of man,
for even when he stands naked, that part is covered." And
as he created each limb, He ordered her, "Be a modest woman,
be a modest woman." Yet in spite of all this, "But ye [i.e.,
Eve] have set at nought all my counsel" . . . "and would
have none of my reproof."[17]

According to the rabbis, Eve's immodesty and lascivious-
ness were paradigmatic of her sex. Leah, Dinah, and the haughty
daughters of Zion condemned by the prophet Isaiah were no better. In one tradition, Leah plays the harlot, thereby setting a bad
example for her daughter, Dinah: "And Leah went out to meet
him" [i.e., Jacob],[18] which means she went out to meet him
adorned like a harlot; therefore "And Dinah went out."[19] The
rabbis associated the "going out" of the mother with the "going
out" of the daughter. Having interpreted the mother's "going
out" as that of a harlot, they inferred that Dinah had behaved in
a similar way. They also noted that Dinah was referred to by
Scripture as "the daughter of Leah."[20] They concluded that she
was not the daughter of Jacob. They pictured Leah as cuckolding
the patriarch Jacob while he studied Torah in the Yeshivah, the
rabbinical academy, of Shem.[21] This fantasy anachronistically assimilates the biblical tale to the preoccupations and the milieu of
the rabbis. The Yeshivah did not exist in the days of the patriarchs.

The rabbinic treatment of the rape of Dinah by Shechem
is especially revealing. The biblical account of the incident is
rather terse:

> And Dinah the daughter of Leah, whom she had borne unto
> Jacob, went out to see the daughters of the land. And Shechem,
> the son of Hamor the Hivite, the prince of the land, saw her,
> and he took her, and lay with her, and humbled her.[22]

There is little in the Bible to suggest that Dinah's behavior was
unseemly. The rabbis stressed Dinah's guilt. Her misfortune is
interpreted as appropriate retribution for her unseemly conduct.

Dinah's wanton conduct is also linked to Eve's, thereby stressing the prototypical nature of Eve's behavior.[23]

Some traditions use Dinah's rape as illustrative of the verse, "And whoso breaketh through a fence, a serpent shall bite him."[24] Dinah broke a moral fence by seductively walking about while her father and her brothers were studying Torah in a *Beth ha-Midrash*, a rabbinic house of learning. While Jacob and his sons engaged in the most hallowed of all rabbinic activities, religious study, Dinah dallied and attracted so much attention to herself that a foreign prince, the "prince of the land," abused her sexually. This repeats and re-emphasizes the fantasy of Leah's adulterous behavior.

The rabbis imputed further guilt to Dinah by their interpretation of the verse "And Dinah went out to see the daughters of the land." They interpreted the verse as if it were "And Dinah went out to be seen among the daughters of the land." This was done by altering the vocalization of the Hebrew verb.[25] A subtle change in vocalization sharpened the theme of Dinah's guilt.

Every conquered people must deal with the problem of the relations between their women and the conquerors who regard females as one of the spoils of war. This problem was faced by the Jewish community during and after the Judaeo-Roman wars. In the long run, the Jewish community succeeded in maintaining its family structure against overwhelming odds. This success had its price. There was always the latent suspicion that the conquered women had enjoyed and even invited being taken more than they could later admit.

Rabbinic legend betrays much hostility toward women. This was undoubtedly due in part to the natural hostility between the sexes. Some of the hostility must have arisen as a result of the anguish of the conquered. When the rabbis studied the story of Dinah's misfortune in Scripture, they noticed that she had been abused by a foreign ruler. Their own feelings about the relations between their women and the Romans were in all likelihood reflected in the way they retold the story.

The disloyalty of some women before the rapacity of

foreign conquerors was also reflected in rabbinic legends concerning the daughters of Zion whom Isaiah condemned. The prophet denounced their proud and haughty ways: "Because the daughters of Zion are haughty, and walk with stretched forth necks and wanton eyes, walking and mincing as they go . . ."[26] The prophet does not remotely suggest that the women took up with the enemy. At worst, they were pardonably vain. In the Aggadah, the daughters of Zion seek lovers among the conquerors. The rabbis enlarged upon the encounter of Isaiah and the women:

> Isaiah said to them: "Repent before the enemy comes upon you." They answered: "If enemies come, what will they be able to do to us? . . . A general will see me and take me! A governor will see me and take me" . . . When their iniquities increased and the enemy came, they adorned themselves and went out to meet them like harlots. A general saw them and took them . . .[27]

Every conquered nation has had the problem. Rabbinic Jews were no exception.

The natural biological and social limitations of being a woman were interpreted by the rabbis as God's punishment of Eve and her sex. This is already implicit in the Bible. As with Adam, Eve's life before the Fall was one of effortless gratification. After her sin, God says to Eve: "I will greatly multiply thy pain and thy travail. In pain shalt thou bring forth children and thy desire shall be to thy husband"[28] The theme of Eve's punishments was homiletically embellished by R. Eleazer ben Simeon and R. Isaac ben Abdimi. R. Eleazar ben Simeon held that the sufferings of miscarriage are among Eve's punishments.[29] R. Isaac ben Abdimi stressed the punitive character of the feminine aspects of Eve's life:

> Eve was cursed with ten curses, since it was written: "Unto woman He said: I will greatly multiply," which refers to the two drops of blood, one being that of menstruation and

the other that of virginity; "Thy pain" refers to the pain of conception; "in pain shalt thou bring forth children" is to be understood in its literal meaning; "and thy desire shall be to thy husband" teaches that while the wife solicits with the heart, the husband does so with the mouth . . .[30]

Another rabbinic tradition asserts that women grow long hair like Lilith, sit while passing water like beasts, and serve as bolsters for their husbands. R. Isaac ben Abdimi's contention that menstruation was punitively inflicted upon Eve has parallels in other sources.[31] Other punishments include the nine-month period for childbirth, a twelve-month period for nursing, the rule of her husband over her, her husband's jealousy lest she speak to other men, her tendency to age quickly, the fact that her capacity for childbirth is of shorter duration than her husband's ability to beget children, her restriction against showing herself in public or going to the market unless her head is covered like a mourner (in rabbinic times), and, above all, the fact that if she lives truly in accordance with religious tradition, her husband will bury her as Abraham, Isaac, and Jacob buried their wives.[32]

The fantasies of divine retaliation against Adam's body are repeated with Eve. Apparently, the rabbis could not accept the facts of human biology, mortality, or sexuality simply as natural phenomena. They had no sense of the sheer givenness of the world. This was undoubtedly a corollary of their belief that God had created the universe meaningfully and purposefully. Neither they nor Paul regarded existence simply as what is there, what is at hand. They felt compelled to place all natural phenomena within a web of meaning. For the rabbis this web centered on the issue of man's relationship with his Creator. Whatever seemed unpleasant or distasteful was usually treated as the result of God's displeasure at the conduct of rebellious man.

There were very good sociological reasons why the rabbis saw feminine existence as more punitive than masculine existence. Rabbinic society was a community in which men had far greater prerogatives than women. Its liturgy included the well-known prayer in which the traditional Jew thanks God that he has not been made a woman. Women simply thanked God that they had been made according to His will. This prayer continues to be recited every morning in traditional synagogues.[33] There were great differences in the mobility, privileges, and status between men and women. Masculine advantage reinforced the rabbinic view that being a woman was the result of being especially punished.

There is a strong masculine bias both in the Bible and in the Aggadah. One of the most striking examples of that bias is found in the biblical tradition that Eve was created from one of Adam's "ribs." We have already cited the homily of R. Joshua of Siknin in the name of R. Levi in which God is depicted as declaring that he will create Eve after the "modest part of man, for even when he stands naked, that part is covered . . ." It is impossible to prove explicitly that in this tradition Eve is created out of Adam's penis. Nevertheless, this seems to be the meaning. The legend sharpens the biblical story, in which the normal order of human reproduction is reversed. In the Bible woman comes forth from man. There was an enormous overestimation of the status and the prerogative of the male throughout rabbinic Judaism. The reasons for this must have been extremely complex. No explanation which fails to include the stresses of defeat, conquest, and minority status upon male Jews will have any degree of adequacy. Jewish masculinity was decisively challenged by the defeats of Roman times and perhaps earlier. After defeat by the Romans and the alienation of the Jewish community from its ancestral territory, Jewish men lacked the capacity to defend or assure possession of their own women. Many of the problems to which their community was exposed were similar to the problems faced with far greater intensity by the American Negro. One difference between the historic dilemmas of the Jew and the identity problems suffered by the American Negro was that the Jew always resided in communities in which he was normally regarded as a person with rights under the law. The American Negro had no

such recourse under slavery.[34] He has frequently had little recourse since 1865. Nevertheless, laws did not always protect the
Jew. In Roman and Christian times, violence against the Jewish
community often broke through the slender network of legal
status. The Jew reacted to the external threat to his masculinity by
asserting it with extra insistence within his own community. The
social structure and the balance between the sexes within rabbinic
Judaism cannot be understood without taking account of the mili-
tarily impotent condition of Jews throughout most of their
history.

The powerlessness of the Jew and his estrangement from
those in power have often been praised as indispensable for maintaining the monotheistic and ethical purity of Judaism. The Ger-
man-Jewish thinker, Franz Rosenzweig, saw the homelessness
and powerlessness of the Jewish community as a special virtue.[35]
It enabled the community to maintain its eternal fellowship with
God, uncorrupted by the vicissitudes of power that afflicted the
other nations. After the extermination of six million Jews, one
can legitimately ask whether a condition of such radical powerlessness has anything to recommend itself. Apart from this issue,
neither Rosenzweig nor his American Jewish followers have
noted the cost of Jewish powerlessness in terms of the male-fe-
male balance and the stresses experienced by the Jewish male in
his attempt to assure the safety of his community under constant
conditions of radical threat. The response of the Jew to his minority status has too often been elevated to the status of an eternal
principle of morality. The Jewish family structure and the overstress on masculinity were functional, given the terms under
which the Jew had to exist. It would be stretching matters to
exaggerate the universal significance of these responses under
other conditions. There is no special virtue in powerlessness.

The serpent is the third member of the original group in
the Bible and the Aggadah. The serpent legends are also paradigmatic. They contain intuitive reflections on the origins of the
human community. There are some sources in which the serpent is

identified with Satan; in others he is Satan's agent.[36] The Bible does not explicitly state that the serpent was male. The rabbinic traditions take this for granted. The most interesting tradition is an old Palestinian legend that the serpent originally possessed the upright posture of a man. He was destined to rule over all the other animals save man. In consequence of his sin God cut off his arms and legs. The rabbis interpret the verse "Upon thy belly shalt thou go" as evidence that before sinning the serpent had more adequate means of locomotion.[37]

According to the rabbis, the serpent was moved by the desire to displace Adam, rule over the world in his stead, and possess Eve. This is evident in a very important Palestinian tradition which exists in a number of variants:

> What was the wicked serpent contemplating at the time? He thought: "I shall go and kill Adam and wed his wife, and I shall be king over all the earth. I shall walk with upright posture and eat all of the world's dainties." Said the Holy One, blessed be He, to him: Thy thought was, I shall kill Adam and wed Eve; therefore, "I will put enmity between thee and the woman."
>
> Thy thought was, I shall be king over the whole world; therefore "Cursed art thou from among all cattle." Thy thought was, I shall walk with upright posture; therefore "Upon thy belly shalt thou go." Thy thought was, I shall eat of the world's dainties; therefore "Dust shalt thou eat all the days of thy life."[38]

The serpent is principally moved by his desire to displace the primal father. The sexual theme is present but not predominant. The serpent wants to enjoy Adam's prerogatives, one of which is sexual possession of Eve. The Promethean element is very strong. The serpent seeks dominion over the earth in Adam's stead. Scripture speaks of the serpent's cunning. It does not specify his motives. They are specified by the rabbis. They assimilate the serpent's tale to a conflict with strong Oedipal overtones.

It is very likely that, here as elsewhere, the rabbis unconsciously restore an archaic element to these legends which had been lost in the Bible. The Bible suppresses a mythological content which the Aggadah seems to reinstate. This becomes evident in a comparison of the rabbinic legends with the psychoanalytic interpretation of the Fall. The rabbinic legends of the serpent's punitive mutilation have been overlooked in the psychoanalytic interpretations. Theodore Reik follows Freud. He depicts Adam as the primal son in rebellion against God, the primal father, for the possession of the primal mother.[39] His interpretation reflects Paul's myth of the first and second Adam. It does some violence to the biblical account. In the Bible the serpent is the first rebel, not Adam. There is no hint of any necessity on Adam's part to win Eve. She comes forth from his body to be his proper mate.

Before the expulsion from the garden, sexual feelings are absent in the Bible. This would accord with the idea expressed by both the rabbis and Paul that death came into the world through sin. Adam and Eve become aware of their nakedness only after sinning. Sexuality is humanity's necessary response to the mortality with which Adam is cursed as a result of his offense. Without death men would have no need to procreate. The author of the biblical story intuits the connection between sex and death. Sexuality is not Adam's sin. It follows from his punishment. Freud and Reik see the biblical story of Adam, Eve, and the serpent as a disguised version of the primal crime. Had their research included the rabbinic legends, they might have noticed the greater parallelism between the Aggadah and *Totem and Taboo*. In the Bible, the serpent's motive is unclear. In the Aggadah his motive is the same as that of the sons in *Totem and Taboo*, displacement of the primal father and possession of the forbidden female. The Aggadah lacks only a specific reference to the serpent as the primal son to make the parallel altogether explicit. Even without it, the rabbinic legend of the serpent as the original rebel more closely parallels the myth of the primal crime than Freud and Reik's forced interpretation of Adam as the first rebel.

The rabbinic legends of Adam, Eve, and the serpent

mythically depict some of the principal anxieties as well as the temptations of the Oedipal conflict. Freud maintained that the son is deterred from acting out his desire to possess the mother by the unconscious anxiety that he will be castrated by the father. Freud also held that there is no distinction between thought and deed in the unconscious.[40] In the Aggadah the serpent is mutilated in consequence of his *intended* destruction of the primal father and possession of Eve. Thought and deed are equated. There is no explicit reference to castration. Nevertheless, the mutilation of all of the serpent's appendages can hardly be interpreted in any other light. A manlike creature whose appendages are completely removed would be functionally castrated, even if explicit reference to castration is absent from the legend.

The parallels between the rabbinic legends and *Totem and Taboo* concerning the primal crime do not necessarily validate Freud's hypothesis. They do add a note of corroboration to a suggestion I made about both the Aggadah and Freud. I suggested that the Aggadah is an excellent window to the fantasy world of rabbinic Judaism. Insofar as the unconscious dimension of rabbinic thought was given verbal expression, it was through the instrumentality of the Aggadah. The legends were a veritable repository of the rabbinic unconscious. The rabbinic fantasies of the first conflict within the human family offer intuitive and non-conceptual images which significantly parallel the Oedipal conflict as described by Freud. What Freud made conceptually explicit was expressed by the rabbis in legendary images whose psychological accuracy was heightened just because they were free-flowing and untied to the rigidities of an *a priori* conceptual structure.

Had Freud known of the rabbinic traditions of the serpent's attempt to displace Adam and his subsequent mutilation, he might have contended that the tradition represented a partial uncovering of an unconscious racial memory of the dire event with which civilization had its origins. There is no necessity to postulate an unconscious racial memory in order to understand the relevance of either the rabbis' myth or Freud's. The value of both myths lies in their ability to rehearse and dramatize some of the continuing conflicts which draw men to religion in every age. The Oedipal conflict is inescapable as long as men are barred from the first object of love by male parental figures upon whom they depend and whom they seek to emulate. Man is a creature divided against himself. He can neither abide nor dispense with the limitations inherent in his social institutions. No human institution can compare with the family in terms of its biological and emotional primacy. It is not surprising that both Freud and the rabbis saw the first human community as beset with many of the same dilemmas of love, hate, ambivalence, and rebelliousness.

There is one element in Freud's myth which rings far less true than the account of Adam, Eve, and the serpent in the Aggadah. In his tale of the envious parricides, Freud says nothing concerning what the women were up to. It is inconceivable that so decisive a conflict about the possession of the females could have taken place entirely without their participation. The rabbinic account may have had an antifeminine bias, but it at least suggested that no member of the original family was entirely without a measure of responsibility.

4 / The Tenth Plague

THE MOST DECISIVE SEQUENCE of events in Israelite history was the redemption from Egyptian bondage and the wilderness experience under Moses. These events are relived by the Jewish community throughout the cycle of its religious calendar. They comprise the principal historical setting of four of the five books of the Torah. These books are read and expounded in the synagogue every week. Every Sabbath and Holy Day is thought of as a "remembrance of the going out of Egypt."

The Exodus was the redemptive experience of the Jewish people par excellence. Moses is the prototypical redeemer. Israel's Messiah will be of the lineage of David, but he will be a second Moses. As Moses led Israel from slavery to freedom, the second Moses will lead Israel into the final redemption. He will complete what the first Moses began.[1] The final redemption will perfect the Egyptian redemption.

The Exodus was preceded by the ten plagues. The last and the most terrible plague was the smiting of the first-born of Egypt. Of all the plagues visited upon the Egyptians before the departure of the Israelites, none engraved itself so deeply upon the psyche of the Jewish people as the tenth plague. As retold in the Aggadah, the story contains significant details which are totally absent from the Bible. In one oft-repeated tradition, the first-born are described as bringing their fate upon themselves. When they heard that they would be destroyed because of their elders' refusal to permit Israel to depart, they appealed to Pharaoh to send Israel forth, thus ending their danger. Pharaoh refused. The first-born returned to their homes. In anger, they slew their own fathers. Only after they had become parricides did God reveal Himself and slaughter them:

> The first-born of Egypt came and said to their fathers: "All that Moses promised, he has brought upon us. If you wish us to remain alive, go and send the Hebrews out of our midst. For if you do not send them forth, we shall die." The fathers answered saying: "Even if all the Egyptians die, the Hebrews shall not go hence." What did the first-born do? All the first-born went to Pharaoh and cried out to Pharaoh: "We beseech thee, O Pharaoh! Send forth this people on whose account evil will come upon us and Thee also!" But Pharaoh said to his servants: "Go and beat these people [i.e., the first-born] until they are humpbacked." What did the first-born then do? They went out at once, and each one of them took his sword, and slew his own father, for it is said "To Him that smote Egypt *with* their first-born."[2] Scripture does not say "To Him that smote the first-born of Egypt," but says "To Him that smote Egypt *with* their first-born." And the first-born of Egypt slew myriads of their fathers.[3]

There is no explicit suggestion in the Bible that the father-son conflict is involved in the tenth plague. The Aggadah assimilates the slaughter to that conflict. The Oedipal conflict becomes decisive in the Aggadah.

In reality, the conflict between the generations is by no means absent from the biblical account of the first Passover. Passover was the oldest Israelite festival. The Bible indicates that it was known to the Hebrews before they left Egypt.[4] Roland de Vaux has succinctly described the archaic character of the Passover sacrifice: "No other Israelite sacrifice is more like the sacrifices of the ancient Arabs. There is no priest, no altar, and the use of blood is most important."[5] In ancient times, a lamb without blemish was selected on the tenth of Nisan. On the fourteenth of Nisan between twilight and dark the victim was publicly slaughtered. Its blood was taken and smeared with a bunch of hyssop on the doorposts of the houses. The animal was roasted whole and entirely consumed, together with matzoth and bitter herbs. The meal was required to be eaten in haste. Whatever remained over in the morning had to be burned.[6]

The Passover offering was a *zebah,* a sacrifice in which the slaughtered victim was consumed for food at a sacred meal. The *zebah* greatly resembled the archaic totem feast.[7] There is at least a hint that the paschal sacrifice was in some sense a surrogate for a human victim. God promises to pass over the homes of the children of Israel provided they exhibit the blood of a sacrificial animal. If they fail to do so, the first-born will be slaughtered.[8] The threat is clear: either the blood of the lamb or the first-born. The blood of the sacrifice alone assures the safety of the Israelite first-born. The Egyptians have no surrogate. Their first-born are struck down.

The story of God passing over the first-born of Israel contains one of the oldest and most persistent of all Jewish religious motifs. From time immemorial normative Judaism has handled the temptation to homicidal sacrifice by utilizing an animal or a monetary surrogate. This is apparent in the Passover story. The rejection of the human or the divine-human sacrifice is a constantly reiterated theme throughout Jewish religious history. The Torah reading on Rosh Hashana describes how God commanded Abraham to offer Isaac as a human sacrifice and then permitted the substitution of the ram.[9] The point of the reading is that it was not necessary for Abraham to offer his first-born. The animal was acceptable. Nevertheless, the necessity to emphasize the acceptability of a surrogate makes sense only if the homicidal temptation was originally very strong and/or remains unconsciously potent to this day.

We know that the oldest traditions of prehistoric Israel involved infant sacrifice. Traces of the most archaic traditions are to be found in such oft-quoted passages as: "The first-born of your sons you shall give to me. You shall do likewise with your oxen and with your sheep: seven days it shall be with its dam; on the eighth day you shall give it to me."[10] Also: "Sanctify unto me all the first-born, whatever openeth the womb among the Israelites, both of the men and of beast; it is mine."[11] No distinction is made between animal and human first-fruits. As Johannes Pedersen pointed out, a distinction is made at a later stage when only the animal first-born are devoted to slaughter. The first-born male is redeemed: "All the first-born of your sons you shall redeem."[12]

In spite of this, in the time of Jeremiah and Ezekiel, Israelites once again practiced sacrificial infanticide. Both prophets condemned the practice. Jeremiah denied that God had so commanded Israel. Ezekiel had a more demonic interpretation. He described the slaughter of the first-born as God's punishment for Israel's infidelity:

> Because they had not executed my judgments, but had despised my statutes, and had polluted my sabbaths . . . Wherefore I gave them also statutes that were not good, and judgments whereby they should not live; and I polluted them in their own gifts, in that they caused to pass through the fire all that openeth the womb, that I might make them desolate, to the end that they might know that I am the Lord.[13]

Scholarly opinion favors the interpretation that child sacrifice was basically Canaanite rather than Israelite.[14] Nevertheless, the custom struck a deep enough response among the Israelites to take hold for a while. The manifest practice was finally obliterated.

Some traces of the sacrifice have never been obliterated.

To this day it is obligatory for religious Jews to "redeem" their
first-born males. The father presents his first-born son to a *cohen,*
a hereditary priest, on the thirty-first day of his birth. The father
declares:

> "This my first-born son is the first-born of his mother, and
> the Holy One, blessed be He, hath given a command to re-
> deem him as it is said: 'And those that are to be redeemed of
> them from a month old shalt thou redeem, according to thine
> estimation, for the money of five shekels after the shekel of
> the sanctuary, the shekel being twenty gerahs';[15] and it is said:
> 'Sanctify unto me all the first-born, of man and of beast: It
> is mine'."[16]

The father places five silver dollars before the priest. The money
is regarded as symbolically equivalent to the biblical five shekels.
The priest asks the father: "Which wouldst thou rather give,
thy first-born son, the first-born of his mother, or redeem him
for five *selaim,* which thou art bound to give according to the
Torah?" The father is required to reply: "I desire to redeem my
son, and here thou hast the value of his *redemption,* which I am
bound to give according to the Torah." After reciting the appropriate benedictions, the priest takes the redemption money
and holds it over the child's head. He says: "This instead of that,
this is commutation for that, this in remission of that."[18] The
traditional Jewish interpretation of the ceremony is that in
ancient Israel the first-born of each household was devoted to
the service of God. After the building of the Sanctuary, the sons
of Aaron took this function upon themselves. They were, however, merely taking the place of the first-born. The *pidyon ha-ben,*
or redemption of the first-born, ceremony served to set the first-
born morally and spiritually free from their priestly duties.[17]
This is clearly a rationalizing and a censoring explanation.

    The ceremony can best be understood in terms of the in-
fant sacrifices of ancient Israel and its pagan predecessors. The
ceremony represents a characteristically Jewish way of handling

a socially dysfunctional temptation. It would have been psycho-logically impossible to preach the infanticidal tendency out of existence. Judaism offered a substitute activity. Judaism's genius lay in its recognition of the ineradicable hostility between the generations. The problem was recognized and dealt with. It was not swept under a rug. No pretense was made that it did not exist.

This hostility is largely unconscious. It is nevertheless very potent. It takes years of psychoanalytic probing before such hostility can be effectively recognized and dealt with in our secular culture. The traditional Jewish method of dealing with the problem involves a dramatic ritual in which the hostility is both unconsciously expressed and sublimated by means of a substitute activity. Sublimation is the characteristically Jewish way of handling the stresses of the unconscious.

The unconscious is normally handled differently in Chris-tianity. Unconscious feelings are allowed to surface under strictly controlled conditions. Whether or not we agree with Freud that the Lord's Supper is an unconscious re-enactment of the primal crime, some very strong elements of hostility and aggression are both expressed and dealt with in the ritual.[18] On any interpreta-tion the Holy Communion ritual re-enacts the sacrificial offering of the first-born, God's first-born in Christianity.

I have suggested that Freud's speculation must be taken seriously, at least on the level of myth. In the Fourth Gospel, Jesus is explicitly identified with the Passover lamb. When Jesus appears at the Jordan to be baptized, John the Baptist proclaims: "Behold, the lamb of God, who takes away the sins of the world."[19] This has been incorporated into the liturgy of the Roman Catholic Mass: "Agnus dei, qui tollis peccata mundi . . ." We do not know whether these words were said by John. It hardly matters. They have become part of the psychological in-heritance of the Christian Church. They are an expression of the Church's attempt to define itself in the light of the sacrificial role of the Christ. Jesus is the lamb. The lamb is the hidden anticipation of the sacrificial son of God. For the Church, Jesus is the true lamb made concrete and manifest after having been unconsciously anticipated in Judaism. His death is the externalization of a very specific inner wish.

One of the oldest continuing claims of the Church against Judaism is that Jews do not know how truly to read the Bible. Jews are said to have a veil over their eyes when they read Scripture.[20] According to the Church, Jews cannot see that Scripture's very essence is the anticipation of the full revelation of Jesus as the atoning sacrifice and Redeemer of mankind. Translated psychoanalytically, the Church claims that it brings to the light of consciousness what is unconsciously present in Judaism. This claim would seem to be psychologically valid.[21] It helps to explain why the most archaic sacrificial victim in Judaism, the paschal lamb, becomes identified with the person of the Christ in Christianity.

Elsewhere in the New Testament, Jesus is explicitly identified with the paschal lamb and its blood. The author of I Peter addresses fellow Jews who believe that Jesus is Israel's promised Messiah and its perfect sacrificial offering: "You know that you were ransomed from the futile ways inherited from your fathers . . . with the precious blood of Christ, like that of a lamb without blemish or spot."[22] The lamb was immediately understood by Jewish readers of the time as the paschal offering. Just as the paschal lamb served as a substitute for the Israelite first-born, Jesus serves as a surrogate offering not only for the first-born but for all mankind.[23]

Parricide and infanticide are twin themes. They are inseparable. They are expressions of one of mankind's deepest and most abiding problems, the hostility and rivalry between the generations. According to Theodore Reik, the practice of the sacrificial slaughter of the first-born is the result of the father's unconscious identification with the son. The father unconsciously recalls his own death wishes toward his father. He intuits that the son has or will have the same murderous thoughts toward him.

His homicidal inclination arises out of an unconscious fear of the son's Oedipal wishes.[24]

Some scholars have suggested that Freud's emphasis was misplaced. They claim that infanticide is a far greater human problem than parricide.[25] The evidence of the history of religion and the Bible certainly corroborates this contention. Nevertheless, the fundamental insight common to those who see infanticide as the greater threat and those who stress parricide is the same. Human institutions are fundamentally endangered by the ineradicable hostility, aggression, and rivalry of the generations within the most indispensable and intimate unit of human civilization, the family. The oldest and the most decisive myths and rituals of mankind are devoted to giving expression to and limiting the destructiveness of this problem. The two great rival religions of the Western world do not part company on their intuitive recognition of the potential for violence within the family. Both seek to contain the destructiveness. They offer mankind radically different psychodynamic instrumentalities with which to cope with the problem. Needless to say, the utilization of different media for dramatizing and overcoming parricide, matricide, fratricide, and infanticide result in radically different personality types.

The tradition in the Aggadah of the Egyptian first-born as parricides helps to fill a gap in both Jewish and Christian theology. The sin for which the first-born are endangered is not specified in Exodus. The sin for which Jesus atones by his death is not explicitly specified in the New Testament. The Aggadah is quite specific. The conviction that without the atoning sacrifice the human victim would be required is basic to both traditions. We do not have to take the rabbinic legend literally. We need only note that when some of the rabbis meditated on the story of the slaughter of the first-born, their fantasies led them intuitively to postulate parricide as the crime which warranted God's retribution at the Passover season.

It is not necessary to assume Freud's phylogenetic memory to see parricidal and infanticidal elements at work in both the Passover and Easter festivals. Patriarchal societies are always endangered by the potential hostility between fathers and sons. In every generation fathers will see their sons as both their continuation and their deadly rivals. They will see their own deaths prefigured in their sons' vitality. Sons will regard fathers as the decisive models for identification and as the hated authorities who must murderously be overcome. In spite of all rational efforts at cooperation and order, some measure of ambivalence will never disappear. This ambivalence is more often unconscious than conscious. It is felt most strongly at the primary process level. The sense of guilt is heightened because the conflicts are so largely unconscious. The unconscious wish to kill a father or a son leads to almost as great a measure of guilt as actual violence. At times the sense of guilt can become intolerable. Sublimation can only prevent the actual deed. This is Judaism's strength. Sublimation can do little or nothing to mollify the sense of unconscious guilt. If anything it only makes matters worse, as Paul observed when he complained: "What shall we say then? Is the Law sin? God forbid. Nay, I had not known sin, but by the Law; for I had not known lust, except the Law had said, Thou shalt not covet. But sin taking occasion by the commandment, wrought in me all manner of concupiscence . . ."[26]

The Law taught Paul what to avoid. There is good evidence that Paul rejected what he had been commanded to avoid. Nevertheless, Paul could not escape a painful sense of guilt for his often unconscious wish to violate the commandments. The success of the commandments in lessening Paul's conscious guilt was joined with their tendency to heighten his unconscious guilt for acts committed in fantasy. This problem did not concern rabbinic Judaism to the degree to which it concerned primitive Christianity. In the Sermon on the Mount, Jesus specified the difference between his view of righteousness and that of the rabbis or Pharisees: "For I say unto you, that except your righteousness shall exceed the righteousness of the Pharisees, ye shall in no case enter the kingdom of heaven."[27] The actions of the best

Pharisees were exemplary; Jesus was not referring to their conscious acts. He continues:

> You have heard that it was said by them of old time, Thou shalt not kill; and whosoever shall kill shall be in danger of judgment:
> But I say unto you, That whoever is angry with his brother without a cause shall be in danger of judgment . . . Ye have heard that it was said by them of old time, Thou shalt not commit adultery: But I say unto you, That whosoever looketh on a woman to lust after her hath committed adultery with her already in his heart.[28]

Judaism rested content with the control of conscious actions.[29] It valued proper intention but did not insist upon it. Jesus led Christianity in insisting on absolute purity of thought and feeling. It is far easier to control deeds. It is quite possible to lust after a woman, yet refrain from doing anything about it. The very knowledge that an action is prohibited could incite to deeper temptation. By equating thought, feeling, and deed, primitive Christianity made sublimation untenable as a means of overcoming unconscious guilt. If the very temptation made a man guilty, the quest for substitute activities was futile. The early Christians needed a far more dramatic assurance that their guilt had been absolved than the mere knowledge that they had not offended in actuality. Once crimes of feeling and fantasy were equated with reality, Paul was absolutely correct in suggesting that no human action (i.e., the Law) could undo his sense of sin (we would call it the feeling of guilt).

The hostility between the generations was a serious matter in the Jewish community. Nevertheless, it was manageable. Jewish law prescribed the norms incumbent upon fathers and sons. It also provided rituals to deal with the moments of crisis in the relations between the generations, such as circumcision, the *pidyon ha-ben* ceremony, and, in modern times, *bar mitzvah*. Each of these rituals had the effect of recognizing and overcoming the antagonism within the family at a particular moment in the life cycle.

Once guilt for fantasy was equated with guilt for actual deeds, the matter required a more radical cure. In Christianity that cure was psychological identification with the divine-human sacrificial victim. Since guilt for homicidal feelings was unavoidable in Christianity, there had to be punishment. By identifying with the Christ, the Christian believer dramatized, confessed, and expiated his guilt. In Judaism guilt was not inevitable because feelings alone did not make the believer guilty.

Hatred and love are the twin foundations upon which both Judaism and Christianity rest. Without the enormous potentiality for aggression inherent in the dynamics of the human family, neither religion would have come into existence. Religious institutions such as circumcision, the Passover *seder,* Easter Sunday, and Holy Communion would never have developed in the special way they did. Both Judaism and Christianity rest upon a vast impulse to hatred and aggression which requires greater and more difficult containment in man than in any other animal.[30] Nevertheless, the development of the characteristic institutions of religion is testament to the greater power of human love. The destructive potentialities of the human family were recognized and given nondestructive expression. Each of the great traditions is the fruit of the resolve that hatred not be the final word spoken by mankind. The aspects of the family rooted in the impulse toward love and nurture were permitted to develop with least impediment from the power of human hate.

It is not surprising that Freud located the origins of religion in the conflicts and aspirations of the family. What is surprising is how long it has taken before the obvious could be given conceptual formulation. In the Bible the tenth plague is the final prelude to Israel's redemption. In a deeper sense, the tenth plague symbolizes that from which men must be redeemed in every age, the destructiveness which forever threatens the most intimate and indispensable of all human institutions, the family.

5 / The Meaning of Anxiety
in Rabbinic Judaism

THE PHENOMENON of anxiety has been of increasing interest to philosophers, psychologists and theologians from the time of publication of *The Concept of Dread* by Søren Kierkegaard.[1] A thinker's understanding of the nature of anxiety has often served to illuminate his fundamental point of view. This was especially true of Sigmund Freud. Castration anxiety was the anxiety par excellence for Freud.[2] There was considerable development in Freud's conception of anxiety. As Rollo May has suggested, the trend in Freud's understanding of castration anxiety was toward an increasingly symbolic interpretation. May emphasizes that, in Freud's thought, anxiety has its ultimate source "in the fear of premature loss of or separation from the mother (or mother's love)." This conception is applicable to castration anxiety. Fear of castration is fear of the loss of that organ with which one would return to the mother or mother-surrogate.[3] Freud's conception of anxiety was particularly relevant to the psychoanalytic interpretation of Judaism. From the perspective of many psychoanalysts, fear of the Lord in Judaism is ultimately fear of the castrating father.[4]

Freud's interpretation of anxiety differed from Tillich's

and Heidegger's. The latter regarded *Urangst,* man's primordial apprehension of the nothingness that forever threatens to envelop him, as primary and irreducible.[5] Freud held that, more often than not, fear of death is a covert form of castration anxiety. He argued that since we have no proper concept of death or nothingness, men are really anxious lest they lose their masculine power when they imagine that they fear death.[6]

Freud maintained that all men unconsciously desire to rid themselves of fathers and parental surrogates. Since the ultimate motive for antipaternal hostility is return to the mother, men are beset by anxiety lest their temptation entail punitive retaliation against the offending male organ. Men internalize their image of the father as the superego or objectify it as God in order to avoid this misfortune. They thus commence a lifelong servitude to one of the earliest objects of their own envy. The temptation which leads to superego formation is sexual. As a result, the deepest unconscious anxiety is said to be that any behavioral deviance will lead to castration.[7]

The importance of castration anxiety has often been stressed in the psychoanalytic interpretation of Judaism.[8] Psychoanalysts have tended to interpret circumcision as symbolic castration.[9] The centrality of circumcision in Judaism is said to have had the effect of greatly reinforcing the castration anxiety of both Jew and gentile.[10]

The tendency to reduce Jewish religious deviance to sexual offense is very old and historically rooted. Insofar as the metaphor of the primal crime is applicable, Freud regarded religion as the result of the desire of the brothers of the primal horde to prevent a repetition of the murderous and deicidal deed. There was a consistent tendency in biblical Judaism to regard idolatry and rebellion against God as forms of sexual sin. The prophets insistently inveighed against those who went "awhoring" after other gods. Sins which were interpreted as sexual offenses engendered the fear of sexual retaliation. This was heightened by the fact that rabbinic Judaism explicitly accepted the measure-for-measure principle, the idea that punitive retaliation is directed against the offending organ.[11]

There are relatively few explicit instances of punitive castration invented or cited by the rabbis in the Aggadah. Nevertheless, they can be found. The most explicit traditions in which the sinner is thus punished concern the biblical characters Potiphar and the couple Zimri and Cozbi.

According to the rabbis, Potiphar hardly deserved a better wife than the one he possessed. They regarded him as a homosexual who purchased Joseph for his own purposes. In retaliation, they maintain, God castrated him. The tradition that he was castrated is dependent upon their interpretation of the biblical word *saris* as "castrate" or "eunuch." Scripture refers to him as "Potiphar, a *saris* of Pharaoh."[12] Usually, *saris* is translated as "officer." It can be translated as "eunuch" or "castrate." The story of his misfortune is given in the Aggadah:

> "A *saris* of Pharaoh." This indicates that he was castrated, thus teaching that he [Potiphar] purchased him [Joseph] for the purpose of sexual abuse whereupon the Holy One, blessed be He, emasculated him . . . Hence it is written, "For the Lord loveth justice and forsaketh not His saints,"[13] which is actually written "His saint"[14] and refers to Joseph: "They are preserved forever: but the seed of the wicked shall be cut off"[15]—[meaning]—that God emasculated him.[16]

This legend takes an ambiguous biblical tale and assimilates it to one in which God Himself causes the sinner to be castrated. The verse "The seed of the wicked shall be cut off" would normally mean that the wicked shall fail of progeny. The rabbis take it to mean that they shall fail through punitive castration.

Even if the rabbis were correct in interpreting *saris* as eunuch, nothing in the Bible suggests that God castrated Potiphar in retaliation for his homosexual designs on Joseph. This detail originates in the rabbinic imagination. In most rabbinic sources God Himself castrates Potiphar. An agent does the deed on God's behalf in one tradition.[17]

Castration is also explicit in the legends concerning Zimri and Cozbi. According to Scripture, immediately after Israel's idolatry with Baal Peor, Phinehas, the priest and nephew of Moses, sought to avenge the Lord by punishing the chief sinners. Among the offenders were Zimri the son of Salu, a prince of the house of Simeon, and Cozbi, his idolatrous Midianite paramour. In the biblical account, Phinehas thrust his javelin at the couple in such a way that it went through the man and the "belly" of the offending woman. The plague sent by God against the entire camp of Israel was thus stayed.[18]

This tale reflects one of the most difficult problems of ancient Israel: the attraction of the more permissive non-Israelite cults and the consequent difficulties inherent in the interdict against intermarriage. The biblical story is terse and demands homiletic embellishment. As the rabbis retell the story, Cozbi is no longer merely the foreign paramour of Zimri. She is the daughter of Balak, the Midianite king, who, on the advice of Balaam, is prepared to prostitute his own daughter in order to bring about the downfall of Moses. Zimri demands that Cozbi surrender herself to him. She replies that her father commanded her to yield only to Moses, Israel's greatest man. Zimri thereupon seizes her hair and declares that he is greater than Moses. This introduces a hint of sexual rivalry between the leader and a rebellious member of his flock. After a time, Phinehas went out to punish the couple. There are a number of variations in the rabbinic description of what transpired. One is stated on the authority of Rabbi Johanan:

> Six miracles were wrought for Phinehas: Zimri should have withdrawn from Cozbi, but did not; he should have cried out [for help] but didn't; [Phinehas] *succeeded in driving his spear exactly through the sex organs of the man and the*

> *woman:* an angel came and lifted up the lintel; an angel came
> and wrought destruction among the people.[19]
> (italics mine)

In another source, Phinehas pierces both offenders while they lie
coupled together. Rabbi Johanan's six miracles became twelve.[20]
The new tradition may represent a later stage in the development
of the story. In the embellished legend the couple are kept locked
in intercourse long after they would normally have separated.
The spear enters Cozbi's belly so that it catches Zimri's genitals.
God did this so that no one would think that Phinehas had acted
out of motives of personal hatred. The locked couple did not
slide down when the spear was held aloft. Their sinful conduct
was thus apparent to all. Finally, God preserved their spirits alive
while they were suspended. This prevented Phinehas the priest
from being ritually defiled as he held the spear. Had the couple
perished Phinehas would have been under a priestly prohibition
against touching the corpses.[21]

There is also a vast overestimation of Zimri's sexual capacities in related traditions:

> R. Nahman said . . . That wicked man [i.e., Zimri] co-
> habited four hundred and twenty-four times that day, and
> Phinehas waited for his strength to weaken . . . In a Baraitha
> we learnt: Sixty [times] until he became like an addled egg,
> whilst she became like a furrow filled with water. R. Kahana
> said: And her seat was a *beth seah* (i.e., she became very
> bloated). R. Joseph learned: Her womb was open a cubit.[22]

Apart from the specific issue of castration anxiety, the
Zimri-Cozbi stories are interesting because of the association of
unbridled sexuality and rebellion against authority figures in this
rabbinic fantasy. This element is present in the Bible. It is greatly
sharpened in the legends. The punitive elements are also greatly
emphasized by the rabbis.

On the basis of psychoanalytic insight, it may be surmised that the biblical "belly" is a euphemism for genitals. This is made explicit in the Aggadah. Here again it is to be noted that the Aggadah frequently retells a story so that the primary process meaning is restored in contrast to that in the often rationalized and censored biblical source. The rabbinic myths restore an unconscious dimension. This is in all probability the result of rabbinic free association on the biblical text.

Another element in this legend related to castration anxiety is the hint at the idea of the *vagina dentata*. Phinehas' inability to withdraw from the sexual posture is explicitly stated, as we have seen, in one of the traditions.

The rabbis also inserted an explicit reference to castration in the tale of the ten plagues God bestowed upon the Egyptians. The Bible says very little concerning the discomfiting of the Egyptians by the frogs. In the legends, the frogs are pictured as leaping at the genitals of the Egyptian noblemen and ripping them off:

> This was one of nine occasions when the Holy One, blessed be He, gave the frail mastery over the tough. Whenever a frog would come and declare: "I am the emissary of the Holy One, blessed be He," the marble [of the Egyptian nobles' houses] would split open forthwith, and the frog would get up into the house. With reference to this, it is said: "The frog which destroyed them,"[23] that is, wrung their privy parts.[24]

The reference to punitive castration is explicit. The frogs act only as God's agents. There is no warrant for this in Scripture.

The final legend in which the rabbis added the idea of punitive castration to a biblical tale was the one about Ham's castration of Noah. In the Bible, Ham merely uncovers the nakedness of his father.[25] In the rabbinic traditions, Ham desires to prevent his father from cohabiting with his mother. He castrates Noah.[26] Usually, the rabbis interpreted Noah's misfortune as

God's retaliation for failing expeditiously to fulfill the commandment that he be fruitful and multiply.[27] There is also a related
tradition that Noah was sexually incapacitated when he left the
ark.[28] In both traditions, a sin of phallic omission is taken as the
reason for divinely inflicted castration.

To the best of my knowledge, there are few, if any, other
traditions in the vast corpus of legends known as the Aggadah
in which castration is an actual punishment of a sinner. I have
attempted diligently to search out all of the relevant traditions
concerning sin and punishment in rabbinic legend. I have examined thousand of such legends. I know of no other *explicit*
reference to the punitive castration of the sinner. There is one
other legend in which God appears explicitly as a castrator. According to one rabbinic tradition God castrated the primeval
monster Leviathan in order to prevent its fantastic ability to
multiply from rendering the world uninhabitable.[29] There is,
however, no punitive element.

In addition to explicit legends concerning punitive castration, there are many in which castration is hinted at in thinly
disguised form. In the psychoanalytic description of the onset of
the castration complex, the child's masturbatory activity is accompanied by the fear that the organ will be punished measure
for measure. At the primary process level of mental functioning, thought and deed are equivalent. The deviant is said to fear
measure-for-measure retaliation for his guilty wishes. The
measure-for-measure principle is the principle of punitive equity
in the unconscious. It was also the principle operative in the
Aggadah.

The measure-for-measure principle was regarded as the
fundamental principle of punitive equity in both the legal
(Halakah) and the mythic (Aggadah) parts of rabbinic literature. It is explicitly enunciated in the Mishnah, the definitive
codification of Jewish religious law compiled in Palestine in the
early part of the third century: "In the measure with which a
man measures, it is meted out to him."[30]

The most interesting application of the measure-for-measure principle in this source is that of the *sotah*, the woman suspected of adultery who is compelled to submit to the biblical test of drinking the bitter waters:

> She bedecked herself for transgression—the Almighty brought her to shame; she laid herself bare for transgression—the Almighty likewise laid her bare; she began transgression with the thigh first—therefore the thigh shall suffer first and afterward the belly; *neither shall ought else of the body go free.*[31] (italics mine)

The conception of punitive retaliation against the offending organ is explicit. Although nothing is said about masculine sexual offenses, there is a clear implication that offenses committed with the male organ would be punished by castration. The application of the talion principle is widespread in rabbinic thought. Many rabbinic comments on the plagues visited upon the Egyptians and other offenders attempt to justify a particular punishment by asserting that it was peculiarly appropriate because of the nature of the offense committed.

This tendency is especially visible in the Mekilta. A number of examples are given to illustrate the statement "For with the very thing which the Egyptians planned to destroy Israel, He [God] destroyed them."[32] The Nile was made bloody because Jewish women were prohibited by the Egyptians from purifying themselves after their menstrual periods.[33] The frogs were a punishment because the Egyptians forced the Jews to handle ritually impure reptiles.[34] The Egyptian first-born were slain because of Egyptian violence against the Israelite first-born and the crime of parricide.[35] The rabbis assimilated the biblical stories of the ten plagues to their own conception of punitive equity. These stories project the rabbinic unconscious more graphically than most. The rabbis invented the details that have been discussed. They never doubted the talion principle, the fundamental presupposition of castration anxiety.

No evaluation of the significance of castration anxiety in

the Aggadah would be complete without reference to those legends in which punitive violence is visited upon female sinners. The afflictions visited upon Eve and her daughters have already been alluded to.[36] These traditions express the extent to which genital violence against both sexes was regarded in rabbinic fantasy as the appropriate retribution for sexual sin.

There are a number of other traditions which hint at castration. Already noted are the traditions in which the serpent was originally a manlike creature whose appendages were cut off in retaliation for his designs against Eve.[37] His serpentine form is the result of punitive mutilation. Nothing is explicitly said about castration. Nevertheless, it is difficult to regard the serpent's mutilation in any other way.

The Joseph legends corroborate the view that mutilation of the appendages was regarded as equivalent to castration in the rabbinic imagination. According to the rabbis, Joseph came perilously close to succumbing to Potiphar's wife. In one tradition, he avoided intercourse by digging his hands into the ground and allowing his semen to pass harmlessly out of his body through his fingers.[38] Here the fingers are regarded as phallus-like appendages.

According to one well-known tradition, as Joseph was about to commit the act, he saw a vision of his father's face "and his blood was cooled."[39] There are variants in which he sees both parents.[40] This tradition parallels the psychoanalytic conception of the superego as the introjected image of parental authority.

Another legend suggests that Joseph tried to sin but proved impotent. Rabbi Samuel ben Nahman interpreted the verse "And it came to pass on a certain day, when he went into the house to do his work: and there was not a man of the house there within:[41] "R. Samuel b. Nahman said: 'To do his work' is meant literally, but that 'and there was not a man'—on examination he did not find himself a man, for R. Samuel said: 'The bow was drawn but it relaxed . . .' "[42]

In another tradition, Joseph attempts sexual intercourse

but suffers premature ejaculation.[43] Thus, Joseph's intended
offense is deterred either by the censoring vision of his parents
or by impairment of his sexual capacity. Nothing in the Bible
offers the slightest support for these legends. The Aggadah reflects the rabbis' feelings about Joseph's predicament.

Impotence and premature ejaculation are Joseph's misfortunes. They are temporary forms of deprivation of sexual capacity. From the psychoanalytic point of view, both are normally
rooted in unconscious castration anxiety which impairs normal
sexual functioning.[44] The Joseph traditions must be included
among those which reflect castration anxiety without explicitly
stating it.

The Aggadah also contains a number of traditions in
which a sexual offense is punished by the impairment of the male
organ's capacity to function. These include the parallel traditions
in which Abimelech, the Philistine king, and Pharaoh take Sarah
away from Abram for a night. In the Bible, God punishes
Abimelech by closing up the wombs of all the members of his
household.[45] In the rabbinic retelling, God closes up every single
orifice of both the males and the females of the house of
Abimelech. One rabbi adds that even the hens of his house did
not lay eggs. This was functionally equivalent to castration. It is
explicitly stated that the king's sexual capacity was impaired.[46]
According to Rabbi Levi, an angel stood over Sarah the entire
night she was with Abimelech, holding a whip (or a drawn
sword in some variants). Whenever she ordered the angel to
strike or to desist, he would obey.[47]

The Bible relates that Pharoah was smitten with "plagues"
for attempting to molest Sarah.[48] The rabbis asserted that
Pharaoh's affliction was leprosy.[49] Leprosy is frequently men-
tioned as a punishment. Leprosy is functionally equivalent to
castration. The fear of leprosy undoubtedly contains some elements of castration anxiety. The terminal stages of leprosy involve the spontaneous amputation of the appendages. Even
before that, the leper is hardly capable of leading a meaningful

sex life. Nevertheless, leprosy also reflects older and more decisive anxieties than castration. Leprosy attacks the skin, the oldest erogenous zone of the organism. Leprosy includes castration anxiety. It also reflects the oldest and most primal anxieties of the organism as well.[50] As a matter of fact, the frequent references in the Aggadah to leprosy go back beyond the Oedipal and the phallic stage to the pre-Oedipal stage. When I began this study, I was struck by the enormous number of tales of leprous punishment that the rabbis invented, but that have no explicit warrant in Scripture. I assumed that leprous retaliation must reflect castration anxiety in rabbinic Judaism. In one sense, I have never departed from this view. However, I no longer see how the evidence can be interpreted so that legends in which the sinner is punished by leprosy can be understood as reflecting *only* castration anxiety.

Leprosy seems functionally equivalent to castration in the legend of Pharaoh's attempted possession of Sarah. The Bible tells of Pharaoh's misfortune. The rabbis sharpen the element of functional impairment. Rabbi Simeon ben Lakish held that the plague with which Pharaoh had been smitten was *ra'athan,* a skin-boil disease.[51] This is identified by Margulies, an Israeli scholar responsible for the critical edition of the text, as leprosy.[52] In rabbinic times *ra'athan* was thought to have an especially debilitating effect on sexual capacity. One rabbi lists twenty-four different kinds of skin disease, all of which are worsened by sexual intercourse. *Ra'athan* was reputed to have the most injurious effects of all.[53] Another rabbi lists twenty-four such diseases and comments that *only ra'athan* is sexually injurious.[54] Pharaoh was punished by a particularly injurious type of skin disease which resulted in functional castration. Some rabbinic traditions maintain that all of the injuries which befell Pharaoh also were visited upon Abimelech.[55]

There is another type of impairment of sexual capacity in the Aggadah. The rabbis depicted Nebuchadnezzar as a rapacious libertine and homosexual. In one tradition, Nebuchadnezzar seeks

to use Zedekiah, the captive Jewish king, homosexually. In retaliation, God causes Nebuchadnezzar's uncircumcised *membrum*
to be extended to the length of three hundred cubits. It then wags
about before all those present. Too much is functionally equivalent to too little.[56]

The Aggadah does contain a goodly number of traditions
in which sexual offenses are punished by castration, often directly
by God Himself. It also contains other traditions in which a
functional equivalent of castration is suggested as the sinner's
punishment and in which punitive genital violence is directed
against female offenders. The Eve traditions hint, but do not
explicitly assert, that women are castrates.[57] The special character of female existence is, in any event, regarded as punitive.

These tales were told and retold for centuries in the
synagogue, the school, and everyday conversation. Incidentally,
these stories made their way into Christian exegesis with surprising frequency. As a result, the rabbinic legends were not
without decisive influence on the religious development of the
Western world.[58] The telling of these tales reinforced the tendency to conform in sexual matters and heightened the anxiety
lest nonconformity have dire consequences. Castration anxiety
was projected into these traditions by the rabbis. It was self-
reinforcing and self-perpetuating in rabbinic Judaism. It is impossible to avoid the conclusion that the Aggadah offers much
evidence of the existence of castration anxiety and what could,
for want of a better term, be regarded as a decidedly "phallic
Weltanschauung" in rabbinic Judaism.

It would be misleading to rest content at this point. If
anxiety is the reaction of the organism to the possibility of loss,
castration anxiety in some form is inevitable among *all* men.
Furthermore, any society which asserts masculine prerogatives
probably intensifies castration anxiety. In such societies, castration means more than loss of sexual capacity. It means the loss
of one's place within the social structure.

Those who stress the decisive character of the Oedipal

project in the individual will probably regard castration anxiety as the most important source of anxiety in rabbinic Judaism. An examination of the rabbinic legends does not validate this view. On the contrary, the Aggadah reflects a far greater preponderance of pre-Oedipal as opposed to Oedipal strivings. I have cited the vast majority of traditions that contain an explicit or an implicit suggestion of punitive castration. They are numerically as well as psychologically overwhelmed by another body of punitive misfortunes.

Leprosy occurs far more frequently in the legends than does castration, either expressed or implied. Most of the leprosy traditions were invented by the rabbis. They do not occur in the Bible. Though leprosy attacks the genital organs, its central and primary attack is on the skin as such. The skin is the oldest erogenous zone. It is the first area of contact with the external environment as well as the first source of pleasure and pain. The ego is in a sense a psychic extension of the skin's relatedness to the external world. The erogeneity of the skin develops at the same time as oral eroticism, to which it is related. Even the later localizing of pleasures to special areas does not cancel out the skin's character as the primary source of erogenous feelings. An attack on the skin constitutes a threat to the organism's oldest source of contact with the external world. Leprosy is a disease which attacks the epidermis most vigorously and with greatest terror to the victim. In so doing, it represents one of the oldest and most feared threats against the organism. This fear was especially great in the ancient Middle East where leprosy was a frequent and ever-visible occurrence. By contrast, fear of castration, though admittedly important, represents a late and localized anxiety. Although the castrative element of leprosy is stressed in the tales concerning Pharaoh and Abimelech, this element is not present in most of the other leprosy traditions.

One of the most frequent sins for which leprosy is suggested as a punishment by the rabbis is verbal wrongdoing—the sins of the mouth.[59] At first glance, this seems like an inordinately

severe punishment. Thus, the spies who returned from the
Promised Land with a false report were, according to the rabbis,
smitten with leprosy.[60] This accords with Scripture.[61] In one tradition, it is explicitly stated that the limbs of the spies dropped
off as a result of leprosy.[62] The rabbis dwell upon the fact that
the sin of the spies was a sin of the mouth. There are also traditions in which the tongues of the spies are elongated until they
reach down to and penetrate the navel, whence the tongues are
attacked by worms.[63] In other traditions, they die of croup, a
disease affecting the larynx.[64] Even the serpent's scales are said
to be leprous. They are God's punishment for a sin of the mouth.
The serpent is regarded as guilty of having slandered God.[65]

There is a tradition in which an offender who sins with
his mouth is depicted as punished by God's causing his limbs to
fall off one by one, though no specific mention is made of leprosy.
The tradition concerns Jephthah, the son of Gilead, who made a
vow that were God to grant him victory, he would sacrifice "whatever cometh forth of the doors of my house to meet me . . ."[66]
His daughter was the first to meet him and was sacrificed in fulfillment of the vow.[67]

The Aggadah relates that for this improper vow, limb
after limb fell off his body and was buried separately.[68] Jephthah's
punishment was derived from the verse "And he was buried in
the cities of Gilead . . ."[69] The rabbis noted that Scripture had
not said "*city* of Gilead," but "cities of Gilead." Since nothing in
Scripture could be without meaningful intent, the rabbis concluded that Scripture's purpose was to teach that his limbs fell off
and were buried in different places. In this tradition, spontaneous
amputation is the punitive retaliation for a sin of the mouth.

The best known homilies in which a sinner is punished
for verbal wrongdoing by leprosy are those concerning Miriam.
In the biblical account, she is depicted as being smitten with
leprosy following an incident in which she spoke ill of her
brother Moses.[70] The Bible does not explicitly assert that her
leprosy is the result of her failure to act with propriety. In rabbinic tradition, it was so regarded.[71]

In spite of the seeming severity of the rabbinic assertion that the sins of the mouth are punished by leprosy, the assertion does make psychological sense. What is most striking is the coincidence of the rabbinic assertion and the psychoanalytic conception that anxieties concerning the skin reflect archaic oral strivings. The sins of the mouth are punished by wounding the decisive erogenous zone, if such it can be called, of the archaic oral period. Leprosy is thus only secondarily a reflection of castration anxiety, although it undoubtedly is also that. Its persistence throughout the legends is consistent with the fact that the strivings of the oral stage are by no means less significant in the development of either the individual or the group than those of the later phallic stage.

Fear of damage to the skin surface is apparently more closely related to fear of incorporation than to castration anxiety. Leprosy is a kind of incorporation. There are other anxieties expressed in the Aggadah which are even more explicitly related to incorporation than is leprosy. However, fear of leprosy seems to form the bridge between the phallic and pre-phallic anxieties evident in rabbinic tradition. It contains elements of both castration and incorporation anxiety.

It is not entirely clear whether incorporation anxieties reflect oral or intrauterine regressive strivings.[72] The question is not of decisive importance for us. What is important is that incorporation occurs in the legends as the most feared punishment inflicted by God with far greater frequency than any other punishment. It hardly matters whether such anxieties reflect oral or intrauterine regressive strivings. In either case, the traditions reflect fear of the pre-Oedipal mother rather than the father. This in turn calls into question the so-called dichotomy between matriarchal and patriarchal religions as well as the assertion, repeated to the point of tedium, that rabbinic Judaism reflects fear of a tyrannical, castrating Father in contrast to the more permissive and humane matriarchal religions in which the warm freedom of the Mothers reigned supreme. Apart from the fact that circumcision is not castration but an attempt to ward it off, the God of rabbinic and biblical Judaism demanded circumcision, while Cybele, the *Dea Syria,* demanded literal castration from her *galloi,* the priests who served her.[73] Submission to the Jewish Father God may very well have reflected a defense against a barely hidden greater fear of the pagan mother goddesses.

Intrauterine regressive strivings are evident in some of the Adam traditions, which interpret extrauterine existence as a punitive fall from paradisaical dimensions and perfections. As we have seen, there are traditions that before sinning, Adam knew not death, disease, or travail. After sinning, he was expelled from the garden and subjected to the infirmities of normal human existence.[74] Nothing is said about the womb. Nevertheless, the description of the effortless paradise in which Adam enjoys cosmic dimensions and almost omnipotent strength reflects the fact that every individual at one time experienced an environment utterly lacking in the stresses and limits of our daily preoccupations. The Adam legends treat this environment as a remembrance of things past. In most of the traditions, however, it is the feared end rather than the wistfully recalled beginning.

Many of the incorporation traditions originate in the Bible. This is true of the flood legends. In these legends, the offense is usually phallic. The punishment is drowning, a form of incorporation. The rabbis assert that God sent the flood only after the generation had been guilty of excessive masturbation and homosexuality. In some traditions, the waters of the flood are described as resembling hot semen.[75] The flood traditions are important psychological data. Given the biblical tale of the almost universal drowning of the race, the rabbis tended to assert that masturbation and pederasty were the cause.

There are also traditions in which the sinner is burned to death. Graham Greene calls our attention to the relationship between leprosy and burning in the title of his book *A Burned Out Case.* The leper whose disease is so far advanced that it can go no further is thus designated. Both burning and leprosy attack the skin. Both are related to incorporation. In rabbinic tradition, burning is the punishment most frequently associated with arrogance. Just as the arrogant man seeks to "go up" beyond his station, so his punishment is a "going up" he hardly desires.[76] The generation of the Flood, Korah and his rebellious band, and Dathan and Abiram are said to have been consumed by fire or a fiery substance in addition to having been incorporated in earth or water.[77]

There is a biblical tradition that Nadab and Abihu, the priestly sons of Aaron, offered a "strange fire before the Lord . . . and there went out fire from the Lord, and devoured them, and they died before the Lord."[78] According to one rabbinic interpretation, though fire descended and burned the brothers, it left their bodies intact: "The streams of fire issued from the Holy of Holies, branching off into four, and two entered into each of their nostrils and burned them."[79] Commenting on this statement, an anonymous authority states in the same source that they were burned but their garments remained intact.[80] Similar legends of the burning of the soul while leaving the body intact are found elsewhere in the legends. Rashi, a medieval commentator, maintained that this disaster befell Korah.[81] Rabbi Johanan, a Palestinian Amora, maintained that it overtook Doeg, after which his ashes were scattered in the synagogues and schools.[82]

Ferenczi had an interesting speculation concerning the dual identification of earth and water with the maternal principle in dreams, myth, and religion. He maintained that the identification of the maternal principle with water represented the situation of fetus *in utero*. The identification with the earth represented the later situation of the suckling child at the mother's breast. He maintained that there was also a phylogenetic parallel in the original oceanic home of the species and its later less suitable land habitat after the "catastrophe" which drove them from the water. For Ferenczi, fear of earth-incorporation would reflect anxieties arising from the child's fear of retaliation for his cannibalistic attempts to achieve reunion orally with his maternal environment. Fear of drowning would reflect even older anxieties.[83]

The sinner is incorporated by means of the opening up of the "mouth" of the earth in the legends concerning Korah, Dathan, and Abiram.[84] In spite of the extraordinary importance of the story of Korah's rebellion, castration is never suggested as a punishment of the rebels. The biblical and rabbinic use of the term "mouth of the earth" indicates that religious tradition employed the metaphors of incorporation and orality long before psychoanalytic theory gave the matter objectivity and precision.

The incorporation of the rebels was so complete that no trace remained. This is a haunting anticipation of the nameless obliteration of European Jewry in the twentieth century. R. Samuel ben Nahman commented on the verse "They and all that pertained to them went down alive into the pit."[85] He held that even a needle borrowed from another Israelite was drawn after them.[86] One tradition maintained that the clothes they had deposited in the laundry rolled after them and were swallowed up.[87] In another legend there is an archaic confusion of the verbal and the concrete. Even the names of the band disappeared (or flew up) from all the documents containing them.[88]

There is also a tradition that they were eternally burned in Gehinom "as one turns flesh in a pot."[89] This resembles the legend in which Balaam boils forever in semen.[90] In another legend the "enemies of Israel" (perhaps Jesus) boil eternally in excrement.[91] These fantasies may have been originally polemic in intent. This would by no means reduce their psychological relevance. In psychoanalytic terminology, the fantasy of Korah boiling like flesh in a pot reflects oral sadism. The image of the "enemies of Israel" boiling in excrement probably reflects both oral and anal sadism.

Incorporation through drowning is the principal punishment of the Egyptians when they attempt to overtake Israel at the Red Sea.[92]

The rabbis speculated on the divine attack on Moses at

the inn, which Zipporah forestalled by circumcising their son and
throwing his foreskin at Moses' feet, declaring that Moses was
a "bridegroom of blood" unto her.[93] Many rabbinic interpretations of the incident suggest that its purpose was to stress the
utter indispensability of circumcision. God's homicidal reaction
to Moses for his failure to circumcise his son provided the rabbis
with a homiletic defense against the two most important challenges to circumcision that confronted Judaism in the first centuries of the Christian era, the anticircumcision polemic of the
rival Christian Church and the proscription of circumcision by
the Emperor Hadrian shortly before the Judaeo-Roman war of
132-35 C.E.[94]

According to Rabbi Eleazar of Modi'im, Moses unwisely
acceded to Jethro's demand that Moses' first son be raised as a
pagan in exchange for the hand of his daughter Zipporah. In
retaliation, the angel sought to slay him. This was deterred by
Zipporah's quick action in circumcising the child.[95]

The same source contains a number of comments on the
great value of circumcision. The burden of the remarks is that
circumcision is so important that even the merits of Moses could
not delay his punishment for neglecting it. Moses' hazard became an object lesson in the potential dangers involved in the
neglect of circumcision.

An extremely interesting interpretation of the incident
appears in late Babylonian and post-Talmudic sources. Rabbi
Judah ben Bizna is quoted:

> When Moses was lax in the performance of circumcision,
> *Af* and *Hemah* came and swallowed him up, leaving nothing
> but his legs. Thereupon immediately "Zipporah took a sharp
> stone and cut off the foreskin of her son," straightway "He
> let him alone."[96]

The tradition that Moses was swallowed up to his feet
seems to be a euphemism for his having been swallowed up to

his penis. This is the opinion of an important medieval commentator, Rabbi Nissim ben Reuben of Gerona. He accepted the tradition of Rabbi Simon ben Gamaliel that the angel's anger was directed against the child rather than Moses. He maintained that Rabbi Judah ben Biznah's statement meant that the child was swallowed up so that "the place of circumcision" was the only visible part of his body.[97] Rabbi Samuel Edels (d. Posen, 1641) cited an opinion supporting Rabbi Nissim's contention. He argued that Zipporah could not have known that circumcision was the issue between Moses and God, were it not that the extent of Moses' incorporation had made this apparent. He also maintained that Moses rather than the child must have been swallowed, else Moses rather than Zipporah would have performed the circumcision.[98] The tradition that Moses was swallowed up to the tip of the penis is stated explicitly in *Midrash ha-Gadol* on Exodus as well as in *Sh'moth Rabbah*.[99] The rabbis reasoned that Moses was the victim because he would have performed the circumcision had he been able.

This legend contains both castrative and incorporative elements. It illustrates my contention that fear of incorporation is more decisive than castration anxiety.[100] In the Flood legends, a biblical tale of the incorporation of a sinful world by water elicited from the rabbis a catalog of phallic sins as the reason for the incorporation. Here a phallic omission, the failure to circumcise, leads to the swallowing of the sinner, an oral retaliation. Castration is not stressed. The swallowing of the victim *up to* the penis may very well suggest an inversion which contains a definite idea of castration. The fundamental image remains one of incorporation.

Incorporative elements also predominate in the story of Absalom, the rebellious son of David. His fate is used as an illustration of the measure-for-measure principle. Scripture states that Absalom took unto himself ten of his father's concubines. He was slain by ten young men of Joab's troop. There is no explicit association of the two episodes.[101] The rabbis associate the offense with the misfortune.

In the Aggadah, Absalom glories in his hair. His punishment is to be hung by the hair from a terebinth. When Absalom seeks to cut himself down, the netherworld opens up to swallow him. He is left suspended from the tree.[102] The rabbis add the threat of incorporation. The threat of incorporation makes Absalom prefer the lesser pain of hanging. He desists from cutting his hair. This can be seen as a symbolic preference for castration rather than incorporation, in which the cutting of the hair is symbolically equivalent to castration.

Finally, Absalom is included among those who will have no share in the world to come.[103] According to rabbinic tradition, the ultimate punishment awaiting the unrepentant sinner is denial of a share in the world to come. This is worse than the death penalty. A sinner sentenced to death might ultimately be saved. *Perek Helek* of Tractate Sanhedrin (the chapter on the "share") is the Talmudic chapter which contains one of the most important rabbinic discussions concerning the actions and the fate of unrepentant sinners. The discussions revolve very largely around the issue of who is to be denied the world to come and the reasons for their exclusion. The rabbis believed that the righteous would be resurrected to life eternal in the world to come but that the unrepentant sinner would be eternally condemned. The wording of the Mishnah in describing the fate of Korah and his band makes it clear that the final punishment is utter annihilation: "The company of Korah shall not rise again, for it is written, 'And the earth closed upon them,' in this world, 'And they perished from among the assembly,' in the world to come."[104]

As we have seen, Freud was convinced that fear of death was frequently derivative.[105] Fenichel had a similar opinion concerning the fear of incorporation. There can be little doubt that a *morbid* fear of death covers unconscious anxieties other than annihilation. Annihilation and incorporation can mean many things on many levels. Nevertheless, if one understands coitus in terms of thalassic regressive tendencies as did Ferenczi —the desire to return, at least symbolically, to the oceanic bliss of the womb—castration anxiety would ultimately reflect a later developmental aspect of the child's ambivalent feelings toward its earliest maternal environment.

Those existentialists who have explored the phenomenology of anxiety hold that castration anxiety is derivative. They regard *Urangst,* existential anxiety, man's primordial, ineradicable, and unmediated reaction to the nonbeing that forever threatens to envelop him, as primary. They maintain that it is cognitive without being conceptual.[106] However, following Kierkegaard, who referred to anxiety as a "sympathetic antipathy," they too recognize the ambivalent character of the phenomenon.[107] One yearns for the very nothingness against which anxiety is the primordial defense.

The existentialists' perspective is phenomenological; that of psychoanalysis is dynamic and developmental. The difference is rooted in differences of perspective. In phenomenological description, there is a very strong reluctance to go beyond the given and the apparent. The dynamic approach of psychoanalysis is not without merit. Clinical experience frequently reveals that a regression to earlier modes of behavior, a flight from the phallic to the oral, for example, is motivated by a flight from later conflicts.[108] Strong castration anxieties could express themselves as if they were earlier oral anxieties. Our evidence cannot rule out the possibility that the incorporation anxieties evident in the Aggadah may contain disguised phallic elements. Nevertheless, the phallic elements do not exclude the earlier oral conflicts that are so evident in rabbinic legends.

There is probably less distance between the existentialist and the Freudian views than is sometimes supposed, at least with regard to the primary object of anxiety. Freud posited a universal yearning of all life to return to the inorganic security which preceded the ecstasy of existence.[109] "The goal of life is death" in Freud's formulation. The last anxiety, the anxiety lest one be utterly annihilated, expresses both the earliest anxiety and the oldest yearning. In the final analysis, we yearn most deeply for that which we fear most insistently. Death is as much return to the source as goal and final end. Fear of and yearning for annihilation and incorporation are related to the organism's oldest strivings, the infant's yearning to return to the womb and its concurrent fear that it will be consumed by the cannibal mother.[110]

There is a basis for equating incorporation, the predominating punishment in the rabbinic legends, with annihilation, the punishment meted out to the most unrepentant sinners according to the rabbis. Both annihilation and incorporation involve the terminal riddance of reality. Death is a reincorporation of the organism by the earth. It was thus understood by many preliterate groups whose unconscious perceptions were often more accurate and closer to the surface than modern man's. Burial in the fetal position is not uncommon.[111] Death dissolves the ego and ends its capacity to resist the environment. This is evident in the coldness of the corpse and in its biological vulnerability.

The rabbis had no illusions about what happened to the body in death. They had no doubt about its return to the earth.[112] They faced the reality of death with an almost total lack of illusion. Nevertheless, they did not regard death as necessarily equivalent to *final* annihilation. Only denial of a share in the world to come was absolutely final. Death, even for the unrepentant sinner, could be the entrance into the world to come. The rabbis believed that God would ultimately resurrect the dead and so alter nature which He Himself had created that there would be no further dying.[113] Only those whom God had utterly rejected were to be totally incorporated into the earth whence they came. One might say that in the rabbinic perspective, the worst punishment of the unrepentant sinner was to be abandoned by the Father and, in consequence, to be finally and completely consumed by the Mother. Here annihilation and denial of the world to come are equivalent to final incorporation.[114]

Among the biblical sinners whom rabbinic tradition assigns no place in the world to come were Jeroboam, Ahab, Manasseh, Balaam, Doeg, Ahitophel, Gehazi, the generation of the

Flood, the generation of the Dispersion (the tower of Babel), the Sodomites, the spies, the generation of the Wilderness, and Korah and his band. These were the sinners par excellence in rabbinic tradition. They served as negative models in the Aggadah. In other traditions, Balaam, the generation of the Flood, the generation of the Dispersion, and the Korahites also suffer punitive incorporation and burning.

Most punishments were partial and subject to revision. Even death could serve as an atonement.[115] There is a pedagogic element in the application of many of the lesser punishments suggested in the Aggadah. The rabbis continually stressed that God did not desire the death of the sinner, but his repentance.[116] It was always hoped that limited punishment would serve as a deterrent against further sin. The conception of punishments as of the *y'surim shel ahavah,* the chastisements of love, contained this idea.[117]

Most punishments serve as a double deterrent. Anxiety lest one be smitten prompts the ego to defend the organism against the pain by avoiding offense. Memory of the actual punishment is a deterrent against further misbehavior. Denial of a share in the world to come is different. It is only meted out to those for whom all possibility of return is excluded. The rabbis distinguished very carefully between sins for which reparation and repentance are possible and sins for which reparation is no longer possible.[118] They directed their special condemnation against those who had led others astray. The gravity of this type of sin stemmed from the fact that, even were the sinner to make reparation, he could only restore himself but could do nothing for those whom he had led astray.[119]

Denial of a share in the world to come could only deter *before* the fact. The matter is in reality extremely complicated. The primordial yearning evident in the Aggadah for the quiescence of the grave is ultimately identical with the most terrible threat envisaged by rabbinic Judaism. For some, the threat of annihilation may actually be an enticement. For the moment, let us recognize that it is the final and ultimate punishment in both the Halakah and the Aggadah. Whatever differences of perspective are to be discerned between the domains of law and legend in Judaism recede at this point. There is unanimity on the question of ultimate punishment. That punishment was not castration. It was annihilation.

The legends cited are but a sample of very many which could be offered to indicate the persistence of prephallic incorporative anxieties in the Aggadah. There can be no doubt that phallic and castrative elements are present. They have been noted.

Whether by accident or intent, Freud's comment that his discovery of the importance of the pre-Oedipal mother came to him with as much of a surprise as the discovery of Minoan-Mycenaean civilization, was pregnant with meaning.[120] He recognized that his own discovery of the decisive character of the archaic elements in the development of the psyche was analogous to the discovery of the significance of the hitherto unrecognized Minoan matriarchal culture for the development of Western civilization.

The fact that incorporation anxieties predominate over castration anxieties in the Aggadah suggests that the dichotomy between matriarchal and patriarchal religions is untenable. Matriarchal religions may not reflect the dilemmas of phallic religion. The archaic strivings they reflect precede and anticipate phallic development. The phallic stage does not cancel out earlier archaic stages in the development of the individual; neither does that stage entirely cancel earlier stages in religious life. No matter how violently patriarchal religions attempt to uproot traces of matriarchal religions, the results are at best only partially successful. The incorporation legends indicate how deeply rooted the older anxieties remained in supposedly phallic rabbinic Judaism. In all likelihood, they had a greater capacity to deter behavioral deviance than the traditions which reflected castration anxiety. Historically and psychologically, there was a far more direct involvement of the people in the tales of the

Flood, the demise of the Egyptians, and Korah's rebellion, than in the less significant stories of Ham's violence or the frogs' castration of the Egyptian nobles. The latter were isolated stories; the former were widely told and repeated. The drowning of the Egyptians is rehearsed daily in Jewish liturgy.[121]

Parenthetically, it is interesting to observe that the laws of eating remain to this day the predominating disciplines of traditional Judaism. Among religious Jews, there is a vast concern with what one may and may not eat. This preoccupation is simply without parallel in any other Western religion. Jewish concentration on dietary matters begs for psychoanalytic study in its own right. We must rest content with noting the existence of the phenomenon. The dietary regulations of Judaism constantly remind the Jew with dramatic forcefulness of the importance of what one takes in with the mouth. Oral activities are emotionally overdetermined in Judaism. The dietary laws tend to confirm the hypothesis that, no matter how preoccupied the rabbis were with phallic and Oedipal matters, they were far more insistently and continuously concerned with oral strivings and anxieties.

A psychoanalytic interpretation of Judaism which ignores the centrality of its oral preoccupations must be woefully incomplete. Any attempt to interpret the severe eating disciplines of Judaism only as unconscious attempts on the part of the community to defend its members against the temptation to repeat the primal crime, that is to commit cannibalistic acts against the fathers, will also be incomplete. An examination of the rabbinic tales of the ways in which sinners were punished strongly suggests that there was far greater fear of the mother than of the father in rabbinic Judaism. I must again suggest that the primal crime simply isn't primal enough.

This conclusion seems to be borne out by the evidence of the history of religion. Too frequently, the image of a mother-goddess conjured up by those who contrast the "restrictive" Jewish Father-God with the "permissive" mothers of ancient paganism is that of the compassionate Mother of Sorrows of Roman

Catholicism. Mary, however, represents an Oedipal rather than a pre-Oedipal mother. A far better perspective is attained when we contrast the God of the Aggadah at His angriest and most punitive with such goddesses as Cybele and Kalima. The mother-goddess had two sides. She was the loving giver and sustainer of life. She was also an incomparably hideous and terrifying ogress. She inspires infinitely greater terror than the God of Judaism at His worst. The unmeasured terror inspired by the great cannibal Earth-Mother reflects the child's first confrontation with its environment unaided by previous learning. The child's project is not merely to eat but so to consume its environment that the hideous pains of hunger which thrust it into reality will be appeased and sated. Its greatest unspoken fear, unrefined by experience or concept, is that this nourishing environment will do unto it as it has done. The cannibal child is in terror of a cannibal world, the world of the Mother. It is that world which we see objectified in the religions of the Great Mother. Something of that world never disappears in later life in any of us. It is helpful to compare the punishments in the Aggadah with the misfortunes inflicted by the Great Mother on the fruit of her womb. The predominant fears of incorporation in the Aggadah correspond to the decisive fears of matriarchal religion. This is most vividly evident in the tales of death by earth-incorporation or drowning. This corresponds to the negative side of the Great Mother. It is she as earth, womb, and tomb who consumes her own children. Erich Neumann has described this aspect of the Great Mother with especial forcefulness:

> Just as world, life, nature and soul have been experienced as a generative and nourishing, protective and warming Femininity, so their opposites are also perceived in the image of the Feminine; death and destruction, danger and distress, hunger and nakedness, appear as helplessness in the presence of the Dark and Terrible Mother.
>
> Thus the womb of the earth becomes the deadly devouring maw of the underworld, and beside the fecundating

womb and the protective cave of earth and mountain goes the
abyss of hell, the dark hole of the depths, the devouring womb
of the grave and of death, of darkness without light, of nothingness. For this woman who generates life and all living
things is the same who takes them back into herself. . . . This
Terrible Mother is the hungry earth which devours its own
children and fattens on their corpses; it is . . . the flesh-eating
sarcophagus voraciously licking up the blood seed of men
and beasts, and, once fecundated and sated, casting it out
again in new birth, hurling it to death, and over and over
again to death.[122]

I would not dispute that the God of rabbinic Judaism was
essentially a Father-God and was so regarded by the rabbis. Nevertheless, the evidence of the legends suggests that earlier archaic
feelings toward the mothers were never lost and actually remained a very significant component in the new piety. In reality,
the God of the rabbis was considerably less terrifying than His
female Syrian neighbor, Cybele. She in turn was prototypical of
the best and the worst in the Great Mother.

The God of biblical and rabbinic Judaism demanded
circumcision as His token of loyalty from male worshippers. By
contrast, the *galloi* expressed their priestly worship of *dea Syria,*
the Mother-Goddess of Syria, by castrating themselves and offering their dismembered genitals, rather than just their foreskins,
to their celestial mother.[123] The mother-goddesses permitted a
greater range of license to their faithful, a fact often emphasized.
Nevertheless, this tells us little about the anxiety content of these
activities for those who participated in them. They may indeed
have been fraught with inner fright and terror that Judaeo-
Christian sexual discipline was actually a relief and a defense
against anxiety. It is by no means certain that sexual discipline
produces greater anxiety than sexual license. The ego often uses
repression as a mechanism to defend itself against anxiety induced by unacceptable sexual promptings. Similarly, the religious
disciplines of Judaism were defenses against the permissiveness
of the Mother and the terrible price she exacted for her freedom.

The disciplines of rabbinic Judaism cannot be interpreted as reflecting the prohibitions of the Father-God alone. The prohibitions of the Father-God were a relief in contrast to the unmeasured and uncontained fear of the Great Mother. The mother is the first object of love. She is the object of the later conflicts of father and son. However, the other side of the picture must not be ignored. The mother is the first object of anxiety by any reading of psychoanalytic literature, religious history, or mythology.

Patriarchal religions may very well reflect defenses of the ego, both individually and collectively, against the barely suppressed but infinitely greater fear of the mother-goddesses and the actual maternal figures they presuppose. The defenses of the ego are not necessarily pleasant. Repression is one of the most important of such defenses. Defenses are elected because the ego finds no other way to avoid greater pain or greater conflict. If this interpretation of patriarchal religion has merit, it would seem that many of the characteristic features of rabbinic Judaism are far less projections of the superego, though this element cannot be denied, than defenses of the ego. By extending our conception of the psychogenetic factors operative in Judaism *backward* to include the oral stage, we also extend them *forward* to include the defensive and the integrative functions of the ego. We thus arrive at a psychological interpretation of rabbinic Judaism that is more compatible with the broader aspects of contemporary psychoanalytic ego psychology than the earlier view which stressed the phallic aspects of Judaism almost exclusively.

The *lex talionis*, or measure-for-measure principle, must also be seen in perspective. It is the irrational application of the measure-for-measure principle, rather than the principle itself, which is archaic and harsh. In some respects, the principle must be seen as a principle of mercy and limitation. Punishment is frequently a psychic need of the sinner himself. Equitable punishment was calculable. It allowed for continued effort thereafter. Perhaps, calculable punishment was welcomed by some because it cleared the slate. Much criticism has been needlessly placed on the "barbaric" character of the measure-for-measure principle and on Judaism as an "eye for an eye, a tooth for a tooth" religion. In actuality, the talion principle was by no means the most archaic or barbaric retaliatory norm. The limitation of punishment to no more than a punitive equivalent must have represented a great advance over the old Semitic custom of avenging the crime of an individual many times on his entire clan.[124] In place of Lamech's cry "If Cain shall be avenged sevenfold, surely Lamech seventy and sevenfold,"[125] the talion principle introduced limitation and measure. In the light of archaic Semitic practice, the principle represented a positive advance in both justice and mercy. It is by no means accidental that the principle is associated in the history of religion and psychoanalysis with the Father-God rather than the mother-goddesses. Here again the father even at his most punitive is an agent of limitation and measure in contrast to the unmeasured terrors of the pre-Oedipal mother. The evidence suggests that the turning from the mother to the father in religion was the work of the ego defending itself against infinitely greater archaic fears.

P. J. van der Leeuw has offered a suggestion concerning castration anxiety which accords with my findings in rabbinic legend. He has suggested that castration anxiety is at least partly a defense against earlier and infinitely greater pre-Oedipal anxieties. Following his suggestion, the fantasy-love of the mother in the Oedipal stage may be a way of resolving an intolerable ambivalence.[126] That ambivalence was so great in the religions of the Father-God as to impel His worshippers to attempt to obliterate all traces of the older mother-goddesses. The history of Judaism and Protestantism attests to the violence with which that project was carried out. The evidence of the Aggadah indicates how incessantly she who was repressed returned, not only in the worst fears of the rabbis but also in their deepest yearnings.

I have frequently suggested that the Aggadah preserves or restores archaic insights of the greatest antiquity. The greater importance of incorporation anxiety in these legends may point to one of the most ancient and continuously relevant conceptions of the significance of the Father-God in the history of religion. The Father-God is the *artifex omnium natura*. One of the oldest and most important sources of rabbinic legend, *Bereshith Rabbah*, begins with a discussion of God's role as architect and fashioner of creation.[127] He creates a cosmos out of the primordial wasteland of chaos. He is the author of order, reason, form, and law in both the moral and the physical realms. His creative activity prevents the all too facile return of cosmos to chaos.

In the oldest mythologies, undifferentiated chaos is the abysmal mother out of which earth, sea, and the world of men arise. In the Sumerian myths of the origin of things, the goddess Nammu is referred to as the "mother, who gave birth to heaven and earth" (An and Ki). S. N. Kramer describes Nammu as written with the ideogram for "sea."[128] An and Ki were regarded as the created products of the primordial mother-sea. There are very clear overtones of the womb-birth metaphor in this mythic representation. Chaos becomes truly cosmos only with the organization of the earth. This is the work of the male god En-lil, "who caused the good day to come forth" and who determined "to bring forth seed from the earth."[129] Few activities of the Father-God are as important as His role in creating order out of disorder.

In rabbinic Judaism, the religious Jew was regarded as the partner of God in bringing about the rule of His kingdom. That kingdom is none other than the rule of order, measure, and equity over the ever-present threat of the return of original chaos. The rabbis were aware of the power and the seductive attraction of chaos. Anxiety is cognitive without being conceptual. With its capacity to shake our innermost foundations, it engenders in us a potent awareness of the dissolving nothingness out of which we have come and to which we must return. At one level, the fundamental intent of rabbinic Judaism can be seen as an attempt to create those forms, limitations, and structures which are indispensable to every human activity of significance. For the rabbis,

6/The Meaning of Sin
in Rabbinic Theology

W HAT DOES THE SINNER ULTIMATELY DESIRE? Freud
stressed the yearning to attain sexual possession of the mother.
Sandor Ferenczi regarded this possession as a "thalassal regression," an attempt to return to the undisturbed bliss of the womb,
the place of human origin.[1] The rabbis had their own special
perspectives on the meaning of sin. They did not regard sexual
possession of the mother as the sinner's ultimate goal. They suggested in myth, legend, and homily that the sinner's ultimate
goal was to do away with God in order that the sinner might
himself become God. The rabbinic insight was intuitive. It was
formulated almost two thousand years ago. It remains rich in its
perennial appropriateness.

The Aggadah recognized incest as one of the motives for
sin. Nevertheless, incest is not stressed. This is graphically illustrated in a representative tradition concerning Amon, one of the
most idolatrous kings of biblical Israel. Amon is depicted as committing incest solely as a means of provoking God. He does
not enjoy himself sexually.

R. Eleazar interpreted the verse "For he Amon sinned
very much"[2] to mean that he had sexual intercourse with his

mother. In the legend the king's mother asks him: "Hast thou any pleasure in the place whence thou didst issue?"

Amon replies: "Do I do this for any other purpose than to provoke my Creator?"[3]

Incest is understood as a grave temptation. Nevertheless, it is subordinated here as elsewhere in the Aggadah to the perverse pleasure of provoking God. Amon is more interested in provocation and self-assertive freedom than incest.

The Amon legend is by no means atypical. There are many tales of conflict between fathers and sons in the Aggadah. Sexual jealousy hardly figures in any of them. There is little, if any, emphasis on incest in the vast majority of rabbinic legends dealing with the father-son conflict. There were rabbinic fantasies of the sinner seeking to reach the mother. Nevertheless, the goal of reaching the mother took older, more archaic forms.

The legends concerning the demise of Nadab and Abihu, the priestly sons of Aaron, emphasize the father-son conflict. In the Bible their death is tersely explained as a result of their having placed a "strange fire before the Lord, which he had not commanded them."[4]

The story of Nadab and Abihu is terse and demands interpretation. Furthermore, the terseness assures us that the rabbinic elaborations will tell us more about the feelings of the rabbis than about the actual incident. R. Levi saw Nadab and Abihu as arrogant and possessed of hearts full of intrigue.[5] R. Berekiah held that they were punished for their father Aaron's sin, presumably the Golden Calf.[6] R. Eliezer held that they died because they gave a legal decision in the presence of their teacher Moses.[7] This was regarded as an indefensible usurpation.

R. Levi interpreted the brothers' arrogance to mean that they avoided choosing wives, in keeping with the biblical tradition that they had no children.[8] R. Levi depicts the priestly brothers as saying: "Our father's brother [i.e., Moses] is a king, our mother's brother is a prince, our father is a High Priest and we are Deputy High Priests; what woman is worthy of us?"[9] In these legends, the sexual element is clearly subordinate to other elements, the most important being arrogance, a form of self-aggrandizement.

The brothers' arrogance toward women was matched by their arrogance toward Aaron and Moses. The father-son conflict becomes explicit but it does not reflect a predominance of incest themes. In a number of traditions the young priests hope for the death of their elders as they walk behind them in religious processions, but only because they desire to usurp the priestly office.[10] God is depicted as warning them of the folly of their homicidal wishes: "Many foals have died and their skins were turned into saddle cloths for their mothers' backs!"[11] The Nadab-Abihu traditions suggest that the rabbis did not stress the sexual rivalry of the generations even when they embellished the biblical tale with the suggestion that the young men sought to displace their elders.

Even in biblical traditions with explicitly Oedipal overtones, the rabbis did not stress incest. Absalom is guilty of possessing his father's concubines, but the rabbis emphasize his unreasoning pride in his hair and appearance rather than his possession of the concubines.[12] Little is said concerning Reuben's attachment to Bilhah, his father's concubine, in the Aggadah although this is assuredly incestuous. There is more in the Apocrypha concerning the incident than in the rabbinic legends. There is a very strong rabbinic tendency to mitigate the seriousness of Reuben's offense.[13]

The low status of incest as a goal of the sinner in the Aggadah is also evident in the legends concerning Korah's rebellion. The rebels accuse Moses of committing adultery with their wives. They do not demand sexual freedom for themselves.[14]

Nonincestuous sexual gratification is an important goal of the sinner in the Aggadah. This is evident in a review of the legends. Among the sinners who strive for illicit sexual gratification are Eve, the serpent, Dinah, Leah, the proud daughters of

Zion, Ham, Abimelech, the Pharaoh who sought to entice Sarah, Potiphar, Balaam, Zimri and Cozbi, David, Absalom, Manasseh, Jehoiakin, and Amon.[15] Nevertheless, sexual wrongdoing is seldom the sinner's worst offense. Illicit sex is the center of interest only in the traditions concerning Abimelech, Sarah's Pharaoh, Dinah, Potiphar, David, and Samson. There was little alternative. The biblical stories stressed the sexual element. Wherever the biblical narrative is more ambiguous and invites rabbinic embellishment, self-assertion and rebellion are almost always more prominent in the legends. In the legends concerning the serpent, the generation of the Flood, the Sodomites, Balaam, Zimri and Cozbi, Jehoiakin and Amon, self-assertion is at least as important as sexual desire.

Sexual activity reflects the relational character of existence. In a sense, it is self-annihilating. The goal of sexual tension is its own riddance. It is related to one side of the human polarity, the primordial yearning of all living things to seek reunion and ultimately to put an end to organic separateness. The other side of the polarity is the need to maintain separateness and individual identity.[16] Before the individual seeks sexual gratification, he must strive to maintain his own distinct identity. In neurotics this can sometimes contradict the inherently relational demands of the libido. The polarities of both reunion and separation presuppose that the human organism exists. Fear of the loss of sexual capacity, castration anxiety, is not as ultimate as fear of nonbeing, existentialist *Urangst*. Conversely, the desire to thwart the limitations of existence, which include sexual deprivation, is older and more fundamental than the quest for sexual gratification.

The rabbis placed far more stress on the sinner's desire to rival or displace God than on illicit sexual activity. To be God means to be beyond all existential thwartings including the sexual. The rabbinic legends suggest that the ultimate goal of the worst sinners is to become God, for only in God are the contradictions which beset existence and agonizingly divide the psyche against itself harmonized.

The desire of the sinner to rival God is already present in the biblical tale of Eve's encounter with the serpent. The serpent entices Eve to commit the first sin: "God knows that, as soon as you eat of it, your eyes will be opened and you will be like God, who knows good and evil."[17] The serpent's words were embellished by the rabbis when they retold the story:

> For in the hour when you eat thereof, you will be like Him, a God. Just as He creates and destroys worlds, so you will be able to create and destroy worlds. Just as He slays and brings to life, so also will you be able to kill and bring to life . . .[18]

A similar emphasis on the sinner's desire to rival God is found in the development of the tradition of Satan's original rebellion against God and his subsequent fall. This legend has many problems. The earliest hint of Satan's rebellion is found in Isaiah 14. The prophet announces the downfall of the king of Babylon. He likens the king to Helal ben Shahar (the brilliant one, son of the morning). The Septuagint translation of Helal is *Phosphoros* ("light bringer"), whence we derive *Lucifer* in the Latin and English:

> How art thou fallen from heaven, O Lucifer, son of the morning! How art thou cut down to the ground, which didst weaken the nations.
> For thou hast said in thine heart, I will ascend into heaven, I will exalt my throne above the stars of God: I will sit upon the mount of the congregation, in the sides of the North:
> I will ascend above the heights of the clouds; I will be like the Most High.[19]

There are echoes of an ancient myth in the prophecy. Bamberger has suggested that the poem may carry an allusion to a Canaanite myth of a rebellious titan who sought to displace El, the supreme God.[20]

The rabbis interpreted Isaiah's prophecy as a reference

to Nebuchadnezzar. The verse "I will be like the most high" is used as the Scriptural basis for the rabbinic contention that Nebuchadnezzar asserted his own divinity. According to R. Johanan ben Zakkai, a Heavenly Voice (*bat qol*) came forth and rebuked him.[21] R. Johanan also linked Nebuchadnezzar to Nimrod. In rabbinic tradition Nimrod was the rebellious king under whom the Tower of Babel was constructed. R. Johanan asserted that Nimrod caused the world to rebel (*himrid*) against God.[22] Among the reasons given by the rabbis for the construction of the tower are rebellion, the desire to make war against God, the desire to cleave heaven with an axe and drink its water, and the desire to dwell on high.[23] The motivations are predominantly Promethean rather than sexual.

The Lucifer prophecy of Isaiah formed the basis for Milton's image of Satan in *Paradise Lost*. The rabbis did not stress Satan as the Promethean opponent of God as did Milton:

"... and with ambitious aim,
Against the throne and monarchy of God
Raised impious war in heav'n ..."[24]

They emphasized the desire of human rulers to rival or overthrow God. To the best of my knowledge, there is only one explicit reference to Satan's desire to overthrow God in the literature of ancient Judaism. It is found in II Enoch 29:4-5.[25] Apparently, because of Gnosticism, the rabbis shied away from the conception of a cosmic rival against God.[26] They did not shy away from the idea of earthly rivals. They fully appreciated the desire to rival God as a human temptation.

One of the most puzzling aspects of rabbinic legend was the rabbis' insistence that the fitting punishment of the sinner is some form of degradation. The logic behind the traditions in which the sinner is punitively degraded is that he who offends by seeking to be too much is punished, measure for measure, by being reduced to a status lower than the one he betrayed. The sinner sought to be more than he was created to be; his punishment is to be made less than he was created to be. The terminal expression of the desire to be more than one was created to be is the desire to be God. The conception of sin implicit in these traditions can be described as "ontic self-aggrandizement." It is punished by degradation, a form of "ontic diminution."

The conception of sin as ontic self-aggrandizement and punishment as ontic diminution bears some resemblance to the Greek notion of "hubris," man's sin against his limits. Hubris is inevitably followed by nemesis, a kind of cosmic restoration of equilibrium of the whole against the aggrieving part which has taken more unto itself than its proper domain.[27] Nowhere do the rabbis identify sin as ontic self-aggrandizement. The term is merely a convenient way of conceptualizing the underlying thread that runs through their legends. The rabbinic traditions cited are offered as illustrations of a general trend. Sin was too significant a reality for the rabbis to objectify and conceptualize it. They were compelled to offer their most significant insights through the concrete, nonconceptual media of myth, legend, and homily. There is no alternative but to translate their images into our concepts. In doing so, we must recognize that something vital is inevitably lost.

The legends concerning Nebuchadnezzar illustrate the conception of sin as ontic self-aggrandizement. He was regarded by the rabbis as one of the four kings who asserted their own divinity. The others were Joash, Pharaoh, and Hiram. All are punished by some form of sexual degradation involving homosexual abuse.[28]

Although Nebuchadnezzar was the first foreign conqueror of Israelite Jerusalem, the traditions concerning his degradation do not stress the conquest of Judaea as his sin. His offense is his desire to rival God. One of the most deeply engrained convictions of rabbinic Judaism was that the destroyers of Jerusalem did not act upon their own initiative. They worked unwittingly as God's agents. They were not ultimately responsible for their conquests. They were guilty primarily of failure to ascribe unto God the glory. They were not guilty of any crime against the

Jewish people; they did commit the ultimate crime against God, self-apotheosis.

Joash was the only Israelite king among the four who asserted their own divinity and were punished *modo foeminarum*. Scripture describes Joash as working with Jehoiada the priest to restore the Temple. After Jehoiada's death, his subjects turned away from the worship of the Lord. They were warned against their defection by the prophet Zechariah, the son of Jehoiada. Joash turned against the prophet and had him executed. Shortly thereafter the Syrians invaded his kingdom and "executed judgment against Joash."[29] Sick and left to die, he was murdered by his own servants after the departure of the Syrians. He was not buried in the sepulchre of kings.[30]

The rabbis turned the story of Joash into a fantasy of self-apotheosis and divinely inflicted degradation. They interpret the verse "Now after the death of Jehoiada came the princes of Judah, and prostrated themselves before the king"[31] to mean that Joash allowed his nobles to convince him of his own divinity. They interpreted Scripture so that an act of homage by the nobles became the king's apotheosis.

Hiram and Pharaoh are treated in very much the same way as Joash and Nebuchadnezzar. Their quest for divinity is repeatedly stressed by the rabbis.

The fundamental intent of the legends concerning the four kings is clear. The sinners seek to displace the Creator in the order of things. They receive the only appropriate punishment in the eyes of the rabbis: he who seeks to be more than he is must be degraded to a status less than he needs to be.

The sinner's basic intention to rid himself of divine authority and constraint is a theme which runs through many other traditions. Ahab, Ahaz, and Doeg are depicted as permitting others to indulge in incest.[32] They themselves do not indulge. Manasseh, Jehoiakim, and Amon indulge, but their real goal, according to the rabbis, is provocative and nonsexual in every instance.[33] R. Johanan maintained that the graven image Manasseh placed in the sanctuary originally had one face. Manasseh later changed it to a four-faced figure so that the *Shechinah,* God's Presence, might see it and be provoked.[34] Manasseh is also depicted as attempting to obliterate the Names of God wherever they appeared in th Scrolls of the Torah. This is a symbolic riddance of the Divine. He also broke down the temple altar.[35] The rabbis also indulged in word-play on his name. They related it to the Hebrew root *nashah,* to forget. From this they derived the tradition that he forgot the Torah and caused Israel to forget it.[36]

Jehoiakim sought a similar riddance of the Divine. He is depicted as exclaiming: "My predecessors knew not how to anger Him . . ."[37] Among the ways in which Jehoiakim provoked God's anger was to tatoo God's name on his penis:

> "And the remaining words of Jehoiakim, and the abomination which he wrought, and that which was found upon him . . ."[38] What is meant by "that which was found upon him"? R. Johanan and R. Eliezer differ: One maintained that he engraved the name of an idol upon his penis, and the other that he engraved the name of Heaven [i.e., the Divine Name] thereon.[39]

Having tatoo inscriptions on one's flesh is in itself a violation of Jewish law. The rabbis imagine Jehoiakim intensifying the offense to its limit. According to R. Johanan, Jehoiakim utilized his tatooed organ to commit incest with his mother, his father's wife, and his own daughter-in-law.[40] As in the tradition of Amon's incest, Jehoiakim is seen primarily as a *mumar l'hachis,* one who sins out of spite and provocation against God, rather than as a *mumar l'téavon,* one who sins for the gratification involved in the sin. The rabbis consistently regarded the *mumar l'hachis* as giving far greater offense than the sinner who was compelled to break the rules because of the overwhelming power of desire. The Jehoiakim legends are extremely significant. They illustrate the extent to which sexual sin is subordinated to provocation and rebellion in rabbinic fantasy. The male organ is depicted as a vehicle of protest and provocation rather than as an instrument of sexual pleasure.

Without realizing it, the rabbis portrayed Amon and Jehoiakim as believers in God, thereby revealing how improbable unbelief was to them. One does not provoke or rebel against a God one doesn't believe in. Jean-Paul Sartre has commented that the priest who celebrated the Black Mass in the Middle Ages believed too much rather than too little. He would have been lost without a religious system to deny.[41] The actions ascribed to Amon and Jehoiakim were the rabbis' fantasies of their equivalent of the Black Mass. They were, in effect, saying, "This is what I would do were I a great sinner like Amon or Jehoiakim." The rabbis were apparently incapable of being indifferent to God.

Riddance of divine authority is the dominant note in the Ahaz legends. In the Bible, Ahaz forsook the true worship of the Lord and offered his son as a sacrifice. He also despoiled and trespassed the Temple. He gave a portion of its treasure to the king of Syria.[42] In the Aggadah, Ahaz is one of the five sinners who were such "from first to last."[43]

The rabbis play upon the king's name as evidence of his desire to rid the world of God: "Why was he called Ahaz? Because he seized [*ahaz*] the synagogues and schools."[44] His reasons for shutting the synagogues and schools were:

> If there will be no children, there will be no pupils; if there will be no pupils, there will be no scholars; if there will be no Torah study, there will be neither synagogues nor houses of study; if there are no synagogues and houses of study, the Holy One, blessed be He, will not permit His *Shechinah* to abide in the world.[45]

The Aggadah emphasizes Ahaz' desire to end religious instruction and render the sacrificial institutions unfit as a means of ridding the world of God's presence and influence.

The denial of the primacy of the sexual factor also figures in the legends concerning Ahab. One Babylonian rabbi maintained: "Ahab was frigid by nature so Jezebel painted pictures of two harlots on his chariot, that he might look upon them and become heated."[46] R. Jochanan says that Ahab "wrote upon the gates of Samaria, 'Ahab denies the God of Israel,' "[47] and that "there is no furrow in Palestine upon which Ahab did not plant an idol and worship it."[48] He also sought to enjoy dominion over the whole world.[49] The rabbis regarded those who sought world rule as seeking to displace God.[50]

The tales concerning Amon, Ahaz, Ahab, Manasseh, Jehoiakim, and the other later kings of Judah and Israel were especially important to the rabbis. There was a very strong tendency on the part of the rabbis to identify with these men, whom they regarded as great rabbinic scholars who went astray.[51] The stories concerning the idolatrous kings were of greater personal concern to the rabbis than those of other sinners with whom they did not so readily identify.

In addition to legends about riddance of divine authority and self-apotheosis, there are a number of legends in which the sinner desires to displace or usurp the prerogatives of superior authorities or parental figures. The serpent desires to displace Adam and possess Eve. Possession of Eve is subordinate to his desire to pre-empt Adam's superior role.[52] Cain's sacrifice was rejected because he took the desirable part for himself and left the remainder for God.[53]

In the Bible, when the spies returned from searching out the land of Israel, they caused the congregation to murmur against Moses because of their evil report.[54] Deuteronomy describes the complaint of the people against Moses upon their return: "Because the Lord hated us, He hath brought us out of the land of Egypt, to deliver us into the hand of the Amorites, to destroy us."[55] The rabbis comment that the people revealed their own hatred of God when they spoke of His hatred of them. They cite an old proverb, "Whatsoever a man wishes his neighbor, he believes his neighbor wishes him."[56]

Dathan and Abiram are regarded in the Aggadah as the

most consistent opponents of Moses throughout his career. All of the legends concerning them stress rebellion, disobedience, and the desire to displace the leader. When the spies returned, the people sought to replace Moses with Dathan and Abiram. They are depicted in the Aggadah as telling Moses:

> "On what ground do you lord it over us? What good have you done to us? You have brought us out of Egypt which is like a garden of the Lord. You have not, however, brought us unto the land of Canaan, but behold we are in the wilderness and the plague is continually let loose upon us!"[57]

This paraphrases the complaint of the people against the leadership of Moses in Scripture.[58] The issue behind Dathan and Abiram's desire to displace Moses was the futility of following Moses' leadership. Again the sexual theme does not predominate.

Jean-Paul Sartre has commented that "man fundamentally is the desire to be God."[59] Human consciousness for Sartre is an evanescent nothingness forever seeking the stability of the objects it apprehends. To be human is to be in a state of desire, a condition of need and incompleteness. An end to desire can come about only through an end to the subject who desires. Man therefore quests for the impossible. He seeks the stability of the object-world together with the capacity to enjoy this stability which only consciousness in its insecurity could possess. Only God realizes the ideal of absolute security and stability while possessing the capacity to enjoy this stability. But God exists only as ideal. In fact, He does not exist. Man is therefore a "useless passion" forever seeking to become a nonexistent God: "Thus the passion of man is the reverse of that of Christ, for man loses himself as man in order that God may be born. But the idea of God is contradictory and we lose ourselves in vain. Man is a useless passion."[60]

Sartre expresses his insight into the nature of the human

project in conceptual terms. The rabbis expressed their insights in legendary and mythic images. Nevertheless, both deal with the same human reality. Their fundamental insights greatly resemble each other. Perhaps one of the most succinct descriptions of the terminal goal of the sinner in the Aggadah is that suggested in another context by Norman O. Brown:

> The Oedipal project is not, as Freud's earlier formulations suggest, a natural love of the mother, but as his later writings recognize, a product of the conflict of ambivalence by narcissistic inflation. The essence of the Oedipal conflict is the project of becoming God—in Spinoza's formula, *causa sui*; in Sartre's *être en-soi pour-soi*.[61]

The desire to be *causa sui* is, according to Brown, the child's desire to be father to himself. On this point he quotes Freud approvingly: "All the instincts, the loving, the grateful, the sensual, the defiant, the self-assertive and independent—all are gratified in the wish to be the *father of himself*."[82]

There is an extraordinary resemblance between the statements of Freud, Sartre, and Brown and a midrash in which, after Moses has rehearsed the glories of God to Pharoah, the Egyptian replies: "Ye speak falsely, for it is I that am lord of the world. *I created myself and the Nile.*"[63]

Buchler and others have suggested that the rabbinic imputation of the desire for self-apotheosis to pagan or idolatrous rulers may reflect rabbinic reaction to the Roman apotheosis of the emperor. Buchler is especially mindful of the rabbis' distaste for Caligula.[64] Undoubtedly, this was part of the social context in which the rabbis intuited that the sinner's terminal ambition was to become God. There is a strong likelihood that some rabbis were also motivated by anti-Christian polemic in asserting this to be the sinner's darkest temptation. Nevertheless, the fact that historical events elicit an insight does not mean that that insight has no psychological relevance. On the contrary, there seems to be strong evidence that, in the hyperbolic language of the Aggadah, the rabbis were able to formulate insights pertaining to the character of sin which were of a high order of sophistication.

The legends which tell of the sinner's desire to displace God and reign in his stead cannot be interpreted as reflecting a socio-political or historical reaction to Roman or Christian ideology alone, although they undoubtedly also do that. They are entirely consistent with everything the rabbis have suggested concerning the nature of sin. The sinner always takes upon himself more than he was created to take. Not every sinner seeks a terminal gratification of his desire to be more than he was created to be. However, when the rabbis isolated the terminal aspect of sin, they identified it with the desire to be God.

The desire to cut out the Divine Name (Manasseh), to make war on God (Nimrod), to reject His lordship (Ahaz and most other sinners), all point in one direction: the sinner seeks to overthrow the thwartings which limit his gratifications. Only God is beyond frustration and limit. Only in God does the distinction between need and fulfillment disappear. Ontic self-aggrandizement reaches its terminal expression in the desire to become God. Sexual gratification is only one satisfaction. There are many others. The very need for gratification betokens a condition of dependence upon the domain of the not-self. Only God is entirely sufficient unto Himself. He alone enjoys the perfection of unending and unlimited gratification. To be God is to be all that there is to be and to be impeded by no restraint whatsoever.

Ironically, the goal of the worst sinners in the Aggadah is not unrelated to the greatest anxiety in the legends. In the final analysis, the greatest anxiety and the greatest yearning coincide. The greatest yearning is the sinner's wish to be God: the greatest anxiety, lest his sin bring upon him annihilation as God's terminal retaliation. Both in the legends and in the explicit Halakic statement of Sanhedrin, the terminal punishment of the unrepentant sinner is that "he has no portion in the world to come."[65] Thus both in Halakah and in Aggadah, ultimate annihilation is threatened against the sinner who forsakes repentance. Paradoxically, only in God's perfection and death's nothingness is there a total absence of ungratified strivings. Aristotle spoke of God as an unmoved mover. He knew well that all propulsion implies a need and an imperfection, a seeking for what one does not possess or for what one possesses only potentially.[66] God's perfection is such that He is beyond appetite. He is His own fulfillment; the sinner's goal is the gratification—and consequently the annihilation—of all appetite. To become God is to gratify and thus annihilate appetite. This end is also accomplished in the nothingness of death which the Aggadah posits as the final punishment against deviance.

In the Bible the conviction is frequently expressed that conformity to God's will is the way of life, whereas the way of sin leads to death.

When this conviction is viewed in the light of the rabbis' insistence that ultimately the sinner seeks to displace and become God, its intelligibility and relevance are heightened. Death is, in a very meaningful sense, a consequence of sin. What the sinner ultimately seeks is the destruction of limit and restraint; this is a process which begins with the abolition of a little limit and a little restraint. The rabbis intuited that in the long run the quest for an end to limitation can feed on its own hunger. Ultimately, no limitation is tolerable. The radical sinner obliterates limitation by obliterating his own nature as a finite, created being. This is accomplished in the fullness of Divine Being and the nothingness of death. As Sartre has suggested, the *pour-soi*, human consciousness, pursues the impossible project of becoming the *être en-soi pour-soi*, or God.

The rabbis insisted that the Torah was the possession of flesh and blood rather than of the ministering angels. They clearly understood that, though frustrating limitations had their unpleasant side, they were infinitely to be preferred to all attempts unrealistically to overcome them. The attempted destruction of limit ends with the real destruction of the human condition. When the rabbis spoke of sin as bringing death in its train or hinted at the darkest temptation of the sinner, the desire to be God, they understood what men have all too frequently forgotten: human existence is viable only when man accepts his place and fulfills his responsibilities within the limitations of the created order. The vision of Prometheus returns in each age to tempt men with the hope that they can be more than they were created to be. The rabbis were well aware of the yawning abyss of nothingness which the apocalyptic promise of Prometheus barely disguised. In truth, he who seeks to be more than he was created to be finds his "more" is in reality considerably less. In the last analysis, this "more" turns out to be nothingness. Limitation is finally overcome by overcoming reality. The preference of rabbinic Judaism was always for limitation and life rather than perfection and death.

7 / God's Omnipotence
in Rabbinic Judaism

EW THEOLOGICAL ISSUES are as decisive as the related questions of God's omnipotence and the ultimate source of authority
within a religious community. In rabbinic Judaism final authority
rested with the omnipotent Lord of nature and history. The
religious Jew's most important obligation was obedience to the
norms ordained by his God. The demand for obedience was also
the point of greatest stress on his loyalties. On occasion, it could
elicit very strong feelings of anxiety. Paul's Epistle to the Romans
offers powerful evidence of the extent to which that anxiety was
felt by at least one rabbinic Jew. Although most rabbinic Jews
found Paul's religious solution unacceptable, Paul's inability to
comply with God's norms as he understood them evoked extremely deep anxiety. Paul's anxiety before God was by no means
unexceptional in his own time or throughout Jewish history. For
many Jews, anxiety was accompanied by the conviction that failure to obey the commandments had brought dire misfortune to
the community in the past and would do so again in the future.

The rabbinic legends concerning the biblical tale of
Korah's rebellion against Moses are especially important for an
understanding of the reactions of the rabbis toward the question

of religious authority.[1] Scripture offers ample evidence of the reluctance of the children of Israel to accept the disciplines of Moses. There were constant backslidings. Korah's rebellion was one of the most serious crises faced by Moses in the wilderness. Korah rejected the sacerdotal and the political authority of Moses and Aaron. His protest was the prototype of many subsequent challenges to religious authority in both Judaism and Christianity. Korah contended that the entire congregation was holy and that no special holiness adhered to Moses and Aaron that set them apart from the people. The assertion of the sanctity of the people against the claims of the priesthood has often found an important place in the platform of religious rebels throughout history.

As the rabbis studied the Korah story, they perceived its special relevance to their own situation. They were the leaders of an imperiled community in which religious authority was indispensable. They had qualified for positions of leadership by an extraordinarily difficult pursuit of religious knowledge. There have always been members of the community prepared to deny the value or the relevance of rabbinic authority, as Korah had challenged Moses. The Korah story offers an example of the precarious nature of authority in any society. The large number of traditions in the Aggadah concerning Korah testify to the extent to which the story impressed itself upon the rabbinic imagination.

The rabbis did not attempt to minimize Korah's challenge against Moses. They could have depicted it as the work of a small group of troublemakers who sought to disturb a unified community. Instead, they maintained that the entire community sided with Korah against Moses.[2]

Reading the Aggadah, one is never quite sure whether Korah or Moses is the real villain in the eyes of the rabbis. In some sources, Korah is described as attacking Moses and his Law for being cruel, inequitable, and arbitrary. The rabbis suggested that Korah was moved by envy. Nevertheless, his attacks are extremely telling. Furthermore, Korah's attacks are never answered directly by Moses. Moses seeks to appease Korah. When this fails, he endeavors to overpower him. Moses never refutes Korah. Moses' victory is clearly one of superior numinous power. There is no hint of an answer by Moses which carries the conviction that the Law is in fact equitable and humane. The rabbis had no difficulty in inventing a very effective attack on the Law by Korah which appears nowhere in Scripture. They were either incapable of answering the attack or thought a defense unnecessary.

The Korah episode ends when God uses his power to destroy the rebels. The mouth of the earth opens up to swallow the dissidents. The moral of the Korah legends is plain: one either accepts the Law, irrespective of any human evaluation of its rationality or its equity, or one suffers the most extreme consequences. The rabbis never doubted the Law's rationality or its equity. They did not believe that this conviction required a defense. It was the starting point rather than the conclusion of their religious affirmations. In the Korah legends Moses uses no argument to prove that his doctrine comes from God. He succeeds in calling forth God's power. This alone vindicates God's lordship over the moral and the physical universe. Korah offers extremely telling arguments against the Law but fails. He cannot match Moses' exhibition of power.

Korah's attack on the Law and, implicitly, its Author can be divided into two parts. In the first place it is an attack against the Law as arbitrary. In one tradition, Korah is depicted as asking Moses whether an entirely purple garment requires the addition of a purple fringe in order to fulfill the law in Numbers 15:38. Moses replies that the addition is required. Korah comments sardonically: "A garment which is entirely purple does not suffice to fulfill the commandment, yet four threads suffice!"[3]

Korah then asks if a home full of sacred books suffices to fulfill the commandment that a mezuzah, with its two sections from the Torah, be placed upon the doorpost of every Israelite house. Moses replies that a mezuzah remains necessary. Korah comments ironically that a house full of books does not suffice to fulfill the commandment, yet two small sections from the Torah attached to the door do.[4] This tradition is further elaborated in a legend in which Korah asks whether a man is unclean if his skin shows a small bright (leprous) spot. Moses replies affirmatively. Korah then asks whether such a man would be ritually unclean if the bright spot were to spread over his entire skin. In accordance with the Law, Moses replies that he would be clean.[5] The point of Korah's challenge is to demonstrate the arbitrary and irrational character of the Torah. Elsewhere, Korah is depicted as turning on Moses and exclaiming: "These words were not commanded upon them [the Israelities], but you devised them in your own heart!"[6] Korah also exclaims: "There is no Torah from Heaven and Moses is not a prophet, and Aaron is not a High Priest!"[7]

In addition to challenging the arbitrary character of the Law, Korah is depicted by the rabbis as rebelling against its inequities and its cruelties. In *Midrash Tehillim*, Korah is portrayed as assembling the entire congregation of Israel against Moses and Aaron. He recites the following anecdote:

> "In my neighborhood there was a widow, and with her were two fatherless daughters. The widow had only one field and when she was about to plow, Moses said to her: 'Thou shalt not plow thy field with an ox and an ass together!'[8] When she was about to sow, Moses said to her: 'Thou shalt not sow thy field with two kinds of seed!'[9] When she was about to reap the harvest and to stack the sheaves, Moses said to her: 'Thou shalt not harvest the gleanings, the overlocked sheaves, and the corners of the field.'[10] When she was about to bring the harvest to the granary, Moses said to her: 'Give me the heave-offering, the tithe, and the second-tithe.' She submitted to God's decree and gave them to him. What did the poor woman do then? She sold the field and bought two sheep, so that she might clothe herself in wool shorn from them, and so that she might profit out of the lambs. As soon as the sheep brought forth their young, Aaron came and said to the widow: 'Give me the firstling males, for this is what the Holy One, blessed be He, said to me: 'All the firstling males that are born of thy herd and out of thy flock thou shalt sanctify unto the Lord thy God.' "[11]

Korah continues in the same vein, describing the poor woman's progressive impoverishment because of the Law of Moses. The story ends with Aaron confiscating her sheep, her remaining possession. She and her daughters are left weeping and totally impoverished.[12]

Korah maintains that the Law is cruel and exacts an unnecessary price from those who can afford it least; it also benefits the priests and rulers at the expense of the people. Korah's rejection of the Law on humanitarian grounds cannot be found in Scripture. The rabbis place this argument in the mouth of Korah. This detailed challenge is their invention. They may have been motivated by anti-Christian polemic. Korah's attack reminds one of Jesus' attack before the Pharisees in Mark 7.[13] Nevertheless, it presupposes considerable religious knowledge. It resembles the Aggadic traditions in which Manasseh confounds Isaiah with his own words, seeking to demonstrate that they contradict the words of Moses.[14]

In some traditions the male followers of Korah accuse Moses of having adulterous relations with their wives. The women are compelled to take the biblical test for *sotah,* the woman suspected of adultery.[15] Korah's band adds the complaint of immorality and hypocrisy on the part of the religious leadership to their allegations of cruelty and irrationality on the part of the Law.

The demise of the rebels is preceded by Moses' demand that God manifest His power lest these men die the common death of all men. Moses declares that if the rebels are permitted to live, he too will become an unbeliever and a heretic (*kofer*).[16] The final test is the same for both sides. The issue cannot be settled by argument. In *B'midbar Rabbah,* Moses' demand that God manifest His power is associated with similar demands by Elijah against the priests of Baal.

The end of Korah's band comes when the rebels are swallowed up by the earth.[17] There is considerable elaboration of this theme in the sources. Korah is depicted as descending while crying aloud through the flames: "Moses is King and Aaron is High

Priest and the Torah is given from Heaven."[18] In some legends Korah is depicted as stirred around in Gehenna like flesh in a pot, proclaiming: "Moses is true and the Torah is true and we are liars." Moses is finally vindicated by the flames of hell.

In the legends, even the flames of hell do not convince Korah's companions, Dathan and Abiram. Long before Mozart portrayed Don Giovanni as refusing repentance while the flames consumed him, the rabbis pictured Dathan and Abiram as dancing and blaspheming as they were consumed along with the other members of Korah's band.[19]

The overwhelming power of God is the ultimate source of religious authority in the Korah legends. The point of the legends is that the sign was given to Moses rather than to Korah. This alone settled the matter. Korah's disaster is the final proof of the fallacious character of his claims.

It is interesting to compare the Korah legends with Kierkegaard's homily on the Akedah, the binding of Isaac, in *Fear and Trembling*. Kierkegaard was also concerned with the problem of ultimate religious authority. He contended that in the Akedah there is a radical conflict between ethical values and religious obligation. From a human perspective, Abraham's intended sacrifice of Isaac is murder. It becomes a holy act only because of God's command.

Kierkegaard was a thoroughly skilled dialectician. He deliberately posited an extreme collision between ethical values and the religious. He concluded that in such a situation there is a "teleological suspension of the ethical." Obedience to God takes precedence over ethical considerations for Kierkegaard.[20]

Something of the same clash between the ethical and the religious is present in the Korah legends, though not in the sharpened dialectic form propounded by Kierkegaard. The challenge does not come from God to man to submit to His arbitrary will as it does for Abraham. It comes from a rebel in the midst of an act of disobedience. The arguments placed by the rabbis in the mouth of Korah do not comprise an absolute opposition between the ethical and the religious, as in Kierkegaard's version of the Akedah. Korah uses ethical arguments to discredit religious fidelity. Abraham must violate the ethical to obey God. The conflict between the ethical and the religious is used by Korah to defend rebellion against Moses and his Law.

In both the Korah legends and Kierkegaard's homily, there is a vast distance between the ways of God and the ways of man. Korah's arguments are not given the dignity of a reply in the Aggadah. They are of no consequence in the face of God's overwhelming power.

There were differences between the rabbis and Kierkegaard. These differences were probably largely due to their life situations. Kierkegaard was a solitary. He was alienated from any decisive human community. He had to reject Regina Olsen. Marriage would have involved him in the community of his own time as well as in the chain of generations. He understood faith as the way of the single one, nakedly alone before God and unaided by human wisdom or experience. Resolving the opposition between the ethical and the religious in favor of the religious was hardly a problem for him. The ethical becomes significant only when one experiences the life of the community as indispensable, as did the rabbis. Kierkegaard's rejection of marriage, his radical fideism, and his attack on the Danish ecclesiastical establishment were of a piece. The rabbis placed a high value on marriage. They *were* the religious establishment. In the final analysis, Kierkegaard saw man as standing utterly alone before God. He was compelled to stand with the Christ, as he understood him, even against his own inherited religious community. He saw the tension between Christendom and Christianity as irreconcilable. His "religionless Christianity" anticipates Bonhoeffer.

The rabbis felt the same tension between the religious and the ethical as did Kierkegaard, but a "religionless Judaism" was impossible for them. It remains impossible to this day. The rabbis were the leaders of a fragile and endangered community. They believed Israel's existence was a central concern within the divine scheme. Kierkegaard, the religious solitary, could devalue the religious community. The rabbis could not. They also felt the tension between the ethical and the religious. They could express it only through a discredited rebel. Only in very recent times have Jews been able to face the full force of the tension between the ways of God and the ethical sensibilities of man.

Although Moses was victorious in the Korah traditions by reason of God's power, these legends were hardly likely to offer the rabbis or their community much comfort. This is evident in the writings of Justin Martyr. He was one of the earliest Church Fathers to enunciate a theology of history with an anti-Jewish bias. He used reasoning similar to that employed by the rabbis in the Korah stories to prove that the Jews were rejected by God and that Christianity was the true religion. Justin wrote his anti-Jewish polemic, *The Dialogue with Trypho*, about the time of the Hadrianic War (*ca.* 132-35).[21] The war ended disastrously for the Jews of Palestine. Justin interpreted the Jewish defeat as a manifestation of God's power against them. The Jews had rejected Jesus. According to Justin, God's answer was the devastation of the Jewish community and its sanctuary by the Romans.

Justin employed a point of view that has remained awesomely influential within Christianity to this day. The recent debates within the Second Vatican Council on the Schema concerning the Jews and Judaism were an indication of the extent to which his point of view has continued to be an issue for Christians. There is much irony in the fact that the biblical-rabbinic theology of history, of which the Korah stories are an important example, was devastatingly employed against the Jewish community throughout the history of the Christian Church.

The rabbis used Korah's destruction as proof that his protest against Moses had been discredited. Justin employed the fact of Jewish defeat at the hands of the Romans as proof that Christianity was correct in its claims against Judaism on three crucial issues: circumcision, the Messiah, and the election of Israel. In Justin's time, circumcision was a subject of great controversy between Christians and Jews. By coincidence, shortly before the outbreak of the war of 132-35, the Emperor Hadrian issued a decree prohibiting the practice of castration throughout the Roman empire. Circumcision was legally interpreted as a form of castration. It was also prohibited by the Romans. The prohibition was not directly aimed against the Jews, but it did constitute a grave threat to the survival of Judaism. As such, it was disobeyed by religious Jews. According to scholarly opinion, Hadrian's interdict was one of the most important causes of the Jewish-Roman war.[22]

The Christians saw the emperor's prohibition of circumcision as further evidence that God no longer required it as the rite of initiation into His covenant.[23] When the Jews persisted in observing the ritual, the Christians took the Jewish defeat as further proof that the Christ had initiated a new covenant. Christian logic in the face of Jewish disaster was no different from rabbinic logic in the Korah traditions. God's revelation was validated in each instance by the misfortunes of the religious adversary.

In Christian eyes, the Jewish refusal to abandon circumcision was aggravated by the graver sin of their following a false Messiah after rejecting the true Messiah. During the Hadrianic wars Simon bar Kochba, the Jewish leader, was hailed by R. Akiba ben Joseph, the leading rabbinic authority, as the Messiah.[24] In Christian eyes, this meant that the Jews had compounded the sin of rejecting the Christ by turning futilely after a false Messiah. When the Romans vanquished the Jews, the Christians regarded this defeat as proof of God's judgment against Israel.

Writing shortly after the Jewish defeat, Justin Martyr addressed the rabbinic Jew, Trypho:

> For the circumcision according to the flesh, that was from Abraham, was given for a sign, that ye should be separated from the other nations and from us and that ye alone should suffer the things you are rightly suffering, and that your lands

should be desolate and your cities burned with fire, and that
foreigners should eat up the fruit before your face, and none
of you should go up into Jerusalem. . . . *For none of you, as
I suppose, will dare to say that God was and is not both
possessed of knowledge beforehand of the events to come and
also is preparing beforehand the things that each deserves.*
And therefore all this happened to you rightly and well. . . .
For ye slew the Just One and His prophets before Him, and
now ye reject, and, as far as in you lies, dishonor those that set
their hope on Him, and God Almighty and Maker of˙ the
universe who sent Him, cursing in your synagogue those who
believe in the Christ. . . .[25] (italics mine)

As it is asserted in the legends on the evidence of Korah's
fate that Moses was the true prophet, Christians could point to
the disasters which befell Israel as proof that they were the new
elect of God. From Justin's time down to the twentieth century,
some Christians have given the same interpretation to every
Jewish misfortune. Some Christians may even have wondered
why, in the face of the repeated and overwhelming evidence of
Jewish misfortune, Jews did not exclaim the Christ was the true
Messiah, even as Korah had exclaimed that Moses was true when
the earth consumed him.

There were other ways of interpreting the Jewish community's disaster. Jewish anxiety, guilt, and self-reproach could
be heightened. God had treated Israel like Korah; perhaps they
were equally guilty. If God is the all-powerful author of the
historical drama, the disasters of the Jewish people must ultimately be His doing. The rabbis did not disagree with Justin's
contention that God was punishing their community for its sins.
They differed only on the question of the nature of Israel's sins.

Rabbinic literature is replete with both direct and inferential statements explaining why Jerusalem fell. The main theme
of these traditions is that a sinful, obstinate, faithless, and un-
grateful Israel turned from the true God and went astray after the
yearnings of her corrupt heart. After sending prophets to warn
His people, God sent alien conquerors to punish them. These

conquerors were ignorant of the true character of their mission. Impelled by the basest motives and deluded by success, they mistakenly imputed their victories to their own might and even to their own divinity. They were, in reality, only instruments of God's wrath against His sinful people. Usually there is a hopeful sequel: a remnant will take heed and learn the true meaning of the terrible message. They will return to the Lord and be faithful to His covenant. He will restore them to their land and to fellowship with Him. The theme has variations, but the basic theology of history remains the same in the prophets and in the rabbis.

A terrible sense of guilt is the inescapable corollary of this theology. The rabbis were convinced that they and their community deserved the misfortunes which had befallen them.

Nowhere in the rabbinic literature is their theme more consistently reiterated than in the midrash on Lamentations, *Ekah Rabbah*. The rabbis regarded Lamentations as Jeremiah's dirge on the fall of Jerusalem in his time. It was read, studied, and discussed on *Tishe B'Ab*, the Ninth of Ab, the traditional anniversary of the destruction of the first Jerusalem.

Throughout the first part of *Ekah Rabbah*, the rabbis repeat a statement explaining why the Jews were driven into exile in 586 B.C.E. and in 70: "Since they sinned, they were exiled . . ."[26] Among the sins that the rabbis assert caused the exile were the three cardinal sins of idolatry, immorality, and bloodshed,[27] ritual neglect,[28] disrespect of scholars, and neglect of the Torah.[29] One tradition asserts that the first Jerusalem fell because its priests were all uncircumcised.[30] In the light of the circumcision controversy with the early church, this tradition may have been polemic in origin.

Most of the traditions explaining the fall of Jerusalem in *Ekah Rabbah* refer to the fall of the first Jerusalem. There is, however, evidence that the rabbis equated the earlier misfortune with the one in their own times. Many rabbinic traditions link the first and second disasters. The rabbis assert that the same causes brought both about.[31] There is also a tendency to regard the earlier generation as less guilty: "R. Johanan and R. Eleazar both said: The former ones whose iniquity was revealed had their end revealed [i.e., the end of their captivity], the latter ones whose iniquity was not revealed have their end still not revealed."[32]

Since the Temple was not restored after 70, some rabbis concluded that the later generation was worse than the generation of the first fall of Jerusalem: "The question was put to R. Eleazar: Were the earlier generations better or the latter ones? He answered: 'Look upon the Sanctuary!' Some say he answered: 'The Sanctuary is your witness [in this matter].' "[33]

The details vary but the thought is everywhere the same. There is apparently no other explanation of national misfortune in rabbinic literature.

Since World War II, men have often wondered why the Jews failed to resist the Nazis. Bruno Bettelheim has suggested that the defense mechanism of identification with the aggressor made it impossible for the death camp victims to wrench themselves free of the all-pervasive influence of the S.S. Some prisoners added snatches of German uniforms to their clothing. Others imitated the manners and bearing of the guards.[34]

It is very likely that many Jews failed to resist because of a deeply paralyzing sense of guilt. When the twentieth-century catastrophe occurred, many religious Jews regarded their predicament in exactly the same perspective as had the rabbis in the first century. The Jewish people were again punished by God for their sins. It was futile to resist. Jewish salvation would be assured by neither political nor military action. Only repentance would restore the broken fellowship with God.

Even where such feelings were not explicitly stated, the tendency to regard misfortune as punishment is too deeply rooted in most men not to have been operative. The victim's unconscious sense of guilt can easily turn him into an unwitting accomplice of the aggressor. His own destruction was the inevitable result.

When all political and military explanations of the inevitability of Jewish compliance with the Nazis in their own undoing are exhausted, psychological explanation is still needed. It would be wrong to overstress Jewish self-blame while ignoring the very real horror of the Jewish situation in wartime Europe. Nevertheless, guilt and self-blame were present. Both were constantly reinforced by the Jewish liturgy. Every new moon and festival the religious Jew offered the *mipnei ha-ta-enu* prayer which asserted that "because of our sins we were exiled from our land. . . ." Jewish religious practice constantly reinforced the conviction of Jewish life since the exile was punitive.

Even the Christian contention that the Jews were punished for rejecting Jesus must have strongly affected the Jewish self-image. The oft-noted phenomenon of Jewish self-hate derived from the Jew's unwitting acceptance of the negative evaluation placed upon him by Christian culture. *The Autobiography of Malcolm X* offers striking evidence of how difficult it is for a member of any minority group to extricate himself from the majority's negative images concerning his community.[35] Many Christian cultural values were unconsciously accepted by Jews. The deicide accusation reinforced Jewish self-accusation. As in the case of the rabbis and Justin Martyr, Europe's Jews and Christians were able to agree that Jewish degradation was the result of God's punishment, even when they could not agree upon the nature of the Jewish offense.

One of the most hideous ironies of the Nazi extermination of Europe's Jews was the fact that the instinctively law-abiding character of the Jewish community greatly contributed to its total destruction. For thousands of years, Jews had been disciplined instinctively and unquestioningly to obey the law in every conceivable domain of human behavior. From earliest childhood, generations of Jews have been trained to comply with the religious and secular norms of their society. The tendency to obedience was almost an automatic response.

When the Nazis took over the conquered nations, they were regarded simply as another authority to be obeyed. This was especially true in eastern Europe where anti-Semitic governments were by no means unknown. Whole Jewish communities responded to posted notices of their impending removal with unquestioning obedience.[36] The habit of obeying was too deeply engrained to be overcome. In the legends, Moses never replies to Korah's arguments that the Torah is cruel and arbitrary. Obedience is due the Law irrespective of any human assessment. One obeys simply because God has commanded.

The same unquestioning willingness to comply compounded the difficulties the Jews faced in confronting the Nazis. The Nazis issued the most vicious and despicable decrees. The Jews followed their deepest instincts. They obeyed. They would have been far better off had they not been so law-abiding. Their habits were no longer life-enhancing in the presence of an enemy determined upon their extermination.

Self-reproach was the principal reaction to the destruction of Jerusalem by Vespasian and Hadrian. There were other possible reactions. There was always the temptation to accuse God. In the legends, Dathan and Abiram, Korah's accomplices, accuse Moses of failing to fulfill the glowing promises that prompted the people to follow him into the wilderness.[37] If God is ultimately responsible for history, one can with much justice find many of His actions unworthy by human standards. In the legends, accusation against God is muted and inferential. It is, nevertheless, present.

The protest against God could not be expressed openly in rabbinic times. That was one of the unhappy lessons of the Korah legends. By settling the question of religious authority in favor of God's power, Jews enormously enhanced their feelings of anxiety, guilt, and self-accusation. It was emotionally less distressing to blame oneself than to blame God. The legends reinforced the conviction that before God man is always in the wrong. The Jewish people had been treated like Korah and some of the worst sinners in the Bible. The moral was clear. It was preached and continues to be preached to the congregation of Israel to this day: Mend your ways—"Return O Israel unto the Lord thy God. . . ." The insistence on repentance became very great. The theme of repentance had its origins in the prophets. It was sharpened in rabbinic Judaism. The call for repentance and the proclamation of God's omnipotence reflected deep and abiding feelings of guilt. These feelings predominate in rabbinic literature. They are part and parcel of the Korah story.

There was yet another conceivable reaction. One could, for lack of supporting signs, become an unbeliever and a heretic as Moses had threatened in the legends. Moses' threat was invented by the rabbis. It is indicative of a mood which could only be entertained in fantasy two thousand years ago. The Jewish community was beset and defeated. It was hardly in a position to support the luxury of atheism or extreme heresy. After the Hadrianic war, it was under extordinary pressure to maintain internal unity for the sake of sheer survival. It would have been disastrous to splinter the group even further. The sole remaining method of organizing the community was through religious authority. The community could no longer tolerate the luxury of religious doubt.

There was one religious leader who responded to the terrible sufferings of his people by becoming an unbeliever and a heretic. In the face of the suffering of his people in and immediately after the Hadrianic wars, Elisha ben Abuya proclaimed the sheer absurdity and meaninglessness of existence, *"Leth din v'leth dayan,"* "There is neither judgment nor Judge." He thereupon withdrew from the Jewish community.[38] It was easier for Elisha to leave his community than to find another. The day had yet to come when alienated Jews would become sufficiently numerous to form their own de-Judaized Jewish community.

Elisha ben Abuya was not entirely alone. None of the other rabbis would or could follow him in his rejection of any inner connection between human action and the moral order or in his very contemporary assertion of the ultimate absurdity of existence. Nevertheless, his most important disciple, R. Meir, refused to turn his back on his teacher. Faced with the protests of his colleagues against continuing what they had to regard as an unworthy association, R. Meir maintained his friendship and commented, "I found a pomegranate; I ate its contents and threw away its husk."[39] More than one rabbi, beholding the ruin of Judea and the increasing violence of Christian hostility, undoubtedly was troubled by the same questions that drove Elisha to deny the hallowed Jewish conviction that God acts meaningfully in history.

The conflict between Elisha ben Abuya and his former colleagues resembles the conflict between Dr. Rieux and Father Paneloux in Albert Camus's contemporary novel *The Plague*. When the plague's fury bursts upon Oran in the early 1940's, some men are unable to accept the sheer gratuity of this unwanted eruption of monumental human suffering. Their position is exemplified by Father Paneloux, the scholarly Jesuit, who leaves the quiet of his study to give theological meaning to the plague. Camus intended his novel as an allegory of the experience of European man during World War II. As in the Hadrianic war of 132-35, those imbued with the prophetic view of history could find meaning in the terrible sufferings of their generation only by regarding their agony as God's punishment. Father Paneloux preaches to his congregation in the Cathedral of Oran in much the same vein as the rabbis preached almost two thousand years ago:

> "Calamity has come on you, my brethren, and, my brethren you deserved it . . . from the dawn of recorded history the scourge of God has humbled the proud of heart and laid low those who hardened themselves against Him. . . . The just man need have no fear, but the evildoer has good cause to tremble. For the plague is the flail of God and the world his threshing-floor. . . ."[40]

Father Paneloux bids his flock repent. Only then will the plague's devastation be terminated.

Like Elisha ben Abuya, Camus's protagonist, Dr. Rieux, can see neither meaning nor purpose in the overwhelming suffering that confronts him. He believes neither in God nor in an ultimately meaningful cosmos. The novel's climax comes when a young child dies convulsively of the plague in Father Paneloux's arms. Dr. Rieux angrily reproaches the priest that at least the boy was innocent. Before the concrete reality of an innocent child's suffering, Father Paneloux's abstract theology falters. He is, however, unable to abandon it. He is psychologically incapable of dwelling in an absurd, meaningless cosmos without the God of history. Father Paneloux has lost his world. He is incapable of finding another. He dies, not of the plague, but of the loss of a meaningful world.

God is dead for Dr. Rieux. He lives without hope or solace. Nevertheless, he is not impelled to justify God and reproach the victim in the face of overwhelming misfortune. He elects to be among the healers. He understands that no power in heaven or earth will offer such healing if men refuse the healing vocation. Like Elisha ben Abuya, he refuses to ratify the justice of human misery. Elisha and Rieux, each in his own time, see no alternative to an absurd cosmos if men are to avoid the self-blame and guilt which are the psychological entailments of the Judaeo-Christian theology of history.

Our theologies are ultimately reflections of the kind of men we are. Men had to experience irrational guilt before they could attach their free-floating feelings to objective events, as did the rabbis and Father Paneloux. One of the functions of the rabbinic theology of history was to provide an institutionalized framework within which the individual Jew's irrational guilt could be objectified.

There are men like Dr. Rieux who are not compelled psychologically to interpret misfortune as deserved punishment. They are a distinct minority. No matter how persuasively rabbinic Judaism insisted upon God's grace, mercy, and forgiveness, no Jew could possibly keep all of its commandments. Every Jew was destined to fail to a degree. Such failure often heightened

anxiety and feelings of guilt. This was especially evident in the
career of Paul of Tarsus. His inability to keep the commandments
created an intolerable strain upon him. It was impossible to be a
rabbinic Jew without feeling guilty. When the life situation of
the rabbis became manifestly undesirable, the rabbis tended to see
themselves as chastised by God.

Dr. Rieux's choice of an absurd and meaningless cosmos
may be viable for a few men. It is not viable for most. His position cannot mollify the irrational feelings of guilt that afflict most
men. The roots of neurotic guilt are located in the life history of
the individual. No theology can cause an individual to feel
unrealistically guilty unless he is predisposed to such feelings.
Where such a predisposition exists, a religious system such as
rabbinic Judaism may actually serve to *limit* neurotic guilt and
its self-punitive concomitants by offering a public context in
which guilt may be expressed and shared. Guilt can also be
periodically ameliorated by institutionalized rituals of atonement
and confession. By contrast, the situation of Joseph K. in Franz
Kafka's *The Trial* illustrates the dilemmas of a man afflicted with
irrational guilt in an absurd cosmos. The death of God does not
end neurotic guilt. On the contrary, it may heighten it. Contemporary men may lack both public and private resources for sharing
and objectifying their painful feelings. The rabbinic system was
admittedly harsh. In the long run, it may prove less harsh than
contemporary secular alternatives.

There was yet another reason why the rabbis, and their
followers to this day, had little alternative but to regard their
misfortunes as divinely inflicted. It is impossible for most people
to live in an absurd and meaningless universe. This is why Camus
wisely depicts Father Paneloux as dying, not of the plague, but
of the loss of his psychological universe. In their book, *The
Psychology of Rumor,* Allport and Postman describe the way in
which people pursue an "effort after meaning" so that their
world can somehow prove manageable. On the basis of their
experiments, they suggest that rumors which express blame tend

to justify, relieve, and explain to the subject his painful tensions.[41] In rabbinic Judaism, the all-powerful God is the most convenient object of blame for Jewish disaster. He is ultimately responsible. Nevertheless, there is too much anxiety and tension involved in blaming God. Self-accusation may be bitter, but it is both safer and less anxiety-producing. Self-reproach also relieves an important primary need, the need to counter-aggress against the enemy when the only safe object of aggression is oneself. Above all, self-accusation explains and offers hope. If suffering is to be understood as God's punitive retribution, there is always the hope that a new relationship to Him will set things right. According to Hannah Arendt, one of the worst aspects of the Nazi domination of captive Europe was the deliberately induced irrationality with which Nazi terror was applied. There was absolutely no hope for Jews. The blackest of tyrannies have a certain rationality about them, when they make it clear that submission means safety and rebellion means death. The Nazi death camps permitted no such intrusion of even the rationality of submission and surrender.

The ceding of ultimate power and authority to God's inscrutable will left the religious Jew with two alternatives: he could blame himself for his misfortunes; or he could proclaim the death of the omnipotent Lord of history, reluctantly regarding the cosmos as hopelessly absurd and ultimately gratuitous, as did Elisha ben Abuya and as do such modern existentialists as Sartre and Camus. Had religious Jews rejected God's omnipotence, they would have had to deny any connection between human virtue and human destiny. Allport, Postman, Bartlett, and other psychologists have suggested how difficult it is for most men to accept an absurd existence. The absurdist mentality seems to go completely against the structure of the human psyche. Men do not seem capable of tolerating a disordered world. They tend to create order even where there is none.

Few if any contemporary thinkers have asserted the absurdist position as insistently as Jean-Paul Sartre. Nevertheless, the characters in his plays and novels, Matthieu, Garcin, Inez, Antoine Roquentin, and others, testify to the extraordinary difficulties men meet when they face the challenge of freedom. Freedom for Sartre is in part freedom from the meaning imposed by consciousness upon human existence. Sartre sees the human predicament as absurd and free. He also sees man as inescapably drawn to reject the absurd freedom to which he is condemned. This is the meaning of *mauvaise foi* or bad faith.

It would have been impossible for the rabbis to reject an omnipotent God and affirm an absurd universe. Theirs was not yet the time of the death of God. He who rejects God rejects hope. Hope was precious to the defeated and beset Jewish community after the Roman war. Camus maintained that hope was the worst evil let loose from Pandora's box.[42] His view contrasts with that of the rabbis and prophets, who never tired of preaching hope in the restoration of Israel to the very people whose sins they denounced. No community can live under conditions of defeat without hope. It was impossible for the Jewish community to live without hope or the God of hope.

The path of doubt and denial was not realistic. Self-blame, self-punishment, heightened guilt, and the resolve to make peace with the omnipotent and inscrutable Lord of history offered the only viable option for the Jewish community. It was certainly the only psychologically tenable alternative. Nevertheless, the rabbinic legends of Korah's rebellion reflected issues which were to continue to confront the Jewish people to this day. When the terms of their existence became such that personal autonomy and self-realization became realistic possibilities for the conduct of life, religious sentiment was bound to change. Many Jews were quick to abandon the religious disciplines of Moses while retaining their identities as Jews. Jewish religious practice had been validated throughout Jewish history by the claim that it reflected the will of God. As such, no Jew was entitled to more of a reply to his doubts than Korah received from Moses. When Jews abandoned their religious disciplines, they frequently did so for reasons not unlike those of Elisha ben Abuya or those that the rabbis placed in the mouths of Korah and Dathan and Abiram. Perhaps today, in spite of the extraordinary psychological difficulties suggested above, some Jews have acquired such resources of inner strength that the alternative of an absurd, hopeless, and only partly comprehensible cosmos no longer frightens them. Their need to make an effort after meaning in history and in the cosmos may very well diminish as they find greater personal meaning within their own concrete lives. With this, there may also come a diminution of Israel's pathetic and often disastrous need to blame itself for all of its misfortunes. Before God, man may not be entirely in the wrong.

8 / God and Human Freedom in Rabbinic Theology

O NE OF THE MOST PERSISTENT TENDENCIES among contemporary theologians from Paul Tillich to Thomas J. J. Altizer has been their interpretation of the God of religious theism as the enemy of human freedom par excellence. The theologians have argued that such a God must ultimately reduce man to the status of an object of control and manipulation. Paul Tillich eloquently stated the case of those who reject theism because of its incompatibility with human autonomy in one of his most influential books, *The Courage To Be*:

> This is the God Nietzsche said had to be killed because nobody can tolerate being made into a mere object of absolute knowledge and absolute control. *This is the deepest root of atheism.* It is an atheism which is justified as the reaction against theological theism and its disturbing implications.[1] (italics mine)

Great minds can never anticipate the ultimate effect of their work. Tillich apparently went through a "death-of-God" experience. It is evident on almost every page of *The Courage To Be*. His negative evaluation of the God of theism was a far more important influence on contemporary death-of-God theology than he was prepared to recognize. Tillich's rejection of the God of theism rested largely on the same "either God or man" perspective which pervades the theology of Thomas J. J. Altizer. No contemporary American theologian has maintained that the God of theism is man's ultimate enemy as insistently as Altizer. For example, Altizer has written:

> The death of God does not propel man into an empty darkness, *it liberates him from every alien and opposing other*, and makes possible his transition into what Blake hailed as "The Great Humanity Divine" or the final coming together of God and man.[2] (italics mine)

The question of the alleged incompatibility of a personal, theistic God with human autonomy and self-realization is especially pertinent to classical rabbinic theology. The rabbis believed in a personal, theistic God. They could not imagine existence without Him. They regarded Jewish religious life as ultimately justified by the conviction that it was in conformity with His will. They believed that righteousness consisted in such compliance. They saw wickedness as ultimately a want of conformity with God's will.[3] According to the rabbis, nothing was intrinsically good or evil in itself. All actions and events received their ethical definition from God's commandments. Whatever God desired was good. What He rejected was evil.[4] Critics of theistic religion have tended to regard normative Judaism as a prime example of the religious rejection of human freedom. These same critics have tended to regard the divine-human encounter as essentially similar to the master-slave relationship.[5]

The tendency to equate the divine-human encounter with the master-slave relationship was not shared by the rabbis. They were convinced that obedience to God's norms as revealed in the Torah was a precondition of true freedom. They saw their lives as essentially free and fulfilling. They did not have any sense that their religious careers were fundamentally enslaved. I do not believe that the rabbinic system is viable without modification for twentieth-century Judaism. It is possible that the rabbinic "slave" did not know his own chains. Nevertheless, it is impossible to understand rabbinic Judaism without insight into why the rabbis did not regard their spiritual situation as unfree. This issue concerns Christians as well as Jews. The question of whether the God of theism is to be rejected is pertinent to both Christians and Jews. I believe that such a God must be rejected. I am convinced that if there is an omnipotent, theistic God, He must be the ultimate author of the gratuitous human evil which abounds in our time. I believe that the theistic notion of God's omnipotence contradicts the ascription of ultimate goodness to Him. My conception of divinity does not exclude the beneficence of God. I would, however, stress the dark and demonic aspects of God in His unfathomable holiness rather than His omnipotence over against man. I reject the God of theism, as did Tillich, but not because He is incompatible with human freedom.

In a very real sense, the religious convictions of the rabbis were dependent upon the teaching of the first chapter of Genesis that God is the Creator of the universe. The instincts of those medieval philosophers who regarded the question of *creatio ex nihilo* as the decisive issue between the Greek and Judaeo-Christian world-views were assuredly very sound.[6] The rabbis believed that God is restrained by His own free determination alone. Since He had created the universe, they believed that no order, relationship, arrangement, or happening could ultimately be independent of His will.[7] Nevertheless, the rabbis believed that, of His own free choice and for His own unfathomable reasons, God granted a measure of freedom to His creatures.[8] They believed that all physical relations and natural laws are expressions of God's will. The laws of nature do not constitute a realm of independent necessity in Jewish thought as they did for the ancient Greeks. The rabbis were also convinced that all personal behavioral norms were an expression of God's will.[9]

Sacred Scripture was considered the repository of these norms. The rabbis regarded the Torah, the Five Books of Moses, to have been communicated directly to Moses and to express completely and without contradiction God's teaching concerning the proper conduct of life. The rabbis did not believe that religious tradition could be progressively developmental. They had a very different sense of time than we do. When they referred to biblical personalities as if they were living in typically rabbinic circumstances, they revealed their conviction that things had remained the same or had gotten worse from generation to generation. They regarded the Torah as perfect because it expressed the will of the divine Source of all perfection. The revelation of God's will through the instrumentality of the Torah had a once-and-for-all-time character. The remaining books of the Bible were considered to be dependent upon the Torah. They interpreted, amplified, and restated its message. They neither added nor detracted from its fundamental intent.[10]

The rabbis considered the Torah to be the written repository of God's will. They also believed that God had bestowed upon Moses and his rabbinic successors an organon of interpretation with which the true meaning of the Written Law could be established, taught, and made relevant to every generation. This was the Oral Law.[11] Whenever contradictions seemed to appear in Scripture, they were resolved in accordance with the interpretative perspectives of the Oral Law. According to the rabbis, all that was required to understand the unitary, perfect, and complete character of God's will as expressed in the Torah was proper religious understanding. This understanding was acquired by diligent study of the tradition in the rabbinic schools.

The rabbis emphatically rejected the notion that they were free to determine appropriate behavior in pragmatic or utilitarian terms. They regarded independence of judgment before the demands of religious obligation as an example of extraordinary folly. They did not esteem autonomy or self-determination as we know them. This aspect of rabbinic Judaism has led its critics to regard it as a classic example of superego religion.

This negative evaluation of rabbinic theism rests upon an

assumption the rabbis would never have granted—namely, that the biblical commandments they obeyed were the arbitrary and irrational fiat of an Omnipotent Autocrat. The rabbis emphatically did not regard God in this light. Undoubtedly, Calvin's theology and Kierkegaard's homily on the binding of Isaac in *Fear and Trembling* have been as influential as Hegel and Nietzsche in furthering this view of rabbinic theism.[12]

There is an absolute and fundamental difference between the Creator-creature relationship and the master-slave relationship in rabbinic theology. A creator is not an arbitrary, capricious tyrant. The rabbis did not regard creation as a demonic act perpetrated by an irresponsible autocrat for the purpose of multiplying human misery. Perhaps Freud was fundamentally correct when he suggested that a man's image of God is infused with very large doses of his unconscious image of his own father. I have not attempted to disguise the extent to which the hostility between fathers and sons was both present and psychically operative in rabbinic thought.[13] I have attempted to demonstrate that the hostility was kept within manageable proportions. Nothing in rabbinic Judaism suggests that the rabbis or their followers were unduly driven to excessive antipaternal hostility. At no point in the literature of rabbinic Judaism is it suggested that the sons will vanquish the fathers or the Father-God. Perhaps Judaism was able to remain a Father-God religion precisely because the father-son relationship was kept in bounds. In rabbinic Judaism, the sons ultimately sought to identify with their fathers rather than to overcome them. One of the psychological results was that the rabbis never believed it was necessary to overcome God in order to be free men. They believed that religious obedience was ultimately their response to a divine Author of existence rather than to an alien, hostile, and intruding master. The rabbis did not feel obliged to obey God simply because He was more powerful and would punish, although this element in rabbinic theology cannot be denied.[14] There was yet another reason for religious compliance in rabbinic Judaism. The rabbis

believed God was to be obeyed because He is the Creator of existence itself. They were convinced that it was ultimately impossible to reject the will of the One upon whom all depend for
existence.

If we grant with Freud that our religious ideologies are
very largely the outer projection of our inner world, we may be
drawn to ask what was psychologically at stake between Jesus and
the rabbis. I have already suggested that much of Paul's theology
revolved around the issue of the failure of sublimation as a
method of coping with the anarchic impulses of the unconscious.[15]
One can ask whether Jesus' teaching does not contain strong elements of antipaternal hostility. Few, if any, contemporary Protestant thinkers have emphasized the absolute character of Christian liberty as insistently as Norman O. Brown. He has stressed
the element of fraternity, the preference for a social order based
upon the supremacy of the sons in Christianity.[16] Jesus makes it
clear that his disciples are to forsake the traditions and structure
of the family and follow after him:

> "For I am come to set a man against his father, a daughter
> against her mother, a young wife against her mother-in-law;
> and a man will find his enemies under his own roof.
> "No man is worthy of me who cares more for father
> or mother than for me; no man is worthy of me who cares
> more for son or daughter . . .[17]

With these admonitions Jesus explodes the disciplines of the
family structure as they were known in Judaism. Jesus' words
also offer further corroboration of my contention that what is
unconscious in Judaism rises to the surface in early Christianity.
When Jesus says that "a man will find his enemies under his own
roof,"[18] he brings to consciousness a psychological reality
that Judaism preferred to cope with through discipline and
sublimation.

The antipaternal bias of early Christianity would also
seem to be present in the tradition of the virgin birth. One of

the most persistent fantasies of those who experience difficulty in coming to terms with their real fathers is the delusion that they were sired by an infinitely more powerful figure than their apparent progenitors.[19] The story of Jesus' birth contains a denial of Joseph's role and the assertion that Jesus became coequal with the most powerful of all fathers, God Himself. Joseph humbly accepts the subordinate role. The son triumphs.

The question of antipaternal hostility cannot be excluded from the debate concerning contemporary radical theology. Each death-of-God theologian may find it helpful to ask himself what his proclamation of the death of God means in terms of his own relation to his father. It is not necessary to be explicitly and intimately autobiographical in dealing with the issue before the public. Nevertheless, if Freud is correct about the projective nature of religion, and I see no reason to challenge him on this issue, each theology must be regarded as a refined but nonetheless highly personal projection of the theologian's unconscious. Presumably those theologians who greet the death of God as a redeeming and a fulfilling event are saying something extremely personal. So too are those theologians who acknowledge the death of God but with a large measure of sadness.

I do not raise these questions to suggest that either Judaism or Christianity in their classical or their contemporary forms is the "better" or the "healthier" projection. I regard both Judaism and Christianity as containing strong elements of both illness and health. Religious illness can be compared to that which is induced by a vaccine for the purpose of creating antibodies capable of resisting the full ravages of disease. I inquire concerning the projective nature of theological discourse in order to become aware of the pitfalls that await *any* theologian who cannot face the subjective character of his enterprise. I dwell on the projective element also in the hope that it may prove possible to push beyond religious subjectivity at some level. I have suggested elsewhere that God can best be regarded as the Holy Nothingness.[20] Although some critics have regarded my language as indistinguishable from atheism, my intent has been to stress the utter inadequacy of all verbal formulations before the divine reality. I have in actuality merely returned to a very archaic insight concerning the mystery and the namelessness of God. My critics have also reiterated the very ancient response of those who find the final mystery of God both intolerable and threatening. My conception of God's Nothingness is not that of a void. It is a conception of the plenum out of which the totality of all that has existed, does exist, and will exist is derived. When our religious ideologies finally begin to transcend the intimacy of our childhood memories within the nurturing family, we arrive at the domain of final mystery, before which silence alone is the adequate response.

The rabbinic view that God's will is ultimately to be honored because He is the creator of all that exists is implicit in the conception that God created both the natural and the moral orders through the aid of the Torah, which served as its pattern and archetype. The rabbis did not see the moral and religious realms as separate and distinct from the natural order. Both were the harmonious product of a single creative divine will.[21] Even the miracles did not happen gratuitously. They were stipulated in the cosmically pre-existent Torah.[22] In a sense, the rabbis regarded the moral and religious prescriptions of the Torah as no more arbitrary or irrational than the advice that if a man attempts to fly with his hands, he assuredly will come to grief. Religious commandments were regarded as equally rooted in the structure of existence as physical laws. Both realms were created by one and the same Author. Neither domain was inherently more arbitrary than the other. Sin is more than the sinner's misguided attempt to gain independence against a superior power who is bound to defeat him; sin is a falsification of the sinner's being as a creature. Solomon Schechter has suggested that sin in rabbinic theology is rebellion against God.[23] This notion is accurate up to a point. Nevertheless, it does not carry the matter far enough. Rebellion means something very different in the Creator-creature relationship from what it means in the master-slave relationship. In the master-slave relationship, rebellion places the slave against an alien and hostile power; in the Creator-creature relationship, the sinner usurps a role and a station inappropriate to his proper nature. Sin is thus as much a violation of the sinner's true being as it is a rejection of God's commandments. This is the deepest root of the rabbinic view that sin is slavery.[24]

The rabbinic conception of sin is misunderstood when the divine-human encounter is seen as an intersubjective combat or as the protest of a human nullity against a divine Omnipotence. The rabbis never pictured human beings as nullities. Too frequently the image conjured up when sin is represented as rebellion is that of potentially free men in revolt against a power seeking to enslave them. Those who stress the subject-object character of the theistic divine-human encounter, as have Paul Tillich and Erich Fromm, turn religious obedience into a surrender of potential freedom in the face of superior numinous power. At one level, this criticism represents an unwarranted application of Nietzsche's analysis of the Judaeo-Christian ethic as a slave morality to the understanding of rabbinic theology and to theism in general.[25] Nietzsche's insights concerning the highly problematic morality of religious submission and repression have such merit. His analysis of *ressentiment* as the aggression of the impotent against the strong has been crucial to the self-understanding of modern man.[26] The questions I raise concerning the extent to which rabbinic theology was a psychological reflection of Jewish powerlessness are in large measure dependent upon Nietzsche's insights into the dynamics of powerlessness. Unlike some modern Jewish theologians, I see no special virtue in Jewish powerlessness. It is a fatality the Jewish community has had to learn to live with. Nevertheless, Nietzsche's insights are not as helpful as a critique of theism as Tillich has suggested. The God of theism does not reduce man merely to an object of manipulation and control.

Behind Nietzsche, there stands the even more decisive

influence of Hegel's dialectic of the "unhappy consciousness" *(Unglückliches Bewusstsein)*. In the *Phenomenology,* one of the dialectic results of the fragmentation of consciousness in skepticism is the division of consciousness into two realms: one, the unchanging, permanent, abiding domain of the all-powerful Other; and the second, the realm of man, the evanescent nullity, aware of the impotent and fleeting character of his own reality, who cedes all being and power to an alien, transcendent Master.[27] In other discussions in Hegel's works, the unhappy consciousness is described as typical of medieval Christianity's relation to God, although it is hardly appropriate there. Hegel also asserts that it is prototypical of the servile relationship of Abraham and his progeny to the God of Israel. This is one of the classical sources of the equation of the divine-human encounter with the master-slave relationship.[28]

The rabbis did not see the Jewish religious situation as did Hegel. *The rabbis could not conceive of freedom apart from God because they were utterly incapable of imagining existence without Him.* In rabbinic thought, God primarily specifies the limitations of existence rather than the impediments to human freedom. The first chapter of Genesis is decisive. For the rabbis, rebellion is a turning away from realistic freedom and fulfillment to folly, the existential folly of being too-much. In the Creator-creature relationship, freedom is limited by the nature of created existence. Nevertheless, the aim of the Creator is not to deny freedom to the creature, but to allow as much freedom as in consistent with the inherent limitations and structure of the created order. Hence, the rabbis insisted that true freedom was a concomitant of fulfillment of the Torah. The rabbis felt that men fulfilled their natures as created beings by fulfilling God's will. Religious obedience was seen as an existential fulfillment rather than a self-inflicted defeat.[29]

There is truth in the assertion that the attitude of the rabbis toward God as the Author of existence resembles the attitude of the child to its parents. Here the analogy between God and the superego is very relevant. The problem of the similitude between God and the superego is complex. The superego is more than a hostile and censoring faculty. As ego-ideal, it has its loving and rewarding side. The ego-ideal makes for personal and social growth, development and security. This corresponds to the fact that under normal circumstances the child's relations with its parents are not exclusively marked by slavish submission to a hostile external power. There is submission. Much of it is grudging. Nevertheless, there is also identification and a turning to the parents as the primary source of approval. When the child identifies with the parent and introjects parental standards, he does not internalize an entirely alien reality; he perpetuates, though often beyond the period of its relevance, the fact that he is dependent upon the parents for his very existence and his early nurture.[30]

Creation is an analog of giving birth. The rabbis did not, of course, see the world as the child of the mating of primordial powers. Yet their conviction that the world has a beginning, a time of development, and will have an end, carries over into the cosmic realm the human experience of birth, growth, and decay. This view has at least two justifications. One is that the macrocosmic world cannot be devoid of resemblance to man, the microcosm. Both are ultimately aspects of a unitary cosmos. The other is psychological. The very capacity of the rabbis and all religious people to project their inner world into the cosmic sphere as religious belief was an act of self-therapy and self-cure. It was a way of dealing with much of the inner stress of the psychic world which today can often be successfully managed only through psychotherapeutic delving.

Creation, nurture, and guidance are attributes of God in the rabbinic system as they are attributes of parents in the world of the child. Rabbinic Judaism saw its compliance with God's will as a fulfillment, precisely because the rabbis were keenly aware of the analogy between God's role and that of the parents. The belief that God has His purpose, His plan, and that in the

end there will be a reconciliation between God and man, did not
stem from the incapacity of the rabbis to see reality in its nakedness. It arose out of their conviction that the universe is dependent
upon the guidance and nurture of a cosmic source rather than on
the irrational and opaque arbitrariness of a strange and alien
power.[31]

I have already alluded to the rabbinic conception of the
sinner as attempting to be too-much and his punishment as a reduction to the status of being too-little.[32] I have suggested the
conception of sin as ontic self-aggrandizement and punishment
as ontic diminution in rabbinic Judaism. As such, I have noted
its resemblance to the Greek notions of *hubris* and *nemesis*.[33]
The rabbinic legends concerning the careers of the wicked
strongly suggest that the rabbis considered freedom and self-
fulfillment to consist in the wisdom of knowing the limitations
of one's assigned place in the order of things. At the level of
explicit theological statement as well as mythic hyperbole, the
rabbis did not see the existence of God as a threat to *realistic*
human freedom. Thomas Altizer's call to the Christian to will
the death of God as the prologue to human freedom would have
been emphatically rejected by the rabbis.[34] Were they capable of
responding to Altizer, they would argue that God cannot be an
enemy of human freedom since he is the author of human existence. Without God, there would be no human being to be free,
according to the rabbis.

Perhaps one of the deepest roots of the failure to see the
God of theism as consistent with human freedom is the refusal
to see the act of creation as a gift rather than an impediment.
The fact that creation is limited and circumscribed does not make
it any less a gift or any less free, realistically speaking. On the
contrary, had it been without limit, it would also have been without content. To exist is to be something definite and limited, to
be set apart and defined by the rest of the matrix of existence.
The rabbis were convinced that God did not create in order to enslave but to make free. The creation of a world of slaves in fear

of a cosmic master would have been, in their eyes, an indecent and sadistic mockery. The rabbis were never so overwhelmed by the thought of the existence of God that they had to carry the idea of God's opposition to man to its radical conclusions. Creation meant limit; existence could only be partial. Nevertheless, the reality of human freedom was never in question.

It is entirely possible that the framework of a theistic religious system is not especially relevant to the problems of life in our time. If, however, it is to be rejected, it ought to be encountered on the basis of an understanding of what it did in fact maintain concerning the decisive issues of human existence. The rabbis freely submitted themselves to their inherited traditions. They regarded man as endowed with a limited measure of existence, dignity, and freedom. Though the Law was engraved *(haruth)* on the Tablets, its content for the rabbis was freedom *(héruth)*. Whether we concur fully in their assessment or not, they were utterly convinced that "There is none free save he who occupies himself with the Torah."[35]

9 / Scribes, Pharisees, and Hypocrites
Rabbinic Identification with the Sinner

T HE UNCONSCIOUS was not invented by Freud. Men have sought through drama, legend, myth, and religion to cope with it from time immemorial. The legends of the Aggadah were both the products of the rabbinic unconscious and the rabbis' attempt to cope with its stresses.

Few psychological stresses are as universal as the tendency to negate the very norms which are indispensable to the maintenance and survival of any human community. Judaism was a religious system resting upon a foundation of religious and social law. Nevertheless, the temptation toward antinomianism could never entirely be suppressed even in the most outwardly compliant religious leaders. Throughout the Aggadah, the rabbis tend to identify themselves with the worst sinners of the Bible. This tendency is especially manifest in the rabbinic legends concerning such idolatrous kings as Ahab, Manasseh, and Jeroboam. All three rulers were anachronistically depicted in the Aggadah as great masters of rabbinic learning who went astray. The rabbis unwittingly betray their own sense of guilt and unworthiness in these legends. They often saw themselves as no better than the worst sinners of Israel. Their self-image as reflected in the Aggadah contrasts with the image of the Pharisees as dishonest hypocrites that has become normative in the Western world.

The terms "pharisee" and "pharisaic" have customarily been used as synonyms for religious hypocrisy, concentration on the outer forms of ritual at the expense of inner commitment, and, above all, a pretense to undeserved virtue.[1] This usage reflects a historical controversy between Christianity and Judaism. The Pharisees were the party of the rabbis at the time of the rise of Christianity. All contemporary branches of Judaism are their spiritual heirs. Because of their rejection of the new Christian movement, the Pharisees were understandably treated as enemies by the early Church.

Matthew 23 is one of the most important sources for the normative Christian view of the Pharisees. Jesus offers his view of the Pharisees: "They do all their deeds to be seen by men; for they make their phylacteries broad and their fringes long, and they love the place of honor at feasts and best seats in the synagogues."[2] The denunciation continues with a series of accusations, each of which is introduced by the phrase, "Woe unto you, scribes and Pharisees, hypocrites." The denunciations include:

> "Woe unto you, scribes and Pharisees, hypocrites! for you cleanse the outside of the cup and of the plate, but inside they are full of extortion and rapacity. You blind Pharisee! first cleanse the inside of the cup and of the plate, that the outside also may be clean! . . .
>
> "Woe unto you, scribes and Pharisees, hypocrites! for you are like whitewashed tombs, which outwardly appear beautiful, but within they are full of dead men's bones and all uncleanness. So you also outwardly appear righteous to men, but within you are full of hypocrisy and iniquity. . . .[3]
>
> "You serpents, you brood of vipers, how are you to escape being sentenced to hell? Therefore I send you prophets and wise men and scribes, some of whom you will kill and crucify, and some you will scourge in your synagogues and persecute from town to town. . . ."[4]

The image is exceedingly harsh. The Jewish community has never accepted this negative evaluation of the founders of normative rabbinic Judaism. In the twentieth century, Christian scholars such as George Foote Moore and R. Travers Herford have presented a more sympathetic picture of the Pharisees.[5] Nevertheless, there must have been some Pharisees who partly resembled the New Testament image. The rabbis themselves were often critical of the kind of Pharisee denounced in Matthew.[6] Rabbinic literature reflects little pretense to virtue on the part of the rabbis. The rabbis were intensely anxious that they might fall far short of the righteousness expected of them.

The rabbis believed that there was an ineradicable impulse to do evil in every human being. This was the *yetzer ha-ra,* the evil inclination. The *yetzer ha-ra* resembled the id in certain respects. The rabbis asserted that, without it, the world could not be maintained nor could children be born.[7] Nevertheless, it could easily tempt a man to go astray. The rabbis confessed that they had to struggle with great difficulty against their own inclinations. The saying "The greater the man, the greater his *yetzer ha-ra*"[8] is often cited as evidence of their difficulties in the face of temptation.

This saying occurs in a passage in which Abaye, a Babylonian rabbi, discusses how powerfully he has been affected by the *yetzer ha-ra*:

> Abaye explained: [The *yetzer ha-ra* works] against scholars more than anyone else; as was the case when Abaye heard a certain man say to a certain woman, "Let us arise betimes and go on our way." "I will," said Abaye, "follow them in order to keep them from transgression." And he followed them three or four parsangs across the meadows. When they parted, he heard them say, "Our company is pleasant, the way is long."
>
> "If it were I [literally, "he who hates me"]," said Abaye, "I could not have restrained myself." And so he went and leaned in deep anguish against a doorpost, when a cer-

tain old man came up to him and taught him: "The greater
the man, the greater the *yetzer ha-ra*."[9]

The psychological truth of the incident is apparent. There is an
intuitive recognition of the relationship between sublimated eros
and scholarly accomplishment. Abaye is convinced that he could
not accompany a woman so innocently. The old man in the story
is identified with Elijah. The rabbis used this device to indicate
their estimation of the antiquity and the authority of Abaye's observation. The story is one of a series describing the power of the
yetzer ha-ra.

There was nothing academic about the rabbinic concern
with the *yetzer ha-ra*. The rabbis were profoundly aware of the
power of their own temptations.

Rabbinic identification with the sinner is especially evident in *Perek Helek,* a chapter of Tractate Sanhedrin. The subject matter of this chapter largely concerns the question of those
who are denied a share in the world to come. The chapter includes the tradition that "three kings and four commoners" have
no share in the world to come.[10] The kings are Ahab, Jeroboam,
and Manasseh; the commoners are Doeg, Balaam, Ahitophel,
and Gehazi. All seven are portrayed as great masters of rabbinic
or mystical wisdom. Their sins are ascribed to the misuse of their
great religious knowledge. The traditions illustrate Abaye's conviction that "The greater the man, the greater the *yetzer ha-ra*."[11]
Greatness is depicted as a function of religious knowledge and
wisdom in each instance.

The misuse of religious knowledge by a great scholar is
the theme of the Balaam legends. In the Bible, Balaam is a pagan
prophet who blesses Israel against his own inclinations.[12] The
rabbis depicted Balaam as an inverted, black Moses, a polar opposite of the real Moses. Balaam apparently fascinated the rabbis.
They often pictured him as the greatest of the gentile prophets,
in contrast to Moses, the greatest of the Israelite prophets. According to some scholars, Balaam may be a rabbinic alias for

Jesus.[13] His morals are far worse than Moses', but never his intelligence. Some of Balaam's prophetic gifts were greater than Moses'. Moses was never certain whether he was addressed by God or an angel. Balaam was. Balaam could speak to God directly at will, but not Moses. Furthermore, although Balaam only exceeded Moses in some respects, he surpassed all other Hebrew prophets in every respect.[14] Throughout the Balaam traditions, the rabbis implied that a paramount master of religious lore can perpetrate the greatest evil.

Ahab, Jeroboam, and Manasseh were pictured as great rabbis who turn against the Torah. The rabbis saw a great deal of themselves in the three kings. They asserted that Manasseh was able to interpret Leviticus in fifty-five different ways, Ahab in eighty-five, and Jeroboam in one hundred and three.[15] Even the relatively modest attainments of Manasseh were considered extraordinary.

There is an Aggadic tradition that Jeroboam's rabbinic teacher was Ahijah the Shilonite. According to Rabbi Simeon ben Yohai, his own (Rabbi Simeon's) personal merits combined with those of Ahijah were great enough to intercede on behalf of all of the generations from the days of Abraham to the coming of the Messiah.[16] In the rabbinic imagination, Jeroboam could hardly have had a better or a wiser teacher.

At one time Jeroboam's religious knowledge was said to be equal to Ahijah's. In their time they were the only teachers who knew the inner mysteries of Jewish mystical lore. Even the ministering angels protested to God for bestowing upon Jeroboam so great a degree of mystical wisdom because of the idolatrous acts he was destined to commit. Nevertheless, God refused to punish Jeroboam in spite of His knowledge of the king's future acts. At the time, he was still a pious and righteous king.[17]

Jeroboam's religious scholarship was so great, according to R. Judah, that the people of his realm were prepared to follow him to any extreme. R. Judah depicted Jeroboam as assembling the royal advisers in his chambers to propose that the nation worship idols. The king placed an idolater next to each pious adviser. He then asked the group whether they would grant him unquestioning obedience. The council agreed until the king proposed that they worship idols. The righteous balked. The sinners argued: "Dost thou really think that a man like Jeroboam would serve idols? He wishes to test us, to see whether we would give him full acceptance." Even men such as Jehu and Ahijah were persuaded to follow him.[18]

The most interesting legends of this group concern Manasseh. The Talmud reports that Rab Ashi once concluded his lecture in the *yeshivah,* the rabbinical academy, immediately before the section in Tractate Sanhedrin dealing with the three kings who have no share in the world to come. Referring to the kings, Rab Ashi told his students, "Tomorrow we will commence with our colleagues." That evening Manasseh appeared to Rab Ashi in a dream. The king asked the rabbi: "Thou hast called us thy colleagues and the colleagues of thy father; now from what part of the bread is [the piece for reciting] the *ha-motzi* to be taken?"[19] Rab Ashi was unable to answer. Manasseh chided him for daring to call himself a colleague when he betrayed such ignorance of a ritual question. Rab Ashi asked Manasseh to teach him. He promised that he would offer the teaching in the king's name in the *yeshivah* the next day. Manasseh replied that it was proper to consume the crust when reciting the benediction over bread. The rabbi asked Manasseh why he worshipped idols in view of his great religious knowledge. Manasseh replied: "Wert thou there, thou wouldst have caught my skirt and sped after me!" The next day Rab Ashi began his lecture in the *yeshivah* with a very different reference to the idolatrous kings: "We will commence with our teachers."[20]

The incident is among those which illustrate how deeply the rabbis were affected by the legends of the Bible and the Aggadah. Rab Ashi genuinely admires a man traditionally regarded as one of the most idolatrous kings of Israel. His ambivalence is apparent. Manasseh affected Rab Ashi's psyche so deeply that he not only dreamed about him but felt compelled to relate the incident to others. The tradition could have been censored by the rabbi's successors. Instead, they passed it on from generation to generation. Though there are traditions in which Manasseh repents,[21] the issue here is not imitation of his repentance but of his idolatry.

Had Rab Ashi followed Manasseh's path, he would, according to rabbinic tradition, have imitated a parricide. According to rabbinic tradition, Manasseh was the grandson of Isaiah. He placed the prophet on trial for his life and used his religious scholarship both to condemn him and to prove the triteness of much of the Torah. The tradition has no warrant in Scripture; it does show the capacity of the rabbis to invent heretical arguments against their own traditions. Manasseh is depicted as saying to Isaiah at the trial:

> "Your teacher Moses said: 'Men shall not see me and live,'[22] and you said: 'I saw the Lord sitting on a high throne, high and lifted up.'[23] Your teacher Moses said: 'For what great nation is there that hath God so nigh unto them, as the Lord our God is whenever we call upon Him'[24] [implying all the time]; and you said: 'Seek ye the Lord when He may be found.'[25] Your teacher Moses said: 'The number of days will I fulfill':[26] but you said: 'And I will add unto your days fifteen years!' "[27]

Manasseh's attack contradicts a fundamental rabbinic belief, that the same divine inspiration was operative without contradiction in both Moses and the prophets. Manasseh's heretical words are in reality not the king's. They are the product of the rabbinic imagination. Here as elsewhere, the rabbis were strongly ambivalent concerning their own religious system. They used fantasy as a safety-valve for expressing their own reservations. Just as repressed desires often find symbolic expression in dreams, religious doubts and censored yearnings were often expressed by the rabbis without conscious awareness in the Ag-

gadah. The rabbis were incapable of giving vent explicitly to
doubts in their own name. The Aggadah often permitted the expression of heretical ideas within the context of the rabbinic
system without threatening the stability of the system. As a
safety-valve the Aggadah was an important element in assuring
the long-term stability of rabbinic Judaism.

Ahab is also reported to have appeared to a rabbi in a
dream. After spending two months lecturing in the *yeshivah* on
Ahab's wickedness, R. Levi dreamed that Ahab chided him for
devoting all his time to the first half of the verse "But there
was none like unto Ahab which did see himself to work wickedness in the sight of the Lord . . ."[28] Ahab reproached the rabbi
for excluding the second half of the verse in his exposition of the
king's career: "whom Jezebel his wife stirred up."[29] R. Levi
thereupon spent the next two months expounding the second
half, which identifies Jezebel as the cause of the king's wrongdoing. Although R. Levi does not exhibit the same degree of
admiration for Ahab which Rab Ashi had for Manasseh, he also
was deeply affected by an idolatrous king.[30]

In spite of Ahab's sinfulness, the rabbis found mitigating
circumstances for the king's worst deeds. According to the Bible,
Ahab enjoyed a long and relatively prosperous life. Just as the
rabbis interpreted disaster as the result of sin, they explained
prosperity as evidence of virtue. The rabbis reasoned that because of his good fortune Ahab couldn't have been completely
worthless. Their logic is already implicit in the Bible where God
says to Elijah: "See thou how Ahab humbled himself before me?
Because he humbleth himself before me, I will not bring the evil
in his days. But in his son's days will I bring the evil upon his
house."[31] The biblical theme is taken up and sharpened by the
rabbis.

According to the Aggadah, when Ben Haddad beseiged
Jerusalem, Ahab was willing to accede to all of the Syrian king's
demands until Ben Haddad demanded the surrender of the
Torah. Ahab balked and was ultimately victorious. This was

taught by the same R. Johanan who maintained elsewhere that "The light transgressions which Ahab committed were equal to the gravest committed by Jeroboam."[32] R. Johanan also taught: "There is no furrow in Palestine upon which Ahab did not plant an idol and worship it."[33] Also: "He [Ahab] wrote upon the gates of Samaria, 'Ahab denies the God of Israel.' "[34] Nevertheless, R. Johanan maintained that Ahab merited his reign of twenty-two years because he had honored the Torah. He derived this exegetically:

> R. Johanan said: Why did Ahab merit royalty for twenty-two years? Because he honored the Torah, which was given in twenty-two letters, as it is written: "And he sent messengers to Ahab king of Israel into the city and he said unto him, Thus saith Ben Haddad, Thy silver and thy gold is mine; thy wives also and thy children, even thy goodliest . . . Yet will I send my servants unto thee tomorrow at this time, and they shall search thine house, and the houses of thy servants: and it shall be that *whatsoever is pleasant in thine eyes, they shall put it in their hands*, and take it away. . . . Wherefore he [Ahab] said unto the messengers of Ben Haddad, Tell my Lord the king, All that thou didst send for to thy servant at the first I will do; but this thing I may not do."[35] Now what is meant by "Whatsoever is pleasant in thine eyes"? Surely the Scrolls of the Torah.[36] (italics mine)

According to R. Johanan, though the great idolator was prepared to surrender the wives and children of his realm, he was not prepared to surrender the Torah! There is, of course, no explicit reference to the Torah in the biblical verse. The story is invented by R. Johanan. In his own mind, R. Johanan sharpened the traditions of both Ahab's rebelliousness and his repentance.

There is also a tendency to mitigate Ahab's sinfulness in discussing his violent seizure of Naboth's vineyard and Naboth's death. Following Scripture, the rabbis depict Ahab as a penitent.[37]

The rabbinic image of Ahab was both complex and contradictory. He is regarded as a great religious scholar, yet he publicly proclaims his denial of God. He is liberal with scholars,[38] yet he plants idols in the furrows of every field. Ahab was not a foreign king. His encounter with Elijah cast him into a role of great prominence in the religious history of the Jewish people. He was an important exemplification of the tendency, never entirely suppressed, of the sons of Israel to turn their backs upon the Lord of Israel because of the enticements of Astarte and her daughters. Ahab represented a tendency in ancient Israel. The rabbis apparently intuited in him a symbol of an ineradicable tendency within themselves.

The same tendency to depict the worst sinners as masters of rabbinic learning is also found in the traditions concerning the four commoners who were denied a place in the world to come. I have already alluded to the great prophetic powers of Balaam.[39] I shall consider the traditions concerning Doeg the Edomite.

In the Bible, Doeg the Edomite betrays Ahimelech and the priests of Nob for their hospitality to David when he fled from Saul.[40] In rabbinic tradition, Doeg becomes a persistent enemy of David and a prototype of the great religious scholar who utterly misuses his knowledge.

There are a number of attempts to play on his name, *Doeg ha Edomi.* R. Isaac held that he was so called because he used to redden *(ma'adim)* with shame the faces of all who argued the Law with him. R. Isaac said that whenever a man sought to debate a matter of religious law with Doeg, his arguments were so powerful that all were reduced to silence in his presence.[41] He is also depicted as being the head of the Sanhedrin in his days.[42]

In one tradition, Samuel, a Babylonian teacher, finds Rab Judah, a rabbi of great authority, weeping against a door. Rab Judah told Samuel that the rabbinic knowledge of Doeg and Ahitophel caused him great depression. Rab Judah's scholarly acumen was so great that he was called *shineena* (literally, "sharp one").[43] Nevertheless, he was convinced of the infinitely greater scholarship of Doeg and Ahitophel. Rab Judah rhetorically asked how could he expect redemption if scholars as great as Doeg and Ahitophel had no share in the world to come. Samuel consoled him. He asserted that there was impurity in the hearts of Doeg and Ahitophel. Rab Judah referred to the pair as "the rabbis."[44] The reference resembles Rab Ashi's allusion to Manasseh as his colleague and his teacher.

Doeg is also depicted as using his religious knowledge to put David to shame. David was a person of the greatest religious authority in the traditions of both Judaism and Christianity. Doeg's hostility to David parallels the traditions in which Dathan and Abiram oppose Moses.[45] According to the Bible, David was the grandson of Ruth the Moabitess.[46] In the legends, Doeg argues that David's descent made him ineligible for membership in the community of Israel. Scripture had expressly forbidden either Moabites or Ammonites to enter the congregation unto the tenth generation.[47] Doeg uses his biblical scholarship to protest David's fitness.[48] There is no warrant for this in Scripture.

Not only were the wicked great scholars who had gone astray, but the best and wisest of men were not without blemish in the rabbinic imagination. The Adam-Eve-serpent legends stressed the proclivity of all men for sinful conduct.[49] Even Moses, the supreme model of rabbinic virtue, sinned and was punished.[50] Noah was regarded as righteous in his generation by the rabbis. However, they were quick to point out that his time possessed little virtue. Noah is the object of much censure in the Aggadah.[51] Jacob, one of Israel's patriarchs, is guilty of self-apotheosis.[52] Occasionally there are isolated statements in the Aggadah concerning a few men who were relatively without sin. However, each is described elsewhere as having committed some sins.

The rabbis thus identified themselves with the very men whose patterns of behavior they sought to avoid. They did so largely because of their intuition of their own temptations. This is evident in the stories concerning Abaye, Rab Judah, and Rab Ashi which I have discussed. It is also apparent in the legends in

which R. Meir and R. Akiba were seized by strong sexual temptation. They successfully overcame it only after great struggle.
Both rabbis are described as having been sorely tempted by
Satan. He appeared to them as a seductively beautiful woman.
Each pursued the woman until, at the last moment, Satan re-
sumed his normal guise.[53] There is also the tradition that R. Meir
entered a Roman house of prostitution in order to rescue his
captive sister-in-law.[54]

There were other reasons why the rabbis tended to see
themselves as no better than the worst sinners. I have observed
that the rabbis were firmly convinced Judaea was overwhelmed
by the Romans because of the sins of the Jewish people. They believed that they were sinful members of a sinful people. They
were convinced that an end to Jewish estrangement from God's
Law would result in an end to Jewish alienation from the ancestral homeland.[55] They regarded the continuation of exile as
a result of the continuation of Jewish sinfulness. It was difficult
to separate the personal from the social. Guilt was built into the
ethos of rabbinic Judaism. The minute details of personal behavior were regulated by the Torah. Some religious deviance was
inevitable even on the part of the most pious. Above all, the sinner
rebelled against God in rabbinic Judaism. It is difficult to deviate
from community norms when they are validated by consensus or
inherited tradition. It was infinitely more difficult for the rabbinic Jew to deviate. Every infraction of his religious life was
regarded as willful rebellion against God.

Normally, rabbinic Jews were able to tolerate a measure
of anxiety and guilt over their feelings of estrangement from
God. There was confidence that somehow man and God would
finally be reconciled. This conviction was never lost in normative
Judaism. The power of repentance and God's mercy were strongly
emphasized.[56] We do, however, know of at least one rabbinic
Jew in whom the anxiety over estrangement from God was so
great that he finally despaired of any reconciliation under the
Law. I refer, of course, to Paul of Tarsus. Paul tells us: "There-

fore by the deeds of the Law there shall no flesh be justified in his sight. . . . For all have sinned and come short of the glory of God.[57] Paul's statements about the Law, especially in Romans, are clearly autobiographical. His anxiety was undoubtedly more intense than that of most rabbinic Jews. It was a predictable response to the rabbinic system. It had to happen to someone sooner or later. Paul's anxiety over sin was overcome in the faith that the Christ was the divine atonement for the sins of men. By a historical accident—Christians would call it the wisdom of the divine plan—Paul's inner psychological needs coincided with the moment in history when a group of Jews were convinced that the crucified Jesus was the Messiah and Redeemer of Israel. The Christianity of Paul was the psychological resultant of many of the same dilemmas that led the rabbis to identify with the sinners of Israel in the Aggadah. The rabbis expressed a measure of their guilt through these identifications. They sought to alleviate their sense of guilt through repentance and the resolve to turn to the path of righteousness. Paul was finally convinced that such measures were incapable of ending his anxiety. Only a new and radical solution proved effective for Paul. Psychologically speaking, Paul's insights had much merit. He understood that the rabbinic path of sublimation was a neverending treadmill. The harder one tried to improve one's relation with God, the more one realized how great the distance between God and man remained. Paul reasoned that what man was incapable of doing for himself, God had done for him through the Christ.

It is also possible that the difference between Paul and his former rabbinic colleagues lay in the psychological identifications each made. As we have seen, the rabbis identified in part with the sinners of Israel. Paul tells us very clearly that he identified with the risen Christ:

"Know ye not, that so many of us as were baptized into Jesus Christ were baptized into his death? Therefore we are buried

with him by baptism into death: that like as Christ was raised
up from the dead . . . even so we also should walk in the new-
ness of life. . . .

"Know ye not, brethren (for I speak to them that
know the Law), how that the Law hath dominion over a man
as long as he liveth? For the woman which hath a husband is
bound by the Law to her husband as long as he liveth; but if
the husband is dead, she is loosed from the Law of her husband. . . . Wherefore, my brethren, ye also are become dead to
the Law by the body of Christ; that ye should be married to
another, even to him who is raised from the dead, that we
should bring forth fruit unto God."[58]

Paul does not argue that the Law is old-fashioned or out-
moded. He asserts that the Law is holy.[59] He reasons that he is
united in faith with the Christ. He experienced crucifixion with
Him. He has thus paid his debt to God. As a Christian, he suffered death and was resurrected with the Christ. He became a
new creature.[60] *Arguing from within the Law,* Paul contends
that the Law is only applicable to those who have not yet died.
The Christian has died in and with the Christ. He has therefore
died to the Law which is not binding upon those who have died.
His Christian life is a resurrected life, a life free of the Law and
the anxiety over guilt which inevitably attends it. The rabbis and
Paul had a common problem—their sense of guilt and unworthiness before the Law. Their solutions were radically different.
Nevertheless, both solutions unfolded out of the identical
conviction that the Law of the Lord was perfect and that no man
had proven worthy of it.

Paul's insight that sublimation could not diminish anxiety over guilt and estrangement had much validity. I am less
convinced of the merit of his solution, faith in the sacrificial death
and resurrection of the Christ. It is possible, as Jews have insisted
for two thousand years, that Jesus was merely a Jewish teacher
of his time who died the common death of all men. In any event,
Paul's struggle remains enormously significant. Paul was one of

the first and most authentic intuitive religious psychologists. He understood the inability of the Jewish religious system to overcome the anxiety and guilt it engendered. Luther made a somewhat similar discovery about Catholicism.[61] Today another path is available when sublimation fails, psychoanalytic insight. That path was unavailable to the rabbis, Paul, and Luther. Nevertheless, their candor in revealing their conflicts contributed greatly to the cultural climate that finally resulted in psychoanalytic insight in our time.

Historically, the rabbis and their community have remained committed to the path of sublimation to this day. Given the precarious situation of the Jewish community as a rejected and endangered minority, no other path was practical. The rabbis could only give intuitive expression to their anarchic inclinations through the safety-valve of fantasy.

There is a strong element of moral realism in the rabbinic tendency toward candor in the matter of the *yetzer ha-ra*, the evil inclination, and in their own intuitive identification with the worst sinners of Israel. The rabbis were honest men grappling with the realities of their admittedly complex inner lives. They also served a community with people of every shade of virtue and vice. They were the first to admit the power of the inner forces that troubled them and their own difficulties in mastering these disturbances. Their discussions of the *yetzer ha-ra* had a therapeutic effect on generations of Jews who, in synagogue and classroom, learned that their own moral struggles were neither unique nor abnormal, but the shared predicament of mankind. The old charges of the hypocrisy and moral insensitivity of the Pharisees must be reviewed in the light of the rabbis' expressions in their fantasies of disguised admiration for the worst sinners. The fact that the rabbis could see anything of themselves in sinners such as the three kings and four commoners of Tractate Sanhedrin is an indication of their moral and psychological honesty. This is also true of the very strong ambivalence toward their own religious system which is so evident in the legends. The traditions under discussion point to the extent to which the rabbis were tempted. They also point to the candor with which they defended themselves against acting out the same temptations.

There was more than moral modesty in the capacity of the rabbis to see themselves as they did. The psychotherapeutic process is effective only when the client has the capacity to see the dark side of his own personality. Without such insight it is impossible to develop effective instrumentalities for dealing with the problems of the psyche. This knowledge comes slowly, with much pain, and with more than a little risk. It would be stretching the point to suggest that the rabbinic traditions did all in their day that psychoanalytic insight can do in ours. Nevertheless, the capacity realistically to face oneself is a precondition for effective therapy in any age. Such self-recognition was implicit in the rabbis' capacity to regard their own temptations with candor and to recognize something of themselves in these sinners.

Ambivalence, rebelliousness, candor, moral modesty, and genuine temptation are to be found in the mythic and legendary traditions of the Pharisees. Although the day has long passed when Jews could accept at face value everything the rabbis said or believed, the day may have arrived when a more genuine appreciation is possible of what the rabbis sought to attain and the methods they employed. These men were not solitaries. They were leaders of a defeated and continuously endangered community. This fact cannot be stressed often enough. The theology of rabbinic Judaism must be understood as the theology of a community under constant stress. The rabbis were pathetically aware of the extent to which the power equation weighed against them, especially in the Roman and Christian worlds. They had a paramount task which dwarfed all other considerations. They had to keep themselves and their community intact. They could afford neither the luxury of emotional spontaneity nor the possibilities of moral experimentation. It was not that they found the game unattractive. On the contrary, they were very well aware of the attractions of giving in to the id. They were absolutely precluded from entering this path because of the pressing need to keep themselves from falling apart.

They also had to keep their community together. Judaism did not have to wait until the twentieth century to become problematic. Even in the most rooted and settled of peoples, the human condition does not lack agonizing dilemmas. After the defeats of the Jewish community by the Romans in 70 and 135 C.E., the Jewish community became perhaps the most uprooted and precarious of all human communities until the emergence of the American Negro. Furthermore, the Jewish community's belief that its degradation was the result of God's displeasure dovetailed neatly with the Christian conviction that Jewish persecution was a sign of God's rejection of the deicide people. Perhaps never before in history did one community's (inner) self-criticism correspond so completely to a rival community's mythology about it. Discipline had to be the watchword, not only in order to keep the community together but in order to keep the individual from falling apart. The path of sublimation alone made sense.

There is no sin in the catalog of vice unknown to rabbinic legend. Furthermore, to the extent that righteousness had been practiced, it had not been rewarded by a goodly portion of divine favor. Emotional freedom was a luxury that the hounded could ill afford. When temptation manifested itself, it was expressed with greatest safety in fantasy. It is not surprising that the sinners of the Aggadah were regarded as great rabbinic scholars and masters of religious lore. After all—in the eyes of the rabbis—who knew better the temptations that beset men? They regarded themselves as very much like Jeroboam, Ahab, and Manasseh.

After the destruction of Jewish political authority in Palestine, authority ultimately passed into the hands of the rabbis. This took place during the period when the classical institutions of normative Judaism were being formed. Then as now, Jews were born into a world in which the special disabilities of Jewish life were neither asked for nor welcomed. Those who were religiously knowledgeable were at least capable of avoiding the worst of all pains, the pain of absolutely meaningless and gratuitous suffering. Then as now, the ambivalence of the leaders was vastly overshadowed by a far more pathetic phenomenon: for many Jews, the difficulties of Jewish life were an unwanted and an uncomprehended hurt.

The community had no alternative but to elect the path of extreme discipline. No matter what has been written in criticism of rabbinic tradition as overly meticulous and compulsive, one fact stands out: religious discipline was a psychological necessity. All of the normal counteraggressive outlets of other peoples were denied to Jews. There could be no race riots, no protests, no violence. Jews had to "roll with the punch." This required enormous internal control. That discipline was offered by Jewish religious law. Jewish tradition left absolutely no aspect of human behavior unregulated. Prayer, property, sexual behavior, dress, and eating all came within its effective compass. Never in the history of Western civilization has any community committed to strict regulation so vast a part of its behavior as did the Jews. Because the usual counteraggressive safety-valves were inoperative for the Jews after the Roman victory, intense personal discipline was the only way in which the threatened community could maintain itself.

Solomon Schechter has written convincingly of "the bliss and happiness of living and dying" under the Law.[62] Schechter was undoubtedly correct that the Law was a source of joy for the majority of Jews throughout history. Nevertheless, had Schechter lived to see the vast atrophy of Jewish religious practice that has taken place in the United States since his time, he might have realized that those Jews who cherished the Law as a joy were very frequently making a virtue out of necessity. Once the conditions of Jewish life were secularized and Jewish persecution diminished, if only to a small extent, Jews rushed to abandon a great many of the disciplines of the rabbis. Perhaps nowhere have these norms been as completely ignored as among those Jews who no longer dwell under conditions of exile, the Jews of Israel.

Throughout Jewish history, the tension between Law and liberation from the Law has been deeply felt. Occasionally antinomian tendencies have surfaced, such as the Messianic disturbances that attended the careers of Sabbatai Zvi and Jacob Frank in the seventeenth and eighteenth centuries. In both instances, the belief that the Messiah's advent had brought an end to Jewish alienation and degradation led to a vast abandonment by Jews of traditional religious, moral, and even sexual norms. Moved by the belief that an end had come to the terrible conditions that made Jewish religious discipline necessary, thousands of Jews and their leaders cast off all restraint. They no longer admired Jeroboam, Ahab, and Manasseh in the safety of fantasy. They became their very embodiment—until the inevitable reaction set in.[63]

Here we return to the symbolism of the Freudian primal crime. I have suggested that the real significance of the Freudian speculation lies less in what it reveals about religious origins than in what it suggests concerning the human condition.[64] Every religion which demands intense behavioral discipline, as does Judaism, is forever threatened by the inability of men to accept these disciplines. Something in most men resists restraint. Men frequently resent both the restraints and those who enforce them, no matter how realistic and necessary the impositions may be. Every man carries within him the full potential of personal and social anarchy. The image of the sons futilely murdering the primal father in the hope of liberating themselves from his prohibitions is prototypical of the human condition. So, too, is the image of the sons imposing the father's restraints upon themselves once the father has been disposed of.

The rabbis had to cope with every conceivable temptation. They bore little resemblance to the usual picture of the Pharisees as men whose exterior pretensions to virtue masked an indifferance to the reality of the inner man. As in every community, the Achilles heel of rabbinic Judaism was the reluctance all men experience in accepting the norms without which society cannot survive. The legends of the sinners offered the rabbis a means with which that reluctance could be both expressed and controlled.

Our times are such that we are not prepared greatly to esteem the special virtues of rabbinic Judaism or its exemplars. The best Jewish minds no longer contemplate the inner meaning of the careers of Jeroboam, Ahab, and Manasseh. Few contemporary Jews are willing to restrict their personal behavior to the very stringent limits which the rabbis, against enormously potent inner promptings, imposed upon themselves. After all, the fathers were not very different from the sons in inclination or temptation. Contemporary Jews have benefited greatly from their newly found freedom, a freedom the rabbis might also have prized had they lived in circumstances conducive to it. Nevertheless, it ought never to be forgotten that the freedom available to contemporary Jews was made possible largely because of the two-thousand-year night of rabbinic discipline and restraint.

10 / The Gift of Meaning

ERHAPS THE MOST DIFFICULT BURDEN contemporary man
has had to bear has been the loss of the conviction that his existence is ultimately meaningful. Of all the gifts the Aggadah
bestowed upon the rabbinic Jew, it is likely that none was as
precious as the gift of meaning.

Few philosophers have delineated the consequences of the
contemporary loss of meaning as lucidly as Jean-Paul Sartre. According to Sartre, man's fundamental passion is ontological. Man,
the absurd, contingent being, cannot tolerate his own meaninglessness. He wastes his life in a useless quest for the absolute
security of necessary being. Man yearns to become God, but God
does not exist. Human existence is as an ironic exercise in
futility.[1]

From a human standpoint *The Words* may prove to be
Sartre's most interesting book.[2] In it, Sartre traces his own resolve
to become a writer back to his earliest childhood. Elsewhere
Sartre has described the attempt to locate the origins of adult
projects in the ontological strivings of earliest childhood as
"existential psychoanalysis."[3] *The Words* is Sartre's attempt at
personal existential psychoanalysis. He reveals that he became a

writer largely because he found the burden of his own radical
contingency unbearable. As a writer, he hoped to become a fixed
value and a defined object for others for as long into the future
as he had readers. The shell of words he secreted around himself
during his lifetime would become a fixed Sartre-essence. When
it was completed, he would be an eternally determined, necessary
being.[4] He regarded his entire life as existing in order to be
used up in the process of creating the Sartre-devoid-of-the-last-
remnant-of-contingency, the Sartre who would never change, the
finished dead author. From earliest childhood, Sartre was in dread
of his own gratuitousness. Sartre has consistently exposed the
anguished cost of godless existence devoid of meaning. His autobiography is testament to the fact that he has paid as high a price
as any man for an ultimately absurd life.

    I share much of Sartre's fundamental conviction about
the human condition. When Nietzsche asked, "Do we not stray,
as through infinite nothingness?"[5] he was anticipating the world
of the twentieth century. We cannot restore the lost world of the
rabbinic Aggadah. Nevertheless, we must not permit the irre-
trievability of that world to diminish our appreciation for it or
for the magnitude of the problems we face with its demise and
the destruction of comparable mythic visions in Christianity.

    In a sense, I have written an obituary of the world of the
Aggadah. Every word of appreciation I offer in its praise is verita-
bly a further nail in its coffin. I can appreciate the Aggadah only
functionally—that is, in terms of what it did for those who lived
within the framework of its myths and symbols. By describing
the psychological efficacy of the Aggadah I largely negate that
efficacy. There undoubtedly will arise new and terrible symbols
which men may perhaps come to believe in. Those symbols will
probably be future-oriented. Skepticism and criticism have made
the domains of the past and the transcendent unavailable as objects of faith. The only remaining realm available to human
credulity is the future. It can remain the repository of our deepest
hopes because it is beyond realistic criticism. Perhaps that is why

so many of the ideologies of the twentieth century have been political messianisms. One wonders what will become of mankind when it finally loses faith, as it must, in the future and humanity's vision of itself collapses entirely into the immanence of the present.

Meaning and purpose had yet to disappear in the world of the Aggadah. The illusion is unassailed save by one pathetic dissident, Elisha ben Abuya. Incidentally, it is possible to view much of the literature of primitive Christianity as a specialized form of a new Aggadah. This is particularly true of those parts of the New Testament which are based upon the conviction that Jesus' ministry is in fulfillment of prophecy.

The Aggadah and the Halakah served related but distinct functions. The Halakah served to define and govern objective behavior in rabbinic Judaism. It gave the rabbinic Jew a very extensive idea of what was expected of him in every significant domain of human behavior. It specified the manifest norms and styles of conduct which enabled the rabbinic community to survive effectively in a multiplicity of religious, historical, and cultural settings. The Aggadah served a no less important need. It helped the community to structure a meaningful psychic world. Without it, Jews might long ago have disintegrated morally and psychologically.

The Aggadah had the power to reach the learned and the ignorant alike. Abstract philosophic ideas would make little impression on most men. The Aggadah used concrete images of legendary figures faced with the same personal conflicts as those experienced by many of the members of the community. Its images had the power to move men and women who were incapable of acting on the basis of abstract concepts. The psychic world of the Jew was largely expressed in the imagery of the Aggadah. A Jew who publicly exhibited disdain for religious tradition could, for example, be identified with Jeroboam ben Nabat. The identification classified his dissidence. It also served as an assurance of future retribution. The moral universe of rabbinic Judaism thus maintained its integrity. The quest for an ordered existence was not abruptly disturbed by behavioral or creedal dissent. Even sin and rebellion had their place in the rabbinic order of things. This limited their capacity to spread. A concrete sense of identification with sinners such as Manasseh or Jeroboam could do more as an instrument of internalized social control than a thousand words of abstract discussion concerning the nature of evil. The principle that a picture is worth a thousand words is also applicable to the mental pictures of legend and myth.

As there were models of sin whose misfortunes served as a warning, there were also models of righteousness to be emulated. The virtue of hospitality was taught through the hyperbolic tale of Abraham sitting in his tent which opened in all four directions so that the patriarch might speedily greet the wayfarer.[6] Peace was not abstractly praised. The image of Aaron and his disciples as pursuers of peace gave substance to the ideal.[7] Through the Aggadah, the Bible became a corpus of ego-ideals to be imitated and negative character-types whose example was to be rejected.

These images were largely realistic. They took cognizance of the human situation in depth. There was assurance in the knowledge that even Moses had transgressed. An overscrupulous or an unduly harsh conscience is not likely to develop when temptation is understood as the problem of everyman. When the Aggadah portrayed Moses as blemished, every Jew was assured that his own failings were not private and isolated peculiarities. His feelings did not separate him psychologically from his peers. No man was free of sin. Neither was any Jew regarded as entirely free of the obligation to do his best in keeping the commandments.[8]

As I have stated, the legends also acted as a safety-valve. Offenses could be committed in fantasy which would have been totally unacceptable in reality. Such tales served as a form of emotional catharsis. Legends of wrongdoing offered the Jew a number of potential identifications. By identifying with the righteous, he assured himself that religious fidelity would not ultimately be in vain. By identifying with the sinner, he was able to give expression to his own conscious and unconscious temptations, if only in fantasy. Imaginary enactment of an illicit act permitted a certain discharge of emotion without harmful social consequence. Such identifications were probably often unconscious. They were no less effective on that account. The same mechanism is at work in the contemporary world of fantasy, the arts, the novel, and the motion picture. The archaic fantasy world of rabbinic legend was more effective emotionally because of the sacred environment of synagogue and school in which it was given expression.

In spite of the manifold miseries inflicted upon the Jewish community throughout its history, it was fortunate not to have had to live beyond meaning. There were burdens enough without the supreme burden of meaningless indignity.

We have also seen that the rabbinic quest for meaning was so insistent that the rabbis preferred self-accusation and an overwhelming sense of guilt to meaninglessness.[9] Few tendencies have been as universal in Jewish religious psychology as the psychological transformation of misfortune into punishment. Of all the legacies of the prophets of Israel, this has been the most dubious. Perhaps the most important example was the suffering servant of Isaiah, which rabbinic tradition identified with the community of Israel.[10] In the suffering servant, misfortune ceases to be merely punitive. It becomes redemptive. What a colossal, megalomaniac, and grandiose misreading of a pathetic and defeated community's historic predicament! To this day Jews can be found who delude themselves with the notion that somehow Jewish suffering and powerlessness have redemptive significance for mankind.

Jewish self-blame has had disastrous effects for Jews in ways that were unanticipated at the time of its original expression. The extraordinary deliberations of Vatican II on the attitude of contemporary Christianity to Judaism had its earliest roots in this tradition of Jewish self-blame. The violently condemnatory statements against the Jewish community throughout the New Testament were in the first instance the criticism by some Jews of the ways and traditions of other Jews! Furthermore, primitive Christian condemnation of Judaism and its institutions had its roots in the prophetic tradition of Jewish self-condemnation. We now know that it is impossible to separate current anti-Semitic hostility from its religious roots. The supreme irony is that the oldest source of this antipathy was the work of Jews bitterly critical of the real or imagined failings of their own community!

Nevertheless, self-blame was the most realistic response available to the Jewish community throughout most of its history in spite of its terrible cost. It was a defensive response. It was not necessarily neurotic. Realistic conditions in Jewish life made self-blame and even delusionary overestimation of the redemptive significance of the community's misfortunes indispensable. In his book *Human Behavior in the Concentration Camp,* Elie Cohen maintains that those prisoners who had some spiritual life had the best chances of survival. Cohen defines spiritual life as comprising "all spiritual values in their widest sense, such as morality, knowledge, emotion, intellect, character, religion, etc."[11] Cohen contends that his Zionist ideology was an important factor in his own survival at Auschwitz. He asserts that both Christian and Communist prisoners shared this advantage. They were capable of regarding their ordeal as meaningful. In his own case, Zionism made the otherwise meaningless fact of Auschwitz meaningful. For Cohen, self-blame was the price of the gift of meaning. Cohen tells us that before the war, he refrained from actively following the consequences of his Zionist beliefs. Had he done so, he would have emigrated to Israel convinced that there was no place for a Jew as a member of a despised minority in the Netherlands. He refrained because emigration would have meant a life of hard, physical labor. An intellectual career awaited him in the Netherlands. Because of his choice of a soft career in Holland, he could not escape the conviction that there was some justice in his being at Auschwitz. Cohen tells us:

> *I was often haunted by the reflection that it was all my fault.*
> I reasoned to myself: "If you had not preferred the illusional
> safety of a physician's existence in the Netherlands, but had
> suited your actions to your words, you would not have had to
> go through all this." *Thus, I could not deny a measure of jus-*
> *tice to my fate, and this made my sufferings less difficult to*
> *bear.*[12] (italics mine)

In face of an overwhelmingly gratuitous catastrophe, Cohen
found a measure of relief in self-condemnation.

The Austrian Jewish psychiatrist Viktor Frankl had an
experience in the death camp very similar to Cohen's and that of
the defeated Jewish community under Vespasian and Hadrian.
While in the death camp, Frankl also felt compelled to rescue
himself from the threat of meaninglessness by regarding his
misfortune as if it were punishment for prior guilt.[13] Only by
resorting to the age-old Jewish interpretation of misfortune could
he maintain his sanity. No interpretation of the God of the rabbis
or of the fantasies of His punitive violence against His own people has any psychological merit unless it comprehends the positive psychological value of these traditions. What Frankl calls
"logotherapy" and the "will to meaning" is not unlike the striving for an ordered, meaningful cosmos on the part of the rabbinic
teachers in their own times.[14]

Most men simply cannot live in an ultimately meaningless
and irrational universe. The threat of disaster does not reside in
the painful affect alone. It resides very largely in the extent to
which such a threat upsets the individual's sense of coherence and
structure. Rational, purposeful pain is infinitely more bearable
than irrational misfortune. Mankind has an extraordinary capacity for self-sacrifice to the point of death where sacrifice is
meaningful and ultimately contributes to the individual's wider
goals. Sometimes rational pain is sought when it has a meaningful place in the structured cosmos of the individual. Only
when pain or disaster loses all meaning does it become ultimately
threatening. The gratuity of events rather than their feeling-

tone constitutes the worst threat against which men must steel themselves.

Rabbinic Judaism was incapable of rescuing Jews from intensely painful experiences for almost two thousand years. It was, however, able to reduce their pain by assimilating it to a way of life which was both meaningful and durable. This was one of the most precious and lasting therapeutic gifts of the Aggadah to the Jewish community.   .

We have also seen how the Aggadah gave expression to the deepest archaic yearnings and anxieties of the people in a context of intersubjective sharing. The striving for infantile omnipotence was not a phenomenon uncovered by the individual after years of analytic probing. Free-floating anxiety was not permitted to fester without meaningful relationship to the individual's psychological disposition. It was a reality persistently faced by the community in legend, myth, and religious discipline. The Aggadah was incapable of offering clinically precise analytic insight to individuals concerning the nature of their personal problems. Its concern was largely social. Its effectiveness was admittedly limited. Nevertheless, it functioned so that many of the most difficult individual psychic dilemmas could be managed.

The Aggadah sought to avoid an eruption in the group of such conflicts as have led to the quest for psychotherapeutic insight in modern times. Using such tales as the Flood, Pharaoh's drowning, Korah's demise, and the burning of Nadab and Abihu, the Aggadah gave expression to some of the deepest human anxieties. With its seemingly irrational legends of sinners making war on God or cutting His name out of the Torah, the Aggadah expressed the terrible yearning for self-apotheosis and infantile omnipotence which besets and disturbs human sanity in every age. Long before Freud and Sartre, and in images far easier to understand than concepts such as "infantile omnipotence" and "être en-soi pour-soi," the Aggadah comprehended and exposed mankind's darkest temptation.

The wisdom of accepting one's very limited place comes

hard, if it comes at all, to most men. It contravenes every human being's primal experience of infantile omnipotence. It also contravenes our ineradicable yearning for a return to infantile omnipotence. The fetus in the womb maintains itself without resistance or effort. This is as close as we come to true omnipotence, the beginning of all things and the goal of all striving, the capacity almost completely to fulfill, effortlessly and automatically, all of the organism's needs. By comparison, later life is a maelstrom of imperfection and limitation. I have suggested that the myth of the expulsion from Eden is an attempt to represent something of the contrast between uterine and post-uterine existence. To accept one's limits is to accept a tragic, resistant, ironic, and only partially satisfying place in the nature of things. It is for some a poor substitute for humanity's primordial "remembrance of things past." In a sense, guilt is ontic destiny. Mankind's "memory" of a prenatal paradise of limitless perfection makes it impossible entirely to accept this world of limit and imperfection. Furthermore, since pleasure is ultimately a reduction of painful tension, mankind's final goal remains nirvana. It is at this point that rabbinic and biblical wisdom are most relevant. The rabbis insisted that the Torah was given to men rather than to the ministering angels, that they might accept and do well within the limitations and imperfections which are the inevitable concomitant of existence. When the rabbis speak of the persistence of their *yetzer ha-ra* and of the sinner's desire to rid himself of God, this may be the underlying reality with which they are grappling. The rabbinic legends played a therapeutic role in the life of the Jewish community. One of their most important functions was to give expression to the universal yearning for infantile omnipotence in a medium all could understand, so that the yearning might be dealt with effectively.

Fear of incorporation was the most compelling anxiety manifest in rabbinic legend. The desire for infantile omnipotence, a God-like utopia of gratification, was the decisive yearning. The object of greatest yearning was ultimately the source of

the greatest anxiety. The sinner was deterred by the threat of the
very nothingness which was his deepest quest. The ultimate
equivalence of anxiety and yearning raises a fundamental question. If the deterrent against sin is that for which the sinner
yearns, how can the deterrents deter? I ask the question within the
context of rabbinic legend. It is relevant wherever capital punishment is employed as a deterrent against behavioral deviance. For
some men the death penalty is the final seduction. In an era of
nuclear weapons, we may someday learn to our horror that death
is also the final temptation for some nations as well. Death does
not always deter. The presence of many-time repeaters in our
prisons suggests that some men eagerly seek the very punishments
society utilizes to limit crime.

The question points up the fragile limitations of social
control in any community, including the community of nations.
The whole conception of deterrents breaks down in the face of
the phenomenon of human self-destructiveness. When the
deviant desires, consciously or unconsciously, to harm or destroy
himself, few threats have deterrent efficacy. A murderer (or
a murderer-nation) unconsciously possessed of the desire to do
away with himself will not be deterred by the death penalty.[15]
In murdering the other, he commits the very act which assures
him of his real goal, his own self-destruction.

It would seem that the real deterrent potential of the
threat of annihilation lies in its power, when taken seriously,
to divide the offender against himself. Anna Freud has suggested
that one of the most important functions of the ego is to harmon-
ize the contradictory tendencies and demands of the organism,
so that it can effectively function as a unity.[16] Extreme self-
division is an unbearable burden. It paralyzes action and destroys
personality. A permanently divided psyche is schizophrenic.[17]
A healthy ego is capable of achieving a relative balance of the
opposing forces which together guide the organism. In a sense,
the mystic conception of God as a *coincidenta oppositorum* may
be as relevant to humanity as divinity. Man is a *coincidenta*

oppositorum in the Freudian as well as the Kierkegaardian view.[18] The threat of annihilation, when taken seriously, can upset the precarious psychic harmony achieved by the normal person. The threat pulls and pushes unbearably in opposite directions at the same time. As long as the organism is faced with the possibility of bringing upon itself this ultimate termination, which is both punishment and goal, the ego is split against itself. Only by withdrawing from those conflict situations which call forth both the yearning and the threat can the ego restore its balance.

Death has no power to deter. What the deviant seeks is avoidance of the very live issue of intolerable self-division. No man can take himself further away from nothingness than he is, to use the metaphor of distance. Men can partly remove themselves from their conflicting feelings about nothingness, by removing themselves from the temptations which call forth the intolerable mixture of threat and yearning. In this way, the deterrents do deter. They do so by creating a condition of inner division which can be repaired only by avoiding the temptation which elicited it. When the rabbis told their graphic tales of the sinner's end, they were using a psychic deterrent which was usually effective in its day. Even when skepticism diminished the efficacy of the rabbinic legends at the conscious level, their efficacy at the unconscious level remained for a very long time.

In the twentieth century, we have had a frightening reminder of the continuing power of religious images similar to those of the Aggadah to influence human behavior. There is little doubt that the image of the Jew as deicide in Christianity was an enormously potent factor in creating the racial antipathy which led to the destruction of European Jewry. The images of rabbinic legend had a similar potency for the Jewish community. In our age of calculating, pragmatic rationalism it is sometimes difficult to comprehend the efficacy of these tales. As in the case of the anti-Semitic images of the Jew, the images of the Aggadah were probably most potent under conditions of emotional stress.

Like all human inventions, the power of the rabbinic tales to influence men was at best only partial. Nevertheless, religious tales have not lost their full power in either tradition to this day.

In contradistinction to the popular notion that the Jew, and inferentially any believer in a religion of Judaic origin, was primarily motivated to maintain religious and social discipline out of fear, it becomes apparent that other forces were operative. The sinner avoided the pain of inner division more than feared retaliation. This is in keeping with what we know of the ambivalent character of human motivations. There are very few objects or conditions which are without some element of ambivalence. Few disasters are without some unconscious attraction. Fear played a great role in rabbinic Judaism, but even castration has some element of unconscious attraction for most men.[19] Usually, the realistic capacity for integration rather than fear discourages unacceptable conduct in healthy people. The temptation is rejected because the conflict is too great. Seen in this light, rabbinic Judaism was not primarily a religion of fear. It was a religion in search of meaning.

The quest for understanding has brought us to an ancient wisdom and a modern folly. The odd and ofttimes exaggerated tales of Aggadah called the rabbinic Jew to a realistic assessment of his place in the order of things. Undoubtedly he lacked our critical faculty. This sometimes prevented him from seeing that his legends were not literally true. Our contemporary gain in critical insight cannot compensate for the loss of a medium with which a community was able to express and cope with its underlying strivings and preoccupations. The clock cannot be turned back. We are children of the secular city. Traditional belief is impossible for most men in our generation. Nevertheless, there was more existential and psychological truth in the ancient mythic hyperbole of the rabbis than in contemporary man's critical precision. We have gained vastly in our power to control nature; we have lost much of our ability to deal with our unconscious which religion, myth, and legend once afforded. In psychoanalytic terms, the rabbinic community, imbued with the spirit of the Aggadah and guided by its insights, was never entirely a stranger to its own unconscious roots. It is doubtful that we can say the same of the desacralized communities of our own times.

The Aggadah riveted the attention of the Jew where it belonged. It helped the Jew to formulate a conception of his place in the cosmos, his obligations to his peers and to his God, the meaning of his precarious historical situation, the irrational psychic conflicts which threatened his personal and social order, and the nature of things hoped for in a broken and tragic world. Without the precise terminology of contemporary depth psychology, the Jew was helped to cope with such psychic dilemmas as his archaic oral strivings, his awesomely ambivalent feelings toward the mother, his fear of and need to identify with the father, as well as his conflicts at every level of psychosexual development.

Before the time of psychotherapy, the Aggadah gave men self-perspective, if not self-knowledge. It did so for all segments of the community in an idiom all could comprehend. No man was compelled to face the maelstrom of his own emotional life alone, unaided, or uninstructed. Admittedly, there was much sickness in the legends. Neither the religiously sanctified laws of sexual encounter nor the image of women encouraged the development of mature sexuality. Nevertheless, even when the Aggadah projected neurotic fears, it was better that such fears were objectified and made the common property of the community than left to fester isolated in each individual. What is repressed is infinitely more dangerous than what is given expression. Even the sickness of the Aggadah was a stage on the way to health. In our own times, when the demonic has released itself from its dark and brooding cave in men's hearts and stalks about as if possessed of its own peculiar dignity, it may yet be possible to see the world of the Aggadah as an irreparably lost haven of human truth.

Bibliography
Works Consulted

---

a. *Abbreviations.*

This list does not include customary and well known abbreviations of the names of biblical books. Abbreviations of rabbinic sources are included in the list of rabbinic works consulted. A reference to the abbreviation is the only reference to the particular work in the list.

A.V. Authorized version, the "King James" translation of the Bible. London: Eyre and Spottiswoode, Ltd., undated. (First published: London: 1611.)

BW Freud, Sigmund. The Basic Works of Sigmund Freud. Ed. A. A. Brill. New York: Random House, 1938.

CP Freud, Sigmund. The Collected Papers. 5 vols. Authorized translation under the supervision of Joan Riviere, with translations and editorial supervision by Alix Strachey and James Strachey. London: The Hogarth Press and the Institute for Psychoanalysis, 1924-1950.

JBL Journal of Biblical Literature.

JE The Jewish Encyclopedia. Vols. I-XII. New York: Funk and Wagnalls Co., 1896.

JQR The Jewish Quarterly Review. The abbreviations (OS) and (NS) refer to the Old and New Series of the Review respectively.

REJ   Revue des études juives.

b. *Works Cited by the Author's Name.*

Bacher, William.   Die Agada der Tannaiten. 2 vols. Strassbourg:
   1884-1890.

————.   Agadot ha-Tannaim. Hebrew translation by A. Z. Rabinowitz. 2 vols. in 4. Berlin: D'vir, 1922-36. Unless otherwise stated
   reference to Bacher is to Hebrew translation which restores to
   original the passages cited by Bacher in German. Passages are cited
   by volume, part (each Hebrew volume is divided into two parts
   and separately bound), and page.

Ginzberg, Louis.   The Legends of the Jews. 7 vols. Philadelphia:
   The Jewish Publication Society, 1909-1938.

c. *Rabbinic Sources.*

Aboth.   A tractate of the Mishnah; to be found in printed editions of
   the Mishnah.

Aggadat Bereshit. Ed. Solomon Buber.   Reprint edition with correc-
   tions. New York: Menorah Institute, 1959. Quoted by chapter
   and page.

ARN and *2 ARN.*   Aboth de Rabbi Nathan. Ed. Solomon Schechter.
   Vienna: 1887. Reprinted, New York: 1945. ARN and 2 ARN
   refer to versions 1 and 2 in the Schechter text respectively.

B'midbar R.   Midrash B'midbar Rabbah. In Standard Edition of
   Midrash Rabbah. Vilna: 1887. Quoted by chapter and paragraph.

BR   Midrash Bereshit Rabbah. In Standard Edition of Midrash
   Rabbah. Vilna: 1887, unless specific reference is made to the
   critical edition of J. Theodor and Ch. Albeck. Berlin: 1912-1920.

DR   Midrash D'barim Rabbah. In Standard Edition of Midrash
   Rabbah. Vilna: 1887. Quoted by chapter and paragraph.

Ek. R   Midrash Ekah Rabbah. (The Midrash on Lamentations.) In
   Standard Edition of Midrash Rabbah. Vilna: 1887. Quotations are
   from ed. S. Buber. Vilna: 1899. Quoted by chapter and page.
   (If quotation is from 1887 edition, quotation is by chapter and
   paragraph.)

ER and *EZ*   Seder Eliahu Rabba w'Eliahu Zutta. Ed. M. Friedmann.
   Vienna: 1902. Cited by chapter and page.

Esther R. Midrash Esther Rabbah. (The Midrash on the Book of Esther.) In Standard Edition of Midrash Rabbah. Vilna: 1887. Quoted by chapter and verse.

J. Where the letter J precedes a Talmudic tractate, the reference is to that tractate in the Jerusalem Talmud. Krotoschin: 1866. Corresponding to the edition of Venice: ca. 1523. Quoted by folio and column, the four columns being designated a, b, c, and d, respectively.

Koh. R. or *Kohelet R.* Midrash Kohelet Rabbah. (The Midrash on Ecclesiastes.) In Standard Edition of Midrash Rabbah. Vilna: 1887. Quoted by chapter, page and verse.

M. Where M precedes a tractate, the reference is to the Mishnah of the tractate. Quoted by chapter and sentence.

Machiri Jalkut Machiri zu den Psalmen. Ed. Solomon Buber. Berdyczew: 1899.

Mek. or *Mekilta.* Mekilta de R. Ishmael. If cited by (Ed. F), quotations are from ed. M. Friedmann. Vienna: 1870. Quoted by massekta and folio; if cited by (Ed. L.) quotations are from Mekilta de Rabbi Ishmael. Edited and translated by Jacob Z. Lauterbach. Philadelphia: 1933. Quoted by volume, page, and numbered line on page.

Mekilta RS Mekilta D'Rabbi Sim'on b. Jochai. If cited by (Ed. Epstein) quotations are from ed. J. N. Epstein completed by E. Z. Melamed, Jerusalem: 1955. If cited by (Ed. Hoffmann) then ed. D. Hoffmann. Frankfurt a. M.: 1905. Epstein volume is quoted by page and numbered line. Hoffmann volume is quoted by page.

MHG on Ex. Midrash Ha-gadol on Exodus. Ed. M. Margulies. Jerusalem: 1956. Quoted by page and numbered line.

MHG on Gen. Midrash Ha-gadol on Genesis. In two volumes. Ed. M. Margulies. Jerusalem: 1947. Quoted by volume, page and numbered line.

MHG on Numbers Midrash Ha-gadol on Numbers. Volume I. Ed. S. Fisch. London: 1957. Quoted by chapter and page.

PK Pesikta de R. Kahanna. Ed. S. Buber. Lyck: 1860. Quoted by piska and folio.

PR Midrash Pesikta Rabbati. Ed. M. Friedmann. Vienna: 1880. Quoted by pesikta and folio.

PRE Pirke R. Eliezer. Ed. D. Luria. Warsaw: 1852. Reprinted New York: 1946. Quoted by chapter.

Ruth R. Midrash Ruth Rabbah. (Ed.). Vilna: 1867. Quoted by chapter and verse.

Sechel Tov Midrash Sechel Tov. Ed. S. Buber. 2 vols. Revised edition. New York: Menorah Institute, 1959. Cited by reference to Scriptural chapter and verse.

Shir Ha-shirim R. Midrash Shir Ha-shirim Rabbah. Vilna: 1887. (The Midrash on Song of Songs.) Quoted by chapter and paragraph.

ShR. Midrash Sh'moth Rabbah. Vilna. 1887. Quoted by chapter and paragraph.

Sifre D. and *N. Sifre D'Be Rab* (on Deuteronomy (D) and Numbers (N)). Ed. M. Friedmann. Vienna: 1864. Reprinted New York: 1948. Quoted by numbered paragraph.

Tan. Midrash Tanhumma. Vilna: 1833. Quoted by parasha and paragraph. This is printed non-critical edition of Tanhumma.

Tan. B. Midrash Tanhumma. Ed. S. Buber. Vilna: 1883. In five books. Quoted by book and page. This is the critical edition.

Tannaim Midrash Tannaim zum Deuteronomium. Ed. David Hoffmann. Berlin: 1909. Cited by page.

Tehillim Midrash Tehillim. Ed. S. Buber. Vilna: 1891. Quoted by chapter and page. English Translation. (The Midrash on Psalms.) Translated by William G. Braude. 2 vols. New Haven: Yale University Press: 1959.

T. or *Tosefta* Ed. Zuckermandel. Pasewalk: 1881. Quoted by chapter and sentence.

WR Midrash Wa-yikra Rabbah. Ed. M. Margulies. 4 vols. Jerusalem: 1933-58. Quoted by volume, page, numbered line. Where reference is made to Standard Edition of Vilna: 1887, quotations are by chapter and paragraph.

Yalkut Yalkut Sh'moni. In two volumes. Frankfurt a.M.: 1687. Reprinted New York: 1944. Quoted by volume, page, and biblical verse to which homily is attached.

Abbreviations of Talmudic Tractates

AZ—*Avodah Zarah*
BK—*Baba Kammah*
BM—*Baba Metziah*
BB—*Baba Bathrah*
MK—*Me'ed Katan*

d. *English Translations of Rabbinic Sources.*

Unless specifically stated to the contrary, all translations of rabbinic sources cited in the text are taken from the standard English translations where such are available.

Aboth de Rabbi Nathan. The Fathers According to Rabbi Nathan. Trans. Judah Goldin. New Haven: Yale University Press, 1955.

Midrash Rabbah. The Midrash. Ed. H. Freedman and M. Simon. 10 vols. London and Bournemouth: Soncino Press, 1939.

Midrash Tehillim. The Midrash on Psalms. Ed. and trans. William G. Braude. 2 vols. New Haven: Yale University Press, 1959.

The Mishnah. Trans. Herbert Danby. London: Oxford University Press, 1933.

Pirke de Rabbi Eliezer. Trans. Gerald Friedlander, London: 1916. Reprinted, New York: Herman Press, 1965.

The Talmud. The Babylonian Talmud, translated under the editorship of I. Epstein. 37 vols. London and Bournemouth: Soncino Press: 1935-52.

e. *Secondary Sources.*

Abraham, Karl. Clinical Papers and Essays on Psychoanalysis. Ed. Hilda Abraham and D. R. Ellison. New York: Basic Books, 1955.

Alexander, Franz. Dynamic Psychiatry. Chicago: University of Chicago Press: 1952.

Allport, Gordon W. Becoming. New Haven: Yale University Press, 1960 (1955).

————. The Individual and His Religion. New York: Macmillan, 1960 (1950).

————. The Nature of Prejudice. Abridged Edition. New York: Anchor Books, 1958 (1954).

————. Personality: A Psychological Interpretation. New York: Henry Holt and Co., 1937.

Allport, Gordon and *Postman, Leo.* The Psychology of Rumor. New York: Henry Holt and Co., 1947.

Almansi, Renato. "A Psychoanalytic Interpretation of the Menorah," Journal of the Hillside Hospital. II (1953), 80-95.

————. "A Further Contribution to the Psychoanalytic Interpretation of the Menorah," Journal of the Hillside Hospital, III, 3-31.

————. "Religions, Mythology, and Folklore," The Annual Survey of Psychoanalysis, IV (1957), 340-355.

Altizer, Thomas J. J. The Gospel of Christian Atheism, Philadelphia: Westminster Press, 1966.

————. Mircea Eliade and the Dialectic of the Sacred. Philadelphia: Westminster Press, 1963.

————, and *Hamilton, William.* Radical Theology and the Death of God, New York and Indianapolis: Bobbs-Merrill, 1966.

Apt, L. and *Bellak, L.* (ed.). Projective Psychology: Clinical Approaches to the Total Personality. New York: Alfred A. Knopf, 1950.

Arendt, Hannah. The Origins of Totalitarianism, New York: Harcourt, Brace, 1951.

Aristotle. Physics in The Basic Works of Aristotle. Ed. Richard McKeon. New York: Random House, 1941.

Arlow, Jacob. "A Psychoanalytic Study of a Religious Initiation Rite: Bar Mitzvah," The Psychoanalytic Study of the Child, VI, 353-374.

————. "Applied Psychoanalysis: Religion," The Annual Survey of Psychoanalysis, II (1954), 538-553.

Bacher, W. Die Agada der Babylonischen Amoräer. Budapest: 1878.

————. Die Agada der Palästinischen Amoräer. 3 vols. Strassbourg: 1892-1899.

————. Die Exegetische Terminologie der Jüdischen Traditionsliteratur. 2 vols. Leipzig: 1899-1905.

————. Translated into Hebrew as 'Arche Midrash' by A. Z. Rabinowitz. Tel Aviv: 1923.

————. "Biblical Exegesis," JE, Vol. III.

Baeck, Leo. This People Israel. Trans. Albert H. Friedlander. New York: Holt, Rinehart and Winston. 1964.

Bakan, David. The Duality of Human Existence. Chicago: Rand, McNally and Co. 1966.

————. Sigmund Freud and the Jewish Mystical Tradition. New York: Van Nostrand, 1958.

Bamberger, Bernard J. Fallen Angels. Philadelphia: The Jewish Publication Society, 1952.

Baron, Salo. A Social and Religious History of the Jews. Vols. I and II. New York: Columbia University Press, 1952.

Bartlett, Frederick C. Remembering. Cambridge: Cambridge University Press, 1932.

Bergler, Edmund. The Basic Neurosis: Oral Regression and Psychic Masochism. New York: Grune and Stratton, 1949.

————. The Battle of the Conscience: A Psychiatric Study of the Inner Working of the Conscience. Washington: Washington Institute of Medicine, 1948.

Berelson, Bernard. "Content Analysis," Handbook of Social Psychology. Vol. I, 1954.

Beres, D. "Vicissitudes of Superego Functions and Superego Precursors in Childhood," The Psychoanalytic Study of the Child, XIII (1958), 324-351.

Berlin, Isaiah. The Hedgehog and the Fox: An Essay on Tolstoy's View of History. New York: Mentor Books, 1957.

Bettelheim, Bruno. Symbolic Wounds. Glencoe, Ill.: Free Press, 1954.

Blackman, E. C. Marcion and His Influence. London: S.P.C.K., 1948.

Bowers, Margaretta K. Conflicts of the Clergy. New York: Thomas Nelson and Sons, 1963.

Brown, Norman O. Life Against Death: The Psychoanalytic Meaning of History. Middletown, Conn.: Wesleyan University Press, 1959.

————. Love's Body, New York: Random House, 1966.

Brunswick, Ruth M. "The Preoedipal Phase of Libido Development," The Psychoanalytic Quarterly, IX, 293-319.

Buchler, Adolph. Studies in Sin and Atonement in the Rabbinic Literature of the First Century. London: Oxford University Press, 1928.

Bultmann, Rudolph. Gnosis: Bible Key Words from Gerhard Kittel's Theologisches Wörterbuch zum Neuen Testament. Trans. and ed. J. R. Coates. London: Adam and Charles Black, 1952.

Campbell, Joseph. The Masks of God: Primitive Mythology. New York: Viking Press, 1959.

Chajes, Z. H. Mebo ha-Talmud. Trans. and ed. Jacob Schachter as The Student's Guide Through the Talmud. London: East and West Library, 1952.

Cohen, Elie A. Human Behavior in the Concentration Camp. Trans. M. H. Braaksma, M.D. New York: W. W. Norton and Co., 1953.

Cohen, Gerson D. "The Talmudic Age," in Great Ages and Ideas of the Jewish People. Ed. Leo Schwartz. New York: Random House, 1956.

Dempsey, Peter J. R. Freud, Psychoanalysis and Catholicism. Chicago: Henry Regnery, 1956.

De Vaux, Roland. Ancient Israel. New York: McGraw-Hill, 1961.

English, Horace B. and English, Ava C. A Comprehensive Dictionary of Psychological and Psychoanalytic Terms. New York: Longmans, Green and Co., 1958.

Enslin, M. S. "Justin Martyr: An Appreciation," JQR (NS) XXXIV, 179-205.

Erikson, Erik N. Childhood and Society. New York: W. W. Norton, 1947.

————. Young Man Luther, New York: W. W. Norton and Co., 1958.

Fenichel, Otto. The Psychoanalytic Theory of Neurosis. New York: W. W. Norton and Co., 1945.

Ferenczi, Sandor. Thalassa: A Theory of Genitality. Trans. H. A. Bunker. New York: The Psychoanalytic Quarterly, 1938.

Findlay, J. H. Hegel: A Re-examination. London: Routledge and Kegan Paul, 1957.

Fingeret, H. H. "A Psychoanalytic Study of the Minor Prophet, Jonah," Psychoanalytic Review, XLI (1954), 55-98.

Fletcher, John M. "Homeostasis as an Explanatory Principle in Psychology" in Psychological Review, XLIX (1942), 80-87.

Frankfort, Henri. Kingship and the Gods. Chicago: University of Chicago Press, 1948.

Frankl, Viktor. From Death Camp to Existentialism. Boston: Beacon Press, 1959.

Freud, Anna. The Ego and the Mechanisms of Defense. Trans. Cecil Baines. London: The Hogarth Press and the Institute for Psychoanalysis, 1954 (1936).

Freud, Sigmund. An Autobiographical Study. New York: W. W. Norton and Co. 1952.

———. Beyond the Pleasure Principle. Trans. James Strachey. New York: Boni and Liveright, 1924. (1920).

———. Civilization and Its Discontents. Trans. Joan Riviere. London: The Hogarth Press and the Institute of Psychoanalysis, 1957.

———. Dostoevsky and Parricide. In CP, Vol. V (1929).

———. The Ego and the Id. New York: W. W. Norton, 1927. (1922)

———. The Future of an Illusion. Trans. W. D. Robson-Scott. New York: Doubleday Anchor Books, 1957. (1928)

———. A General Introduction to Psychoanalysis. Trans. Joan Riviere. Garden City: Permabooks Division, Doubleday and Co., 1956 (1924).

———. Group Psychology and the Analysis of the Ego. Trans. James Strachey. London: The Hogarth Press and the Institute for Psychoanalysis, 1959. (1921)

———. Moses and Monotheism. Trans. Katherine Jones. New York: Vintage Books, 1955. (1939)

———. New Introductory Lectures in Psychoanalysis. Trans. W. J. H. Sprott. New York: W. W. Norton and Co., 1933. (1933)

———. The Problem of Anxiety. Trans. H. A. Bunker. New York: W. W. Norton and Co., 1936. (1927).

———. Three Contributions to a Theory of Sex. in BW. Trans. A. A. Brill. (1905)

———. Totem and Taboo. Trans. James Strachey, New York: W. W. Norton and Co., 1962. (1913)

———. The Acquisition of Power Over Fire. In CP, Vol. V (1932).

———. Analysis of a Phobia in a Five-Year-Old Boy. In CP, Vol. III (1909).

———. "A Child Is Being Beaten." In CP, Vol. II (1919).

———. The Economic Problem in Masochism. In CP, Vol. II (1924).

———. Family Romances. In CP, Vol. V (1909).

———. Female Sexuality. In CP, Vol V (1932).

———. Formulations Regarding the Two Principles in Mental Functioning. In CP, Vol. IV (1911).

———. From the History of an Infantile Neurosis. In CP, Vol. III (1918).

———. The Infantile Genital Organization of the Libido. In CP, Vol. II (1923).

———. Medusa's Head. In CP, Vol. V (1922).

———. The Most Prevalent Form of Degradation in Erotic Life. In CP, Vol. IV (1912).

———. A Neurosis of Demoniacal Possession in the Seventeenth Century. In CP, Vol. IV (1923).

———. Notes Upon a Case of Obsessional Neurosis. In CP, Vol. III (1909).

———. Observations on "Wild" Analysis. In CP, Vol. II (1910).

———. Obsessive Acts and Religious Practices. In CP, Vol. II (1907).

———. The Passing of the Oedipus Complex. In CP, Vol. II (1924).

————. A Religious Experience. In CP, Vol. V (1928).

————. Some Psychological Consequences of the Anatomical Distinctions Between the Sexes. Vol. V (1925).

————. A Special Type of Object Choice Made by Men. In CP, Vol. IV (1910).

————. The Splitting of the Ego in the Defensive Process. In CP, Vol. V (1941).

Friedman, Maurice. Problematic Rebel—An Image of Modern Man. New York: Random House, 1963.

————. To Deny Our Nothingness. New York: Delacorte Press, 1966.

Fromm, Erich. Escape From Freedom. New York: Rinehart and Co., 1941.

————. The Forgotten Language. New York: Grove Press, 1951.

————. Man For Himself. New York: Rinehart and Co., 1947.

Gaster, Theodore. Passover—Its History and Traditions. Boston: Beacon Paperbacks, 1962.

Ginzberg, L. "Some Observations on the Attitude of the Synagogue Towards the Apocalyptic Eschatological Writings." In JBL, Vol. XLI, 1922, pp. 121 ff.

————. Of Jewish Law and Lore. Ed. Arthur Hertzberg. Philadelphia: Jewish Publication Society, 1955.

————. "Critical Review of R. T. Herford's Christianity in Talmud and Midrash." JQR. (OS) Vol. XVII, pp. 171-183 (1905).

Glock, Charles Y. and *Stark, Rodney.* Christian Beliefs and Anti-Semitism. New York: Harper & Row, 1966.

Glover, Edward. Freud or Jung? Cleveland: Meridian Books, 1956.

Graetz, Heinrich. A History of the Jews. Philadelphia: Jewish Publication Society, 1902. Vol. II.

Grant, R. M. Gnosticism and Early Christianity. New York: Columbia University Press, 1966 (1959).

Grollman, Earl. Judaism in Sigmund Freud's World. New York: Appleton-Century-Crofts, 1965.

Guttman, Julius. Philosophies of Judaism. Trans. David Silverman. New York: Holt, Rinehart and Winston, 1964.

Hall, Calvin S. and Linzey, Gardner. "Psychoanalytic Theory and Its Application in the Social Sciences," Handbook of Social Psychology, Vol. I, 1954.

Hegel, G. W. F. Phänomenologie des Geistes. Hamburg: Felix Meiner, 1952. Trans. J. B. Baillie as The Phenomenology of the Mind. London: George Allen and Unwin, Ltd., 1931.

———. "The Spirit of Christianity and Its Fate," Hegel: Early Theological Writings. Trans. T. M. Knox and Richard Knox. Chicago: University of Chicago Press. 1948.

Heinemann, Isaac. Darke Ha-Aggadah. Jerusalem: Magnes Press, 1954.

Helfgott, Benjamin. The Doctrine of Election in Tannaitic Literature. New York: King's Crown Press, 1954.

Herford, R. Travers. Christianity in Talmud and Midrash. London: William and Norgate, 1903.

———. The Pharisees. London: Macmillan, 1924.

Hertz, J. H. (ed.) The Authorized Daily Prayer Book. New York: Bloch Publishing Co., 1957.

Hilberg, Raul. The Destruction of the European Jews. London: W. H. Allen, 1961.

Horovitz, S. "Midrash" in JE, VIII, 548-550.

Hyppolite, Jean. Genèse et structure de la Phénoménologie de l'Esprit de Hegel. Paris: Auber, 1947.

Isaac, Jules. The Teaching of Contempt. Trans. Helen Weaver. New York: Holt, Rinehart and Winston: 1964.

Jonas, Hans. The Gnostic Religion: The Message of the Alien God and the Beginnings of Christianity. Boston: Beacon Press, 1958.

———. "Gnosticism" in Handbook of Christian Theology. New York: Meridian Press, 1958.

Jones, Ernest. The Life and Work of Sigmund Freud. Vol. I-III. New York: Basic Books, 1955-57.

Josephus. Antiquities in The Life and Works of Flavius Josephus. Trans. William Whiston. Philadelphia: The John C. Winston Co., 1957.

Jung, C. G. The Archetypes and the Collective Unconscious. New York: Pantheon Press, 1959.

————. Modern Man in Search of a Soul. New York: Harcourt Brace, 1933.

————. Two Essays on Analytic Psychology. New York: Meridian Books. 1956.

Kadushin, Max. The Theology of Seder Eliahu. New York: Bloch Publishing Company, 1932.

Kierkegaard, Søren Abaye. The Concept of Dread. Trans. Walter Lowrie. Princeton: Princeton University Press. 1944.

————. Fear and Trembling. Trans. Walter Lowrie. Princeton: Princeton University Press, 1941.

Langer, Marie. Maternidad y Sexo. Buenos Aires: Editorial Nova. 1951.

Lewin, Bertram. The Psychoanalysis of Elation. New York: W. W. Norton and Co. 1950.

————. "Sleep, Mouth and the Dream Screen," Psychoanalytic Quarterly, Vol. XV.

Lieberman, Saul. Greek in Jewish Palestine. New York: Jewish Theological Seminary, 1942.

Lorenz, Konrad. On Aggression. Trans. Marjorie K. Wilson, New York: Harcourt, Brace and World, 1966.

McLuhan, Marshall. The Gutenberg Galaxy. Toronto: University of Toronto Press, 1962.

————. Understanding Media: The Extensions of Man. New York: McGraw-Hill, 1965.

Marmorstein, A. Studies in Jewish Theology. London: Oxford University Press, 1950.

May, Rollo. The Meaning of Anxiety. New York: The Ronald Press, 1950.

Menninger, Karl. Man Against Himself. New York: Harcourt, Brace and Co., 1938.

Merton, Robert K. Social Theory and Social Structure. Revised Edition. Glencoe, Ill.: The Free Press, 1957.

Money-Kyrle, R. The Meaning of Sacrifice. London: The Hogarth Press and The Institute for Psychoanalysis, 1930.

Montefiore, Claude and *Loewe, Herbert.* A Rabbinic Anthology. Philadelphia: The Jewish Publication Society, 1960.

Moore, George Foote. Judaism. 3 vols. Cambridge, Mass.: Harvard University Press, 1927.

Mullahy, Patrick. Oedipus: Myth and Complex. New York: Grove Press, 1955.

Neumann, Erich. The Great Mother. Trans. Ralph Mannheim. New York: Pantheon Books, 1955. Bollingen Series XLVII.

————. The Origins and History of Consciousness. Trans. R. F. C. Hull. New York: Pantheon Books, 1954. Bollingen Series XLII.

Nietzsche, Friedrich. The Antichrist. Trans. Walter Kaufmann. The Portable Nietzsche. New York: Viking Press, 1954.

————. The Gay Science. Trans. Walter Kaufmann. *op. cit.*

Nilsson, Martin P. Greek Piety. Trans. Herbert J. Rose, Oxford: Clarendon Press, 1948.

Nunberg, Hermann. Problems of Bisexuality as Reflected in Circumcision. London: Image Publishing Co., Ltd., 1949.

Ostow, Mortimer and *Scharfstein, Ben-Ami.* The Need to Believe: The Psychology of Religion. New York: International Universities Press, 1954.

Parkes, James H. The Conflict of the Church and Synagogue. London: Soncino Press, 1934.

Patai, Raphael. Man and Temple. London: Thomas Nelson, 1947.

Pedersen, Johannes. Israel. Vols. I-IV. Copenhagen and London: Oxford University Press, 1928-1940.

Piers, Gerhardt and *Singer, Milton.* Shame and Guilt. Springfield, Ill.: Charles C. Thomas, 1953.

Rank, Otto. The Myth of the Birth of the Hero and Other Writings. Ed. Philip Freund. New York: Vintage Books, 1959.

————. The Trauma of Birth. New York: Harcourt Brace and Co., 1929.

Rank, Otto and *Sachs, Hanns.* The Significance of Psychoanalysis for the Mental Sciences. Trans. Charles E. Payne. New York: Nervous and Mental Disease Monograph Series, 1916.

Reik, Theodore. The Compulsion to Confess. New York: Farrar, Straus, and Cudahy, 1959.

————. The Creation of Woman. New York: George Braziller, 1960.

————. Dogma and Compulsion: Psychoanalytic Studies of Religion and Myth. Trans. Bernard Miall. New York: International Universities Press, 1951.

————. Masochism and Modern Man. Reprinted New York: Grove Press, 1956. (1941)

————. Mystery on the Mountain. New York: Harper and Brothers, 1959.

————. Myth and Guilt. New York: George Braziller, 1957.

————. Ritual: Psychoanalytic Studies. London: The Hogarth Press and The Institute of Psychoanalysis, 1931.

Roellenbeck, E. Magna Mater im Alten Testament. Darmstadt: Classen and Raether, 1949.

Roheim, Geza. The Gates of the Dream. New York: International Universities Press, 1958.

Rosenfeld, Eva M. "The Pan-Headed Moses—A Parallel," International Journal of Psychoanalysis, Vol. 32.

Rubenstein, Richard L. After Auschwitz: Radical Theology and Contemporary Judaism. New York: Bobbs-Merrill, 1966.

————. "Freud and Judaism: A Review Article," Journal of Religion, Vol. 47, No. 1. (January 1967)

Sachs, Hanns. "The Transformation of Impulses into Obsessional Ritual," American Imago (February, 1946), pp. 67-74.

Sartre, Jean-Paul. Baudelaire. Trans. Martin H. Turnell. New London, Conn.: New Directions Book, 1950.

————. Being and Nothingness. Trans. Hazel Barnes. New York: Philosophic Library, 1956.

————. The Flies. Trans. Stuart Gilbert in No Exit. New York: Vintage Books, 1947.

————. The Words. Trans. Bernard Fechtmann. New York: George Braziller, 1964.

Schafer, Roy. Psychoanalytic Interpretation in Rorschach Testing. New York: Grune and Stratton, 1954.

Schechter, Solomon. Some Aspects of Rabbinic Theology. New York: Behrman House, 1936.

——. Studies in Judaism. First Series. Philadelphia: Jewish Publication Society, 1945.

Schendler, D. "The Signature of Pain," Psychoanalysis, Vol. 2, No. 3.

Scholem, Gershom. Jewish Gnosticism, Merkabah, Mysticism, and Talmudic Tradition. New York: Jewish Theological Seminary. 1960.

——. Major Trends in Jewish Mysticism. New York: Schocken Books, 1946.

Servado, Emilio. "Le Rôle des Conflits Pre-Oedipens," Revue Française de Psychoanalyse, Vol. 18, 1-45.

Silverstone, A. E. Aquila and Onkelos. Manchester University Press, 1931.

Smith, W. Robertson. Kinship and Marriage in Early Arabia. Cambridge: 1885.

——. The Religion of the Semites. Cambridge: 1889. Reprinted, New York: Meridian Press, 1956.

Spitz, René. The First Year of Life. New York: International Universities Press. 1965.

——. "Genèse des premiere rélations objectales: Observations directes sur le nourisson pendant sa première année," Revue Française de Psychoanalyse, Vol. 18, 479-575.

——. No and Yes: On the Genesis of Human Communication. New York: International Universities Press. 1957.

Strack, Hermann L. Introduction to the Talmud and Midrash. Philadelphia: Jewish Publication Society, 1931.

Tarachow, S. "Applied Psychoanalysis: Mythology and Folklore," The Annual Survey of Psychoanalysis, II (1954), 553-568.

Tcherikover, Viktor. Hellenistic Civilization and the Jews. Translated by S. Applebaum. Philadelphia: The Jewish Publication Society, 1959.

Theodor, J. article, "Midrash Haggadah," JE, VIII, pp. 550-568.

————. article "Midrashim, Smaller," JE, VIII, pp. 572-580.

Tillich, Paul. The Courage To Be. New Haven: Yale University Press, 1952.

————. Systematic Theology. Vol. I. London Nisbet and Co., 1953.

Van der Leeuw, P. J. "The Preoedipal Phase of the Male," The Psychoanalytic Study of the Child, XIII, 352-374.

Versenyi, Laszlo. Heidegger, Being, and Truth. New Haven: Yale University Press, 1945.

Wayne, Robert. "Prometheus and Christ," Psychoanalysis and the Social Sciences, III (1951), 201-219.

Weber, Max. The Protestant Ethic and the Spirit of Capitalism. Trans. Talcott Parsons. New York: Charles Scribner's Sons, 1958.

Weigert-Vowinckel, E. "The Cult and Mythology of the Magna Mater from the Standpoint of Psychoanalysis" in Psychiatry, I (1938), 348-353.

Wellisch, Erich. Isaac and Oedipus. London: Routledge and Kegan Paul, 1954.

Weiss, J. H. Dor Dor weDorshaw, Zur Geschichte der Jüdischen Tradition. Vol. II. Vienna: 1871.

White, Robert W. The Abnormal Personality. New York: The Ronald Press, 1948.

Wild, John. The Challenge of Existentialism. Bloomington: Indiana University Press, 1955.

Zeitlin, Solomon. The Rise and Fall of the Judaean State. Vol. II. Philadelphia: Jewish Publication Society, 1967.

Zeligs, Dorothy F. "Abraham and Monotheism," American Imago, Vol. XI.

Zilborg, Gregory and *Hall, J. K.* One Hundred Years of American Psychiatry. New York: Columbia University Press, 1944.

Zimmer, Heinrich. "Die Indische Weltmutter," Ernanos-Jahrbuch. Zurich: 1938.

Zunz, Leopold. Die Gottesdienstlichen Vorträge der Juden. Berlin: 1832.

Notes

Introduction

1. Cf. *Infra.* Chapter 2, page 22.

2. Sigmund Freud, *Totem and Taboo,* trans. James Strachey (London: Routledge and Kegan Paul), 1950.

3. Freud, *op. cit.,* pp. 100 ff.

4. Among the biblical personalities whose legends were studied were: Adam, Eve, the serpent, Cain, the generation of Enosh, the generation of the Flood, Noah, Ham, Nimrod, the generation of the Tower of Babel, the men of Sodom, the Pharaoh who sought to possess Sarah, Abimelech king of the Philistines, Reuben, Joseph, Potiphar, Dinah, Moses, the Pharaoh who opposed Moses, Dathan and Abiram, Nadab and Abihu, Korah and his band, Balaam, Zimri and Cozbi, the Spies and the Murmurers, Jephthah, David and Bathsheba, Doeg the Edomite, Absalom, Jeroboam ben Nebat, Ahab, Gahazi, Joash, Ahaz, Shebnah, Manasseh, Amon, Jehoiakim, Nebuchadnezzar and the first fall of Jerusalem, and Hiram, prince of Tyre. In the course of investigating the legends concerning this group, I investigated a considerably larger body of traditions. The reason why the legends were investigated by personalities rather than by theological topics is explained in some detail in Chapter 2. I

was more interested in determining *how the rabbis felt about what they believed* than in restating what they believed.

5. This theme is of considerable importance to my argument. I am indebted to the contributions of Margaretta K. Bowers for this insight. Cf. her *Conflicts of the Clergy* (New York: Thomas Nelson and Sons, 1963), pp. 57 ff.

6. Jean-Paul Sartre, *Being and Nothingness,* trans. Hazel Barnes (New York: Philosophical Library, 1956), p. 615.

7. Cf. Richard L. Rubenstein, *After Auschwitz: Radical Theology and Contemporary Judaism* (New York and Indianapolis: Bobbs-Merrill, 1966).

8. Cf. Leo Baeck, *This People Israel,* trans. Albert H. Friedlander (New York: Holt, Rinehart and Winston, 1964), pp. 235 ff.

9. Cf. Marshall McLuhan, *The Gutenberg Galaxy* (Toronto: University of Toronto Press, 1962) p. 41. ". . . . if a new technology extends one or more of our senses outside us into the social world, then new ratios among all of our senses will occur in that particular culture." The Roman destruction of the Jerusalem Temple did not create a new technology. It did, however, alter radically the media through which Jewish religious life was expressed. This was related to the changed circumstances of the Jewish community after the defeats. Cf. Salo Baron, *A Social and Religious History of the Jews* (New York: Columbia University Press, 1952), pp. 89 ff.

10. Cf. Raul Hilberg, *The Destruction of the European Jews* (London: W. H. Allen, 1961), pp. 666 ff.

11. Cf. Hilberg, *op. cit.,* pp. 646 ff.

12. Hilberg, *op. cit.,* pp. 760 ff. Hilberg ends his account of the extermination of European Jews with the observation, "The Jews can live more freely now. They can also die more quickly. The summit is within sight. An abyss has opened below." (p. 765.)

13. Maurice Friedman has perhaps expressed this position better than any other contemporary Jewish theologian. Cf. his *Problematic Rebel—An Image of Modern Man* (New York: Random House, 1963), especially pp. 462 ff., and his *To Deny Our Nothingness* (New York: Delacorte Press, 1967), especially pp. 335 ff.

14. David Bakan, *The Duality of Human Existence* (Chicago: Rand, McNally and Company, 1966), p. 5.

Chapter 1

1. David Bakan has traced the role of Jewish mysticism in the formation and the motifs of Freud's psychoanalytic career. Cf. his *Sigmund Freud and the Jewish Mystical Tradition* (New York: Van Nostrand, 1958). Cf. Earl Grollman, *Judaism in Sigmund Freud's World* (New York: Appleton-Century-Crofts, 1965); Cf. Richard L. Rubenstein, "Freud and Judaism: A Review Article," *Journal of Religion*, Vol. 47, No. 1, January 1967.

2. Cf. Sigmund Freud, *Moses and Monotheism*, trans. Katherine Jones (New York: Vintage Books, 1955), pp. 117 ff. Freud's view of the neurotic character of religion has been echoed by many of his followers. Cf. Theodore Reik, *Dogma and Compulsion: Psychoanalytic Studies of Religion and Myth*, trans. Bernard Miall (New York: International Universities Press, 1951); Reik, *Myth and Guilt*, (New York: George Braziller, 1957) p. 381; Hanns Sachs, "The Transformation of Impulses Into Obsessional Ritual," *American Imago* February 1946, pp. 67-74; Karl Abraham, *Clinical Papers and Essays on Psychoanalysis*, ed. Hilda Abraham, trans. Hilda Abraham and D. R. Ellison (New York: Basic Books, 1955) p. 138.

3. Cf. Freud, *The Future of an Illusion*, trans. W. D. Robinson (New York: Liveright Publishing Corp. 1949).

4. "For in our opinion the Oedipus-complex is the actual nucleus of neurosis, and the infantile sexuality which culminates in this complex is the true determinant of neurosis." Sigmund Freud, "A Child Is Being Beaten," in CP, Vol. II, 188-189. Cf. Freud, "Notes on a Case of Obsessional Neurosis," in CP, Vol. III, 345; Freud, "Obsessive Acts and Religious Practices" in CP, Vol. II, 25-35.

5. Freud, *Totem and Taboo*, trans. James Strachey (New York: W. W. Norton and Co., 1962), pp. 146 ff., and Freud, *Moses and Monotheism*, pp. 101 ff.

6. Freud, *Totem and Taboo*, pp. 125 ff.

7. Oddly, Freud does not stress infanticidal sacrifice and the sacri-

ficial peril of the first-born although there is much material on this subject. Cf. Bakan, *op. cit.* pp. 59-60, 210-13, 219. Theodore Reik, *Ritual: Psychoanalytic Studies,* trans. Douglas Bryan, (London: Hogarth Press, 1931), pp. 70 ff. Erich Wellisch, *Isaac and Oedipus* (London: Routledge and Kegan Paul, 1954), pp. 17-23.

8. Freud, *Moses and Monotheism,* p. 127. Freud, *Group Psychology and the Analysis of the Ego* (London: The Hogarth Press and the Institute of Psychoanalysis, 1959), pp. 54-60.

9. Cf. Bruno Bettelheim, *Symbolic Wounds* (Glencoe, Ill.: The Free Press, 1954), pp. 46, 48, 105-114. Bettelheim rejects the psychoanalytic conception of circumcision as a *pars pro toto* surrogate for the entire male organ. However, cf. D. Schendler, "The Signature of Pain" in *Psychoanalysis,* Vol. 2, No. 3 (New York: Winter 1954). Schendler's article is a critical review of Bettelheim. Cf. Freud, *New Introductory Lectures* (New York: W. W. Norton and Co., 1933), pp. 120-121, and Freud, *An Autobiographical Study* (New York: W. W. Norton and Co. 1952), p. 129. Cf. Herman Nunberg, *Problems of Bisexuality as Reflected in Circumcision* (London: Image Publishing Co. Ltd., 1949), for a restatement of the Freudian viewpoint.

10. Freud refers to his primal crime theory as a "scientific myth" in *Group Psychology and the Analysis of the Ego,* p. 112.

11. Freud, *Totem and Taboo,* pp. 141 ff.

12. Cf. Freud, *Moses and Monotheism,* pp. 102 ff.

13. Cf. Bettelheim, *op. cit.,* pp. 144 ff. Norman O. Brown, *Life Against Death—The Psychoanalytic Meaning of History* (New York: Vintage Books, 1959), pp. 121 ff. Cf. Erich Fromm, *The Forgotten Language* (New York: Grove Press, 1951), especially pp. 196 ff. Fromm's interpretation of the Oedipus legend is especially interesting.

14. Freud, *Totem and Taboo,* p. 143.

15. The fraternal parricides lie to themselves in denying the primal crime. They are guilty of *bad faith* in the sense that Sartre uses this conception. Cf. Jean-Paul Sartre, *Being and Nothingness— An Essay on Phenomenological Ontology,* pp. 47 ff.

16. Cf. Sartre, *The Flies,* trans. Stuart Gilbert in *No Exit* (New York: Vintage Books), pp. 126 ff.

17. Freud, *op. cit.* p. 143.

18. Cf. Ernest Jones, *The Life and Work of Sigmund Freud* (New York: Basic Books, 1955), Vol. III, 367.

19. Freud, *op. cit.,* p. 147.

20. Freud, *op. cit.,* pp. 133 ff.

21. Freud, *op. cit.,* pp. 126 ff.

22. Cf. Richard L. Rubenstein, *After Auschwitz,* pp. 104 ff.

23. Graham Greene, *The Heart of the Matter* (New York: Viking Press, 1948).

24. Freud, *op. cit.,* p. 146.

25. Cf. Freud, "The Most Prevalent Form of Degradation in Erotic Life" in CP, Vol. IV, 203 ff.

26. Freud, *Moses and Monotheism,* pp. 113 ff.

27. Freud, *op. cit.,* pp. 148 ff.

28. Freud, *Totem and Taboo,* p. 154.

29. Cf. Freud, *loc. it.*

30. Margaretta K. Bowers has discussed the desecration of the host accusation from the point of view of psychoanalysis. She has written the most compassionate and insightful account of the psychodynamics of Holy Communion I know of. Cf. her *Conflicts of the Clergy,* p. 51.

31. Bowers, *op. cit.*

32. Cf. Reik, *Ritual,* pp. 105 ff.

33. Cf. Bettelheim, *op. cit.* pp. 46 ff., 105-114, 128-133. Cf. Freud, *New Introductory Lectures* (New York: W. W. Norton and Co., 1933), pp. 120-121, "We have conjectured . . . . that in the early days of the human family, castration really was performed on the growing boy by the jealous and cruel father and that circumcision which is so frequently an element in puberty rites is an easily recognizable trace of it."

34. Cf. Calvin S. Hall, *A Primer of Freudian Psychology* (New York: Mentor Books, 1954), pp. 109 ff. Freud, "Some Psychological Consequences of the Anatomical Distinction Between the Sexes" in CP, Vol. V, 186-197.

35. Freud, "The Infantile Genital Organization of the Libido" in CP, Vol. II, 244-49. Freud, "Some Psychological Consequences

of the Anatomical Distinctions Between the Sexes" in CP, Vol. V, 186-197. Freud, "Female Sexuality," in CP, Vol. V, 252-272.

36. Reik, *Mystery on the Mountain* (New York: Harper and Brothers, 1959), pp. 167-170. "God indeed corresponds in collective life to a deified superego projected back into the outer world." (pp. 167 ff.)

37. Freud, *The Ego and the Id* (New York: W. W. Norton and Co., 1960), pp. 21 ff.

38. Freud, "Analysis of a Phobia in a Five-Year-Old Boy" in CP, Vol. III, 149-289. Cf. Freud, *Totem and Taboo,* pp. 128-132.

39. Cf. Brown, *Life Against Death,* pp. 126 ff.

40. Freud, *New Introductory Lectures,* p. 222.

41. Cf. Bettelheim, *op. cit.,* p. 132. Bettelheim sees the shift from Judaism to Christianity with the elimination of circumcision as due to the fact that the "threatening, castrating God" of Judaism takes on "the additional elements of a tender, loving Christ." p. 137. Freud saw castration anxiety as one root of anti-Semitism. He suggested that circumcision elicits from gentiles fear of the dreaded castration the primal father was alleged to have practiced long ago. *Moses and Monotheism,* p. 116.

42. Freud, *Totem and Taboo,* p. 149. "I cannot suggest at what point in this process of development a place is to be found for the great mother-goddesses, who may perhaps have preceded the father-gods."

43. Bettelheim, *op. cit.,* pp. 132 ff.

44. This is especially evident in the work of Theodore Reik. Crucial to Reik's analysis of the psychoanalytic significance of the legends concerning Eve is a midrash which asserts that Eve was created from "the modest part of man, for even when he stands naked, that part is covered." This tradition appears in BR 80.5 in the Theodor-Albeck edition. It is not in the current edition. Reik quotes the tradition as if he were quoting the rabbinic source. In actuality, he quotes Ginzberg's summary in *The Legends of the Jews,* Vol. I, p. 66. Had he checked the source, he might have realized that Ginzberg's term "the chaste part of the body" is a circumlocution. The source strongly suggests that Eve is created from Adam's penis in this tradition. Through-out Reik's treatment of Jewish themes, there is an uncritical re-

liance on secondary sources. For Reik's treatment of the tradition we have cited, cf. his *The Creation of Woman* (New York: George Braziller, 1960), p. 39.

45. Cf. Jacob Arlow in *The Annual Survey of Psychoanalysis*, Vol. II, 553.

46. Erik H. Erikson, *Young Man Luther* (New York: W. W. Norton and Co., 1958).

47. Freud, *Group Psychology and the Analysis of the Ego*, pp. 54 ff. *Totem and Taboo*, p. 139, note 1.

48. Freud, *Group Psychology and the Analysis of the Ego*, pp. 54 ff.

49. Patrick Mullahy, *Oedipus: Myth and Complex* (New York: Grove Press, 1955), pp. 30-50.

50. Freud, "Female Sexuality" in CP, Vol. V, 252-272.

51. Freud, *The Ego and the Id*, pp. 40-44. The mother-child dyad is the matrix out of which all interpersonal relations have their origin. Cf. René A. Spitz, *The First Year of Life* (New York: International Universities Press, 1965), pp. 296 ff.

52. Brown, *op. cit.*, p. 124.

53. Cf. Marie Langer, *Maternidad y Sexo* (Buenos Aires: Editorial Nova, 1951), abstracted in *The Annual Survey of Psychoanalysis*, Vol. II, 645-653; Emilio Servado, "Le Rôle des Conflits Pre-Oedipens" in *Revue Française de Psychoanalyse*, Vol. 18, 1-45; René A. Spitz, "Genèse des première relations objectales: Observations directes sur le nourisson pendant sa première année," in *Revue Française de Psychoanalyse*, Vol. 18, 479-575; P. J. van der Leeuw, "The Preoedipal Phase of the Male" in *The Psychoanalytic Study of the Child* (New York: International Universities Press, 1958), Vol. XIII, 352-374; Ruth M. Brunswick, "The Preoedipal Phase of the Libido Development," in *The Psychoanalytic Quarterly*, Vol. IX, 293-319; Otto Fenichel, *The Psychoanalytic Theory of Neurosis* (New York: W. W. Norton and Co., 1945), pp. 83 ff.; Freud, "Female Sexuality," in CP, Vol. V, 252-272; Brown, *op. cit.*, pp. 119 ff.

54. C. G. Jung, *The Archetypes and the Collective Unconscious* (New York: Pantheon Press, 1959), Bollingen Series, XX, 75-110; Jung, *Two Essays on Analytic Psychology* (New York: Meridian Books, 1956), pp. 120, 241; Erich Neumann, *The*

Origins and History of Consciousness (New York: Pantheon Books, 1954), Bollingen Series, XLII, 39-101; Erich Neumann, *The Great Mother* (New York: Pantheon Books, 1955), Bollingen Series, XLVII, especially pp. 89-210; Joseph Campbell, *The Masks of God: Primitive Mythology* (New York: Viking Press, 1959), 313-333. A similar stress appeared later in the writings of Otto Rank and Erich Fromm. Cf. Fromm, *The Forgotten Language,* pp. 195-235, and Rank, "Forms of Kinship and the Individual's Role in the Family," in *The Myth of the Birth of the Hero and Other Writings,* ed. Philip Freund (New York: Vintage Books, 1959), pp. 298-315.

55. Cf. Bettelheim, *op. cit.,* p. 137. Norman O. Brown, *Love's Body* (New York: Randon House, 1966), pp. 209, 215 ff.

56. Jung, *Modern Man in Search of a Soul* (New York: Harcourt Brace, 1933), p. 122.

57. Peter J. R. Dempsey, *Freud, Psychoanalysis and Catholicism* (Chicago: Henry Regnery, 1956) p. 45.

58. Jung, *loc. cit.*

59. Victor H. White, *God and the Unconscious* (Cleveland: Meridian Books, 1961), p. 45.

60. Freud, *Civilization and Its Discontents* (London: The Hogarth Press, 1930), p. 21.

61. Freud's mother was ninety-five when she died in 1930. At that time Freud was in his seventy-fifth year. In the best of analyses, the problems arising out of the client's earliest encounters with the mother are the most difficult to deal with. Freud was self-analyzed. Seventy-five was hardly an age at which he could have delved into the meaning of Amalie Freud's life and death for his own development.

62. Freud, *The Problem of Anxiety,* tr. Henry A. Bunker (New York: W. W. Norton and Co., 1936).

63. Freud, *Beyond the Pleasure Principle,* tr. James Strachey (New York: Boni and Liverwright, 1924).

64. Freud, *The Ego and the Id.*

65. Arlow, *op. cit.* Renato Almansi in *The Annual Survey of Psychoanalysis,* Vol. IV, 355; S. Tarachow in *op cit., The Annual Survey of Psychoanalysis,* Vol. II, 567.

66. Cf. Ernest F. Jones, *The Life and Work of Sigmund Freud,* Vol. II, 69 ff.

67. Cf. Jones, *op. cit.*, Vol. III 186; Edward Glover, *Freud or Jung?* (Cleveland: Meridian Books, 1956), pp. 150 ff.

68. George Foote Moore, *Judaism* (Cambridge, Mass. Harvard University Press, 1927), 3 Vols.; R. Travers Herford, *The Pharisees* (London: Macmillan, 1924).

69. The special value of Erikson's *Childhood and Society* lies in the questions he asks concerning the cultures he has studied rather than in any slavish attempt to impose Freud's categories on other cultures. Cf. Clyde Kluckhohn, "The Influence of Psychiatry on Anthropology in America during the Past One Hundred Years" in *One Hundred Years of American Psychiatry*, ed. Gregory Zilberg and J. K. Hall (New York: Columbia University Press, 1944). Cf. Margaret Mead, "Some Relationships between Social Anthropology and Psychiatry" in *Dynamic Psychiatry*, ed. Franz Alexander (Chicago: University of Chicago Press, 1952).

Chapter 2

1. J. Theodor, article "Midrash Haggadah," in JE, Vol. VIII, 550-568. Cf. George Foote Moore, *Judaism* (Cambridge, Mass.: Harvard University Press, 1927), Vol. I, 132-134 and 161; J. Z. Lauterbach, *Midrash and Mishnah* (New York: Bloch Publishing Co., 1916), p. 2; S. Horovitz, article "Midrash," in JE, Vol. VIII, 548-550; W. Bacher, article "Bible Exegesis," in JE, Vol. III, 163; Bacher, *Die Exegetische Terminologie der Jüdischen Traditionaliteratur*, I: *Die Bibel-exegetische Terminologie der Tannaiten* (Leipzig: 1905), translated into Hebrew as *Arche Midrash* by A. Z. Rabinowitz (Tel Aviv: 1923), pp. 24-26 and 70.

2. The Scriptural basis for tracing Midrashic activity at least as far back as Ezra is to be found in Ezra 7:10; cf. Lauterbach, *Midrash and Mishnah*, p. 3.

3. J. Shabbat 15c, cited by Moore, *op. cit.*, Vol. I, 163. R. Johanan and R. Nahman who flourished in third-century Palestine were reported to have used such written works. Cf. Gittin 5oa. R. Johanan, however, objected to the use of such books on the ground that if one learns Aggadah out of a book, he will soon forget it. J. Berachot 9a. This comment is important because R. Johanan apparently intuited the importance of the Aggadah

remaining an oral and aural literature rather than a visual literature. For parallel misgivings among the Greeks, cf. Marshall
McLuhan, *The Gutenberg Galaxy* (Toronto: University of
Toronto Press, 1962), pp. 25 ff. In the *Phaedrus*, tr. B. Jowett,
274-75, Socrates complains that writing will have a negative effect: "For this discovery of yours will create forgetfulness in the
learner's soul, because they will not use their memories. . . ."

4.   Sifre D. 49 (Ed. F, 85a).

5.   Solomon Schechter, *Studies in Judaism,* First Series (Philadelphia: Jewish Publication Society, 1945), pp. 196-97.

6.   Salo W. Baron, *A Social and Religious History of the Jews*
(New York: Columbia University Press, 1952), Vol. II, 298.

7.   Cf. Freud's discussion of the capacity of Sophocles' *Oedipus
Rex* to move contemporary audiences as it did the ancients.
Freud, *The Interpretation of Dreams,* pp. 261 ff.

8.   Ruth Munroe, *Schools of Psychoanalytic Thought,* pp. 27 ff.

9.   Munroe, *op. cit.,* pp. 29 ff.

10. Freud, *The Interpretation of Dreams,* pp. 588 ff.

11. Freud, *op. cit.,* pp. 261 ff.

12. Cf. Carl G. Jung, *Man and His Symbols* (Garden City: Doubleday and Company, 1964).

13. Freud, *The Interpretation of Dreams,* pp. 533 ff.

14. Freud, *op. cit.,* p. 549.

15. Munroe, *op. cit.,* pp. 58 ff.

16. Cf. Max Kadushin, *The Theology of Seder Eliahu* (New
York: Bloch Publishing Company, 1932), pp. 17 ff.

17. Ez. 28:2. The rabbinic sources which identify Hiram with the
"prince of Tyre" are Mek. (Ed. L.) Shirata II, p. 61, 1.27-33;
Mek. RS (Ed. H.), p. 66; Mek. RS (Ed. E.), p. 91 ff.

18. ShR 1.29-31; Tan. Shemoth 9-10; DR 2.29.

19. ShR, *loc. cit.*

20. ShR 5.20; Tan Wa-Era 6; Tan. B. II, 20-21.

21. ShR 25.10; Tan Tezaweh 11; Mek. RS (Ed. Epstein) p. 111,
1.21-p.114 1.5 tells the story but does not specify Dathan and
Abiram as do most of the other sources.

22. Tehillim 106,455; Tan. Korah 25; BaR 18.10.

23. Cf. Ginzberg, VI, 35, n. 196.

24. Aboth 6.2.

25. In one tradition, the rabbis picture Manasseh as proving the triteness of some of the sentences in the Torah: "Our Rabbis taught: 'But the soul that doeth ought presumptuously!' (Num. 15:30) This refers to Manasseh . . . who examined (biblical) narratives to prove them worthless. Thus, he jeered, had Moses nothing better to write but, 'And Lotan's sister was Timna' (Gen. 36:22), 'And Timma was concubine to Eliphaz' (Gen. 36:12). . . ." (Sanhedrin 99b. The rabbis could not state explicitly that any sentence in the Torah was without relevance. They could place such ideas in the mouth of an idolatrous king such as Manasseh. Nevertheless, the thought is theirs alone.

    This particular tradition may reflect rabbinic polemic against Gnostic criticisms of the Bible. The rabbis may have known of such criticisms and sought to devalue them by placing them in the mouth of Manasseh in their legends. Cf. A. Marmorstein, *Studies in Jewish Theology* (London: Oxford University Press, 1950). However, I. Heinemann regards this tradition as an instance of dealing with the question of regarding the Bible as a unified work of equal value in all of its parts. He does not raise the issue of Gnostic criticism as does Marmorstein. Cf. I. Heinemann, *Darke Ha-Aggadah* (Jerusalem: Magnes Press, 1954), p. 75.

26. Cf. Roy Schafer, *Psychoanalytic Interpretation in Rorschach Testing* (New York: Grune and Stratten, 1954), pp. 78-82. Schafer discusses the difference between the level of psychic functioning in Rorschach responses and dreams.

27. Cf. Freud, "Observations on 'Wild' Psycho-Analysis" in CP, Vol. II, pp. 297-304. On the problems of interpreting myth and legend, cf. Freud's letter to C. G. Jung dated December 7, 1911, in Ernest Jones, *The Life and Work of Sigmund Freud*, Vol. III, 452-453.

28. Cf. Munroe, *op. cit.*, p. 54.

29. Renato Almansi, "A Psychoanalytic Interpretation of the Menorah" in *Journal of the Hillside Hospital* (New York:

1953), Vol. II, 80-95, and Almansi, "A Further Contribution," JHH, Vol. III, 3-31.

30. H. H. Fingeret, "A Psychoanalytic Study of the Minor Prophet, Jonah," in *Psychoanalytic Review*, 1954, Vol. XLI, 55-98.

31. Gordon Allport and Leo Postman, *The Psychology of Rumor* (New York: Henry Holt and Co., 1947), pp. 162-169.

32. Gen. 9:20. Cf. BR 36.3, 22.5; Tan. Noah 13; MHG on Genesis, Vol. I, p. 185, 1.6-8. On the rabbinic attitude toward wine, cf. Erubin 65a; Sanhedrin 70a where R. Meir holds that Adam's tree was a vine; BR 36.4 WR 12.1. In this source the redness of wine is associated with blood. Its misuse is interpreted as violating rabbinic sexual norms involving blood, such as lusting after a woman during her period.

33. Cf. Margaretta K. Bowers, *op. cit.* p. 57.

34. Allport and Postman, *op. cit.*, p. ix

35. Allport and Postman, *op. cit.*, pp. 43-45.

36. Allport and Postman, *op. cit.*, pp. 33-56.

37. Allport and Postman, *op. cit.*, pp. 75-86.

38. Allport and Postman, *op. cit.*, p. 86.

39. Allport and Postman, *op. cit.*, pp. 56, 97 ff., 102. Closure is related to Bartlett's concept of the "effort after meaning." Bartlett has suggested that the human mind tends to fit all experience into meaningful categories. He regards every human cognitive reaction as an effort after meaning. Cf. F. C. Bartlett, *Remembering* (Cambridge: University Press, 1932), pp. 44 ff.

40. Allport and Postman, *op. cit.*, p. 100.

41. Allport and Postman, *op. cit.*, p. 104.

42. Allport and Postman, *op. cit.*, pp. 105-115.

43. Allport and Postman, *op. cit.*, p. 163.

44. Louis Ginzberg, "Jewish Folklore: East and West," in *Of Jewish Law and Lore* (Philadelphia: Jewish Publication Society, 1955), pp. 61 ff; cf. Ginzberg, preface to *The Legends of the Jews*, Vol. I, vii-xv and Vol. V, vii-xi.

45. Cf. L. Zunz, *Die Gottesdienstlichen Vorträge der Juden* (Berlin: 1832), p. 349; Moore, *op. cit.*, pp. 161 ff.; Hermann L.

Strack, *Introduction to the Talmud and Midrash* (Philadelphia: Jewish Publishing Society, 1931), pp. 201-203; Z. Chajes, *Mebo ha-Talmud,* trans. and ed. Jacob Schachter, as *The Student's Guide Through the Talmud* (London: East and West Library, 1952), pp. 139-147.

46. When authoritatively interpreted, the Written Law is said to yield the Oral Law. There was a tradition that during the period of mourning for Moses, no less than three thousand Mosaic oral traditions deriving from Sinai were lost. Others were forgotten by Joshua. Many of the exegetical proofs were also forgotten. Some were restored by Othniel's acumen. Others were restored by R. Akiba. Cf. Temura 16a and Menahot 29b.

47. II Kings 21:1-18.

48. Berakhoth 4a; Erubin 53b.

49. AZ 4b-5a.

50. I Samuel 18:14.

51. Shabbat 56a; Ketuboth 9b.

52. Allport and Postman, *op cit.,* p. 146.

53. Allport and Postman, *op. cit.,* pp. 145 ff.

54. Schafer, *op. cit.,* pp. 74-139.

55. Leopold Bellak, *"The Thematic Apperception Test In Clinical Use,"* in L. Apt and L. Bellak, *Projective Psychology: Clinical Approaches to the Total Personality* (New York: Alfred A. Knopf, 1950), p. 186.

56. Bellak, *loc. cit.*

57. Bowers, *op cit.,* pp. 41 ff.

Chapter 3

1. Freud, *Moses and Monotheism,* pp. 109 ff.

2. Romans 5:12.

3. Romans 5:18, 19.

4. Freud, *loc. cit.*

5. ARN 1, 6.

6. BR 19.12.

7. Sanhedrin 38b. This tradition is related to the tradition that Adam was born circumcised found in ARN 2, 12. For a detailed bibliography of rabbinic attitudes toward circumcision, cf. Ginzberg, V, 267-269, n. 318.

8. 2 ARN, 42, 116-117; cf. Ginzberg, V, p. 102; cf. 2 ARN, 34, 74.

9. Gen. 3:8

10. BR 19.9 and 12.6; cf. BR 8.1 where a number of views are cited as to Adam's primordial dimensions.

11. Tehillim 92, 412; cf. Shabbat 55b, "The Ministering Angels asked the Holy One. . . . 'Why didst Thou impose the penalty of death upon Adam?' Said He to them, 'I gave him an easy command yet he violated it.' " Cf. Tehillim 92, 403 where R. Levi depicts God as about to destroy Adam when the Sabbath arrived to save him temporarily. Cf. Ginzberg V, pp. 128-131, n. 142.

12. Cf. Ginzberg, *loc. cit.*

13. Shabbat 55a.

14. Gen. 3:2 ff.

15. Yebamoth 103a; cf. Shabbat 146a where the tradition is less explicit and AZ 22b.

16. BR 24.6.

17. Proverbs 1:25 is quoted in this source. The source is BR 80.5 in the Theodor-Albeck edition but not in the current edition; BR 18.2 is a parallel; cf. Tan. B. II, 172 where God's dilemma as to what part he will use to create Eve is recorded. In that source God's dilemma is not resolved. Tan WaYesheb 6 cites a tradition that God created her from "a rib from a hidden place."

18. Gen. 30:16.

19. BR 18.1; cf. Tan. B. I, 171; cf. Archin 17; MHG on Gen. Vol. II, p. 586, 1-6– p. 587, 1.11. This source largely parallels BR 80.1; Tan. WaYishlah 6.

20. Gen. 34:1.

21. Tan. WaYishlah 7; cf. MHG on Gen. II, p. 587, 1.1-11.

22. Gen. 34:1, 2.

23. BR 80.5; BR 18.2.

24. Eccl. 10:8.

25. Tan. WaYishlah 7; Tan. B. II, 172; Tan. B. I, 169 which sharpens the imputation of guilt to Dinah by asserting that she not only displayed herself but violated the Sabbath by going out to be seen with jewels on that day. The vocalization of the Hebrew verb was altered by changing the *qal* or simple form to the *niph'al* or reflexive form.

26. Isaiah 3:16 ff.

27. WR 16.1; cf. Margulies *ad. loc.* comments on this tradition in his critical edition. BR 45.5 contains an unkind description of women in general.

28. Gen. 3:16.

29. BR 20.6. On the Eve legends, cf. Ginzberg, V, 101, n. 85.

30. Erubin 100b.

31. Cf. Ginzberg, V, 101, n. 85.

32. 2 ARN, 42, 117.

33. Joseph H. Hertz (ed.), *The Authorized Daily Prayer Book* (New York: Bloch Publishing Co., 1948), p. 21.

34. Cf. Stanley M. Elkins, *Slavery: A Problem in American Institutional and Intellectual Life* (Chicago: University of Chicago Press, 1959).

35. Cf. Julius Guttmann, *Philosophies of Judaism,* tr. David Silverman (New York: Holt, Rinehart and Winston, 1964), pp. 394 ff.

36. Cf. Ginzberg, V, 123-124, n. 131.

37. Gen. 3:14.

38. The quotation from Scripture is Gen. 3:14. The rabbinic source is ARN 1.5.

39. Theodore Reik, *Myth and Guilt,* pp. 305-335.

40. Freud, "The Unconscious" in CP, Vol. IV, 118 ff.

Chapter 4

1. Cf. Joseph Klausner, *The Messianic Ideal in Israel,* trans. W. F. Stinespring (New York: Macmillan, 1955), pp. 13 ff.

2. Ps. 136: 10.

3. Tehillim 136, 520.

4. Ex. 5:1.

5. Roland de Vaux, *Ancient Israel* (New York: McGraw-Hill Paperbacks, 1965), Vol. II, p. 489.

6. Ex. 12:3 ff. Cf. Theodore Gaster, *Passover—Its History and Traditions* (Boston: Beacon Paperbacks, 1962).

7. W. Robertson-Smith, *The Religion of the Semites* (Cambridge: 1889, reprinted New York: Meridian Press, 1956), pp. 222, 237, 295, 405.

8. Ex. 12:13.

9. Gen. 22:1 ff.

10. Ex. 22:28, 29.

11. Ex. 13:2; cf. Ex. 34:19, 20 and 13:12 ff.

12. Ex. 34:20.

13. Ez. 20:24-26.

14. Cf. Pedersen, *op. cit.*, IV, 320.

15. Num. 18:16.

16. Ex. 13:2. The text of the ritual is to be found in Hertz, *The Authorized Daily Prayer Book,* pp. 1034 ff.

17. Cf. Hertz' *ad. loc.* comments, *op. cit.*, pp. 1034 ff.

18. Cf. Bowers, *op. cit.*, pp. 49 ff.

19. John 1:29; cf. John 1:36.

20. II Cor. 3:15.

21. Freud saw Christianity as a "return of the repressed." Cf. *Moses and Monotheism,* p. 113.

22. I Peter 1:18-19.

23. Jesus is also referred to as the first-born and the first-fruit. Cf. I Cor. 15:23 and Col. 1:15, 18.

24. Reik, *Ritual,* pp. 69-89.

25. Cf. David Bakan, *The Duality of Human Existence,* pp. 205 ff. Erich Wellisch, *Isaac and Oedipus,* pp. 9 ff.

26. Romans 7:7, 8.

27. Mt. 5:20.

28. Mt. 5:21, 22.

29. Cf. Aboth 1:17. "Not learning but doing is the chief thing." The stress in Judaism was on the appropriate action. Motivation was important but it remained subordinate to the religious deed.

30. Cf. Konrad Lorenz, *On Aggression,* trans. Marjorie K. Wilson (New York: Harcourt, Brace and World, 1966), pp. 236 ff.

Chapter 5

1. Søren Kierkegaard, *The Concept of Dread,* trans. Walter Lowrie (Princeton: Princeton University Press, 1944). (Originally published in Danish, 1844.)

2. Freud, *The Problem of Anxiety,* p. 75. "... We assume castration anxiety as the motive force behind the struggles of the ego."

3. Rollo May, *The Meaning of Anxiety* (New York: Ronald Press, 1950), p. 123.

4. Cf. Bettelheim, *Symbolic Wounds,* pp. 128 ff.

5. Paul Tillich, *The Courage To Be* (New Haven: Yale University Press, 1952), p. 38; cf. John Wild, *The Challenge of Existentialism* (Bloomington: Indiana University Press, 1955), pp. 70-71. For an excellent criticism of Heidegger's conception of man as a being-toward-death, cf. Laszlo Versenyi, *Heidegger, Being, and Truth* (New Haven: Yale University Press, 1965), pp. 177 ff.

6. Freud, *The Problem of Anxiety,* p. 105; May, *The Meaning of Anxiety,* pp. 121 ff.

7. Cf. Freud, *The Ego and the Id,* pp. 47 ff.

8. Cf. *supra,* p. 9.

9. Cf. *supra, loc. cit.*

10. Freud, *Moses and Monotheism,* p. 116.

11. M. Sotah 1.7 ff. Cf. J. Peah 21b and Ta'anith 21a in which the teacher of R. Akiba, Nahum of Gamzu, welcomes his extraordinary misfortunes as God's measure-for-measure retaliation for his sins. Cf. Mek. Beshallah, ed. Lauterbach, Vol. I, 243-245, "For with the very thing with which the Egyptians planned to destroy Israel, He (i.e. God) destroyed them." Cf. T. Sotah 3.13; cf. Mt. 5:31, "If your right eye cause you to sin, pluck it out and throw it away. ..."

12. Gen. 39:1.

13. Ps. 37:28.

14. The Masoretic (i.e. official rabbinic) text of the Bible does not have the reading of the midrash. The Masoretic text reads "saints" as in the English translation.

15. Ps. 37:28.

16. BR 86.3.

17. Cf. Sotah 13b where Rab says that Potiphar was emasculated by the angel Gabriel; Targum Jerushalmi on Gen. 39:1; cf. Tan. B. II, 85 where God does the castrating; MHG on Gen., Vol. II, p. 656, 1.13-15 and p. 657, 1.4-7 which parallels Sotah 13b and also quotes Rab.

18. Num. 25:1-18.

19. Sanhedrin 82a-b; cf. J. Sanhedrin 28b-29a; Sifre on Numbers, ed. Friedmann, p. 131; Sh'moth R. 33.5; B'midbar R. 20.24; Tan. B. IV, p. 148; Tsn., Balak 20.

20. B'midbar R. 20.24.

21. B'Midbar R. 20.25; cf. Buber's comments on Tan. IV, p. 148.

22. Sanhedrin 82b.

23. Ps. 1:28.

24. Tehillim 105:452 and 78:350. The latter source describes the frogs as going up through the marble houses but omits the castration story. Cf. Sh'moth R. 10.3, but cf. Buber's *ad. loc.* comments on Tehillim 78:350 where he suggests that the source in Sh'moth R. is medieval.

25. Gen. 9:22.

26. BR 36.7; Sanhedrin 108b; Tan. Noah 12; BR 31.12; BR 34.7; Tan. B. I, 42-43. Tan. B. I, 49-50.

27. BR 35.1.

28. BR 36.4 and MHG on Gen., Vol. I, 189, 1.5-6.

29. Baba Bathra 74 b.

30. M. Sotah 1.7 ff.

31. *Ibid.*

32. Mek. Beshallah (Ed. L.), Vol. I, 243-245. Cf. T. Sotah 3.13;

Mek. (Ed. L.) Amalek, Vol. II, 148, 1.8-11; Mek. (Ed. F.), II, 55a. Cf. Ginzberg, V, 427, n. 172 where Ginzberg discusses the rabbinic passages which assert that the Egyptians were punished measure for measure.

33. ShR 9.10; Tan. WaYera 14; MHG on Ex. 116, 1.16-17. In another tradition it is maintained that the Nile was turned into blood in retaliation for the drowning of the Israelite children. Cf. MHG on Ex., p. 116, 1.15-16.

34. ShR 10.4.

35. Tehillim 136, 520. Cf. *supra*, pp. 58 ff.

36. Cf. *supra, pp.* 47 ff.

37. Cf. *supra,* p. 54.

38. BR 87.7 and 98.20; Sotah 36b; J. Horayoth 2, 46d.

39. BR 87.7

40. MHG on Gen., II, 668, 1.6-7 and 1.9-15. Cf. BR 98.20 where he sees his mother.

41. Gen. 39:11.

42. BR 87.7; cf. BR 98.20 where the tale is slightly less explicit.

43. BR 87.7.

44. Fenichel, *The Psychoanalytic Theory of Neurosis,* pp. 170 ff.

45. Gen. 20:18.

46. BR 52.13.

47. BR 52.13; cf. Tan.B., I, 101, where the tradition omits the angel and the drawn sword; cf. MHG on Gen., Vol. I, 328, 1.15-16 where Gabriel is the angel; PRE 26.

48. Gen. 12:17.

49. BR 40.2 in the current edition. In Theodor's critical edition the tradition appears in chapter 41. Cf. MHG on Gen., Vol. I, 225, 1.6-10 where R. Tarphon is quoted as saying that Pharaoh was smitten with leprosy on the eve of Passover as a hint of the later fate of the Egyptians. PRE 26.

50. Cf. Erikson, *Childhood and Society,* pp. 67-73; Fenichel, *The Psychoanalytic Theory of Neurosis,* pp. 62 ff. For a most interesting discussion of the development of psychotoxic reactions in the skin of eight-month-old babies, cf. René A. Spitz, *The*

First Year of Life (New York: International Universities Press, 1965), pp. 224 ff.

51. WR 16.1.

52. M. Margulies' *ad. loc.* comment on WR 16.1 in his critical edition.

53. Ketuboth 77b; cf. WR 16.1 which contains this tradition and the one cited in n.54. However, Margulies removes this tradition in his *ad. loc.* comments on the text. On *ra'athan* cf. T. Ketuboth 7 *ad. fin.* Cf. MHG on Gen., Vol. I, 225, 1.11-15.

54. BR 41.2.

55. BR 41.2.

56. Shabbat 149b.

57. Cf. *supra.*, pp. 43 ff.

58. Cf. Ginzberg, Vol. VII, 586-598, for an index of Church Fathers and medieval Christian writers using material from the Aggadah. This is by no means an exhaustive list.

59. WR 16.1.

60. Sotah 35 a; Kohelet R. 9.12.

61. Num. 14:37. Scripture refers to the "plague" rather than leprosy. The rabbis understood the plague to be leprosy.

62. Kohelet R. 9.12.

63. Sotah 35a.

64. Sotah 35a.

65. ARN 9, 39.

66. Judges 11:31.

67. Judges 11:34-40.

68. WR 37.4; BR 60.3; Tan. B. III, 112-114; Tan. Behukkotai 5; Kohelet R. 10.15; Ta'anit 4a; Midrash Tannaim 100; Sifre D. 148; ER 11, 55-57.

69. Judges 12:7.

70. Num. 12.10.

71. WR 16.1, ARN 9.39, Shabbat 97a.

72. Cf. Bertram Lewin, *The Psychoanalysis of Elation* (New York:

W. W. Norton and Co., 1950), pp. 109-110; Lewin, "Sleep, Mouth and the Dream Sequence" in *The Psychoanalytic Quarterly*, Vol. XV, 1946, 240; Geza Roheim, *The Gates of the Dream* (New York: International Universities Press, 1958), pp. 88 ff; René Spitz, *No and Yes: On the Genesis of Human Communication* (New York: International Universities Press, 1958), pp. 70-85.

73. Cf. Edith Weigert-Vowinckel, "The Cult and Mythology of the Magna Mater From the Viewpoint of Psychoanalysis" in *Psychiatry*, Vol. I (1938), 348-349; Bettelheim, *Symbolic Wounds*, pp. 154-164.

74. 2 ARN 9, 39.

75. For the flood traditions, cf. Sanhedrin 57a, 108b; WR 7:6, BR 26.4, 5 and 32.7, AZ 23b; Hulin 23a; cf. Ginzberg, V, pp. 182-183.

76. WR 7.6.

77. WR 7.6 and 20.2 Korah is depicted as boiling like "flesh in a pot" in Baba Bathra 74a; cf. Sanhedrin 110a-110b; Tan. B., IV, 94.

78. Lev. 10:1, 2.

79. Sanhedrin 52a.

80. *Ibid.*; cf. Tan. B. I, 50.

81. Rashi on Sanhedrin 110a.

82. Sanhedrin 106b.

83. Sandor Ferenczi, *Thalassa: A Theory of Genitality*, trans. H. A. Bunker (New York: The Psychoanalytic Quarterly, 1938).

84. Num. 16:32, 33.

85. Num. 16:33.

86. B'midbar R. 18:13; Tan. B. IV, 96-97.

87. *Ibid.*

88. J. Sanhedrin 10, 28a which reads 'flew up.'

89. Baba Bathra 74a; Sanhedrin 110a-T n. B. IV, 94.

90. Gittin 56b-57a; cf. AZ 11a and A. E. Silverstone, *Aquila and Onkelos* (Manchester: Manchester University Press, 1931), pp. 1-22 and 148-160.

91. Gittin 56b-57a.

92. Ex. 14:26; Mek. Beshallah (ed. L.), Vol. I, 243, 1.3-p. 244. 1.7,
     Mek. RS, (ed. E.) p. 66, 1.20-44. The story of the Egyptian
     drowning is rehearsed throughout Jewish liturgy. It thus re-
     ceived the widest currency of any of the punishment traditions.

93. Ex. 4:24-27.

94. CF. Salo Baron, *A Religious and Social History of the Jews*
     (New York: Columbia University Press, 1952), Vol. II, 107
     and 374; Justin Martyr, *Dialogue with Trypho,* tr. A. Lukyn
     Williams (London: S.P.C.K., 1930), p. 107; M. S. Enslin,
     "Justin Martyr: An Appreciation," JQR (new series), **XXXIV**,
     179-205; cf. Nedarim 31b-32a and Bacher II a, 22.

95. Mek. Amalek (Ed. L.), Vol. II, 168, 1.93-p. 169 1.105; Mek.
     Jethro (Ed. F.), I, 57b-58a.

96. Ex. 4:25, 26. The rabbinic source is Nedarim 32a.

97. Ran on Nedarim 32a printed in the standard edition of Ayn
     Ya'acob (reprinted, New York: 1953).

98. Mahrsh'a on Nedarim 32a printed in the standard edition of
     Ayn Ya'acob.

99. MHG on Ex., 78, 1.2-4; ShR 5.8.

100. But cf. Fenichel, *op. cit.,* pp. 63 ff and 83 ff. Fenichel tends to
     reduce incorporation anxiety to castration. Nevertheless, his de-
     scription of archaic object relations does not necessarily call for
     that reduction. The intersection of anxiety over castration and
     incorporation is described by Freud in the case of "little Hans."
     CF. Freud, "Analysis of a Phobia in a Five-Year-Old Boy" in
     CP, Vol. III, 149-179.

101. II Sam. 15:1 ff and II Sam 18:15.

102. M. Sotah 1.8.

103. M. Sanhedrin.

104. M. Sanhedrin 10.3.

105. Freud, *The Problem of Anxiety,* p. 105.

106. John Wild, *op. cit.,* pp. 70-71.

107. Søren Kierkegaard, *The Concept of Dread,* pp. 38, 55.

108. Fenichel, *op. cit.,* pp. 206 ff.

109. Freud, *Beyond the Pleasure Principle*, pp. 67 ff.

110. From the point of view of psychoanalysis, one of the earliest anxieties is the archaic anxiety of incorporation. This is stated succinctly by Fenichel: "The content of the primitive ego's idea of anxiety is determined in part directly by its biological nature and in part by its animistic ways of thinking, which make the ego believe that its environment has the same instinctual aims as it has itself (combined with more power). In these animistic misunderstandings the punitive talion principle is at work, according to which any deed may be undone (or must be punished) by a similar deed inflicted on the original doer." Fenichel, *op. cit.*, pp. 43-44. Since one of the fundamental aims of the archaic oral stage is the striving to unite, by means of the mouth, with the predominantly maternal environment, it follows that the anxiety lest one be incorporated is decisive at this stage. Cf. Erikson, *op. cit.*, pp. 67-73.

111. Ferenczi, *op. cit.*, pp. 81-95.

112. Cf. Aboth 3.1 and 4.1.

113. M. Sanhedrin 10.1. There are extremely complicated problems connected with the question of the rabbinic view of the time of the Messiah and the World to Come. R. Johanan held that, though the prophets spoke of the days of the Messiah, nevertheless concerning the World to Come "no eye has seen what God has prepared for those who wait for him." Berachoth 34b. In the present context, what is important is that the rabbis never doubted God's power to make alive and to annihilate. For some views on the problem, cf. Joseph Klausner, *op. cit.*, and Montefiore and Lowe, *A Rabbinic Anthology*, pp. 580-608.

114. The rabbis were mindful of the analogy between the womb and the tomb: R. Tabi further said in the name of R. Josiah: "What is meant by the text, 'There are three things which are never satisfied. . . . the grave and the barren womb'? (Prov. 30:15, 16) How come the grave next to the womb? It is to teach you that just as the womb takes in and gives forth again, so the grave takes in and will give again. . . . Here is a refutation of those who deny that resurrection is taught in the Torah. . . ." Berachoth 15b.

115. For the conception of the sinner's death as atonement, cf. M. Sanhedrin 6.2 and T. Sanhedrin 9.5: "Those who are put to

death by the (rabbinical) court have a share in the world to come, because they confess all their sins."

116. For a succinct summary of rabbinic attitudes toward repentance, cf. Maimonides, *Mishneh Torah*, Hilkoth T'shuvah (reprinted New York: Otzer Harambam, Inc., 1960).

117. Cf. Berachoth, 5a-5b.

118. Cf. Maimonides, *op. cit.*, Hilkoth T'shuvah, 4.2 ff.

119. Maimonides, *loc. cit.*

120. Freud, "Female Sexuality" in CP, Vol. V, 254.

121. Cf. Hertz, *The Authorized Daily Prayer Book*, pp. 101 and 129.

122. Erich Neumann, *The Great Mother*, trans. Ralph Mannheim (New York: Pantheon Books, 1955), pp. 149 ff. Cf. Heinrich Zimmer's description of the bloody worship of Kali-ma quoted by Neumann (p. 152). Cf. Heinrich Zimmer, "Die Indische Weltmutter" in *Ernanos-Jahrbuch* (Zurich: 1938), pp. 179 ff. The entire issue of the *Ernanos-Jahrbuch* for 1938 is devoted to the problem of the Great Mother.

123. Weigert-Vowinckel, *loc. cit.*

124. Cf. W. Robertson Smith, *Kinship and Marriage in Early Arabia* (Cambridge: 1885), pp. 22 f.

125. Gen. 4:24.

126. P. J. van der Leeuw, "The Preoedipal Stage of the Male" in *The Psychoanalytic Study of the Child*, Vol. XIII, 352-374. Cf. Edmund Bergler, *The Basic Neurosis: Oral Regression and Psychic Masochism* (New York: Grune and Stratton, 1949), p. 16.

127. BR 1.1.

128. Samuel N. Kramer, *Sumerian Mythology* (New York: Harper Torchbooks, 1961), p. 39.

129. Kramer, *op. cit.*, p. 42.

Chapter 6

1.   Cf. Ferenczi, *op. cit.*

2.   2 Chron. 33:23.

3. Sanhedrin 103b.

4. Lev. 10:1, 2.

5. WR, ed. M. Margulies, 20.2; PK ed. S. Buber, 170a; Tan. Achare Moth, 2; Tan. B., III, 7.

6. WR 20.6; PK 172a; Tan. Achare Moth 5; Tan. B. III, 61; MHG on Lev. p. 195.

7. WR 20.6; Erubin 63a; Yoma 53a; MHG on Lev. p. 187. R. Eliezer's interpretation is related in connection with his remark to his wife Imma Shalom that one of his disciples would not live out the year because the disciple had improperly offered a legal opinion in R. Eliezer's presence. This incident is indicative of the way the life-situations of the rabbis were often relevant to the character of their interpretative insights.

8. Num. 3:4.

9. WR 20.9; PK 172b; Tan. Achare Moth 6; Tan. B. III, 63; MHG on Lev. p. 192.

10. WR 20.10; Sanhedrin 52a.

11. WR 20.10. Cf. the *ad. loc.* comment of M. Margulies in his critical edition of WR. Margulies maintains that this was a proverbial saying directed against young men who waited hopefully for the death of their elders.

12. M. Sotah 1.8; Sanhedrin 103b; Sotah 10b; B'Midbar Rabbah 9.24.

13. Cf. W. Bacher, *Die Agada der Tannaiten* (Strassbourg: 1884-1890), translated into Hebrew as *Agadot ha-Tannaim* by A. Z. Rabinowitz (Berlin: D'vir, 1922-6). Page reference is to the Hebrew translation which restores the cited material to its original language. Hereafter cited as Bacher. Vol. I a, 94, n. 2. Cf. Ginzberg, Legends, Vol. V. 331, n. 60. For attempts to exculpate Reuben, cf. Shabbat 55b where R. Eliezer and R. Joshua b. Hanania hold that he sinned. R. Gamaliel, R. Eleazar of Modi'im and R. Jeremiah b. Abba maintain that he avoided sin. R. Nathan exculpates him. Cf. PK 25, 159a-159b where R. Eleazar holds that Reuben was in sackcloth and was fasting. Cf. Sifre D. 344 where R. Hanina b. Gamaliel maintained that, while one's wicked deeds are not normally cancelled out by good deeds, they were in the case of Reuben. Cf. MHG on Gen.

Vol. II 936, 1.1-p. 938, 1.18. A veritable compendium of rabbinic opinions on Reuben are offered in this source.

14. Cf. Tan. Korah 2; Tan. B. IV, 85-86; J. Sanhedrin 10, 27d-
28a; Midrash Tehillim I, 14.

15. For traditions concerning *Eve's* illicit sexual gratification, cf.
Yebamoth 103a, "R. Johanan stated: When the serpent copulated with Eve, he infused her with lust"; Cf. Shabbat 146a
and AZ 22b for less explicit traditions. Cf. BR 24.6 where it
is held that night sprites were made ardent by Eve during the
one hundred and thirty years that Adam held aloof from her.
She is supposed to have borne children as a result of these unions.
The serpent: ARN 1.5. *Dinah*: 2 ARN (text b in the Schechter
ed.) 3, 14; Koh. R. 10.8; BR 80.5; MHG on Gen. Vol. II, 587,
1.18-19; Yoma 77b; Sechel Tov on Gen. 34:2, p. 189. *Leah*:
BR 80.1; Tan. B. I, 171. Cf. MHG on Gen. Vol. II, 586, 1.6-
p. 587, 1.11 which largely parallels BR 80.1; Tan. WaYishlah
6. *The Daughters of Zion*: BR 45.5 and WR 16.1. Cf. Margulies
ad. loc. comments on WR 16.1. *Ham*: BR 36.7; Sanhedrin 108b;
Tan. Noah 12. *Abimelech:* BR 52.13; Tan. B. I, lol; MHG on
Gen. Vol. I, 328, 1.15-16. PRE 26. *The Pharaoh who sought to
entice Sarah:* BR 40.2 in current edition. In Theodor's critical
edition, this tradition is in chapter 41; MHG on. Gen. Vol. I,
225, 1.6-10; BR 41.1 and 2. *Potiphar:* BR 86.3; Sotah 13b;
MHG on Gen. Vol. II, 656, 1.13-15 and p. 657 1.4-7 which
parallels the Sotah account. *Balaam:* Sanhedrin 105a. He was
thought by the rabbis to have had decidedly peculiar sexual
tastes. *Zimri and Cozbi: B'midbar Rabbah* 20:23 and 24; Tan.
B. IV, 148; Tan. Balak 19; Sanhedrin 82a-b; J. Sanhedrin 28d-
29a; Sifre on Numbers, p. 131; Sh'moth Rabbah 3.5. *David:*
AZ 4b-5a where it is maintained that David was not the sort
of man to commit adultery but that God predestined the matter
to teach the power of repentance; Shabbat 56a; Ketuboth 9b;
Cf. Sanhedrin 107a, "The school of R. Ishmael taught . . .: She
was worthy (i.e.) predestined for David from the six days of
Creation, but that he enjoyed her before she was ripe." Cf. the
comments of Saul Lieberman on this tradition in his *Greek in
Jewish Palestine* (New York: Jewish Theological Seminary,
1942), p. 163, and Ginzberg, *Legends,* VI, 265, n. 93. *Absalom:* M. Sotah 1.8; *Manasseh:* Sanhedrin 103b; *Jehoiakin*

Sanhedrin 103b; WR 19.6; Tan. B. I, 154; *Amon:* Sanhedrin 103b. This is a partial but a representative listing.

16. This is well expressed in Paul Tillich, *Systematic Theology* (London: Nisbet and Co., 1953), Vol. I, 220-224.

17. Gen. 3:5.

18. PRE 13; Cf. BR 19.3-4. The Promethean note is stressed by R. Joshua of Siknin in the name of R. Levi who depicts the serpent as telling Eve: "Of this tree did He eat and then create the world; hence He orders you, ye shall not eat thereof, so that you may not create other worlds, for every person hates his fellow craftsman."

19. Is. 14:12-14.

20. Bernard Bamberger, *Fallen Angels* (Philadelphia: Jewish Publishing Society, 1952), pp. 9 ff.

21. For rabbinic interpretations of Isaiah 14:12-14 as referring to Nebuchadnezzar, cf. Mekilta Shirata (Ed. L.), Vol. II, 18, 1.84-86; p. 46 ff., 1.49-58; Mekilta RS (Ed. H.), p. 58; Mekilta RS (Ed. Epstein), p. 75; Mek. RS (Ed. H.) p. 66; T. Sotah 3.18.

22. Pesahim 94a-94b; cf. Bacher Ia 30; Hulin 89a; AZ 53b where one rabbi calls the Tower of Babel "the house of Nimrod."

23. Cf. BR 23.7 and 26.4; MHG on Gen. Vol. I, 198, 1.9-12; Sanhedrin 109a; MHG on Gen. Vol. I, 199, 1.1-12; Tan. B. I, 55.

24. John Milton, *Paradise Lost*, Book I.

25. Cf. Ginzberg, V, 84, n. 35.

26. Cf. Bernard Bamberger, *Fallen Angels*, pp. 54 ff.

27. Cf. Martin P. Nilsson, *Greek Piety*, trans. Herbert J. Rose (Oxford: Clarendon Press, 1948), pp. 52-59.

28. Cf. Tan. B. II, 23, 31, 33; Tan WaEra 14; Sh'meth Rabbah 8.2; Megillah 11 a. Mek. (Ed. L.) Amalek, II, 138, 1.40-43; Machiri on Ps. 9, p. 59. J. H. Weiss saw a covert reference to Roman homosexuality in these passages. Cf. his *Dor, Dor we-Dorshaw, Zur Geschichte der Judischen Tradition*, Vol. II (Vienna: 1871), 21. Cf. Ginzberg, VI, 426, n. 107.

29. II Chron. 24:24.

30. II Chron. 24:1-26; II Kings 12:1-10.

31. II Chron. 24:17.

32. *Ahab:* Sanhedrin 102b. *Ahaz:* WR 11.7; BR 42.3; J. Sanhedrin 10, 28b; Sanhedrin 103b. *Doeg:* BR 32.1 and 38.1.

33. *Manasseh:* Sanhedrin 103b. *Jehoiakim: ibid. Amon: ibid.*

34. Sanhedrin 103b; EZ 9, p. 188; DR 2.20; Cf. Apocalypse of Baruch 64:3 which asserts that Manasseh made a five-faced figure with one of the images facing heavenward to offend God.

35. Sanhedrin 103b.

36. Sanhedrin 102b.

37. Sanhedrin 103b.

38. II Chron. 36:8.

39. Sanhedrin 103b.

40. It is said of Jehoiakim that "he entered the very gateway whence he came out." WR 19.6; Tan. B. I, 154.

41. Jean-Paul Sartre, *Baudelaire,* trans. Martin H. Turnell (New London, Conn.: New Directions Books, 1950), pp. 71 ff.

42. II Kings 16:2-20; II Chron. 28:1-7.

43. Megillah 11a; Esther R. 1.2; Midrash Tehillim 105, 449. The other sinners were Dathan and Abiram, Nimrod, Esau, and Ahasuerus.

44. BR 42.3; J. Sanhedrin 28b; EZ p. 187; Sanhedrin 103b where it says that "he sealed up the Torah" but does not explicitly play on his name; WR 11.7.

45. WR 11.7; BR 42.3; J. Sanhedrin 10, 28b.

46. Sanhedrin 39b.

47. Sanhedrin 102b.

48. *Ibid.*

49. Cf. Ginzberg, VI, 310, n. 31.

50. The irony of rabbinic legend is evident in the traditions in which Nebuchadnezzar is depicted as seeking to displace God by ruling the entire world but was actually an ugly dwarf. He sought to

enjoy the cosmos but could not enjoy his own body. Tan. B. II, 90; Tan. Terumah 4; BR 16.4; PK 13, 112a; PR 31, 144a, but cf. Buber's *ad. loc.* comments on PK, PR and Tan. B. as to textual difficulties with the word for dwarf.

51. Cf. infra., pp. 151 ff.

52. Yebamoth 103a; Shabbat 146a; AZ 22b.

53. BR 22.5.

54. Num. 13:15 ff.

55. Deut. 1:27.

56. Sifre D. 24; Tan. B. IV, 84; Midrash Tannaim 12.

57. BaR 18.10.

58. Num. 16:13, 14.

59. Jean-Paul Sartre, *Being and Nothingness*, pp. 556 ff.

60. Sartre, *op. cit.*, p. 615.

61. Norman O. Brown, *Life Against Death: The Psychoanalytic Meaning of History* (Middletown, Conn.: Wesleyan University Press, 1959), p. 118.

62. Sigmund Freud, "A Special Type of Object-Choice" in CP, Vol. IV, 201. Cf. Freud, *New Introductory Lectures on Psychoanalysis*, p. 154.

63. Tan WaEra 5. Pharaoh's reply is a direct quote from Ez. 29:3. It would thus seem that the insight that the sinner desires to displace God is pre-rabbinic.

64. Adolph Buchler, *Studies in Sin and Atonement in the Rabbinic Literature of the First Century* (London: Oxford University Press, 1928), p. 54.

65. M. Sanhedrin 10.1 ff.

66. Aristotle, *Physics*, Bk. III, Ch. 1.

Chapter 7

1. The biblical story is to be found in Num. 16:1-35.

2. B'midbar R. 18.10, 11; Tan. Korah 6-7; Tan. B., IV, 90-91.

3. Tan. Korah 2; Tan. B., IV, 85-86.

4.   *Ibid.*

5.   J. Sanhedrin 10, 27d-28a.

6.   Tan. Korah 2; Tan. B., IV, 85-86.

7.   J. Sanhedrin 27d-28a. Rab is the authority.

8.   Deut. 22:10.

9.   Lev. 19:19.

10. Lev. 19:9; cf. Deut. 24:19.

11. Deut. 15:19.

12. Tehillim 1, 14.

13. It may also have been a reaction to Gnostic criticism of the Bible. Cf. A. Marmorstein, *Studies in Jewish Theology*, pp. 1-71 and 93-105; cf. Gershom Scholem, *Major Trends in Jewish Mysticism* (New York: Schocken, 1946), pp. 40-79 on Jewish Gnosticism.

14. Yebamoth 49b; PR 4:14.

15. Vd. Num: 5.14; B'midbar R. 18.20; Tehillim 106, 455; cf. Tan. B., IV, 94; Tan. Korah 10.

16. B'midbar R. 18.12; Tan. B., IV, 96.

17. Num. 16:32 ff.

18. Tan. B., IV, 97; cf. Targum Yerushalmi on Num. 16:22-34.

19. B'midbar R. 18.10.

20. Søren Kierkegaard, *Fear and Trembling,* trans. Walter Lowrie (Princeton: Princeton University Press, 1941).

21. Justin Martyr, *The Dialogue with Trypho,* trans. A. Lukyn Williams (London: SPCK, 1930).

22. Salo Baron, *A Religious and Social History of the Jews,* Vol. II, 374. n. 22.

23. Justin Martyr, *op. cit.,* XVI.

24. Baron, *op. cit.,* Vol. II, 121 ff.

25. Justin Martyr, *loc. cit.*

26. Ekah R., Proem 6, 8, 9, 12, 14, 22, 23, 26, 30, 31, 32 and 33. This is not an exhaustive count.

27. Yoma 9b.

28. B'midbar R. 9.7.

29. Shabbat 119b.

30. Ekah R. 1.9, 37; J. Sanhedrin 10, 29c.

31. Cf. Ginzberg, VI, p. 391, n. 24.

32. Yoma 9b.

33. *Ibid.*

34. Bruno Bettelheim, *The Informed Heart* (Glencoe: The Free Press, 1960), pp. 171 ff.

35. Malcolm X, *The Autobiography of Malcolm X* (New York: Grove Press, 1964).

36. Hilberg, *op. cit.*, pp. 312 ff.

37. B'midbar R. 18.10.

38. According to tradition, Elisha b. Abuya became an apostate when he saw one man lose his life while fulfilling a commandment for which the Torah promised long life. At the same time he knew of another man who broke the law and was not hurt. The law was Deut. 22:7. Cf. Kiddushin 39b and BR 26.6.

39. Hagigah 15b.

40. Albert Camus, *The Plague*, trans. Stuart Gilbert (New York: Knopf, 1948), pp. 86 f.

41. Allport and Postman, *op. cit.*, pp. 56, 97 ff., 102.

42. Albert Camus, "Summer In Algiers," in *The Myth of Sysyphus and Other Essays*, trans. Justin O'Brien (New York: Vintage Books, 1960), pp. 104-113.

Chapter 8

1. Paul Tillich, *The Courage To Be* (New Haven: Yale University Press, 1952), p. 185.

2. Thomas J. J. Altizer, *The Gospel of Christian Atheism* (Philadelphia: Westminster Press, 1966), p. 107.

3. Cf. George Foote Moore, *Judaism*, Vol. I, 460 ff. Moore cites the Westminster Shorter Catechism as summarizing succinctly the rabbinic doctrine of sin. He identifies sin in rabbinic Judaism

as "any want of conformity unto, or transgression of, the law of God." Cf. Schechter, *Some Aspects of Rabbinic Theology*, pp. 219-241.

4.   *Ibid.*

5.   Hegel's analysis of Judaism as servitude of the human slave to the divine master has been extremely influential. Cf. G. W. F. Hegel, "The Spirit of Christianity and Its Fate," in the English translation of T. M. Knox and Richard Kroner, *Hegel: Early Theological Writings* (Chicago: University of Chicago Press, 1948), pp. 182-205. Cf. Jean Hyppolite, *Genèse et structure de la Phénoménologie de l' Esprit de Hegel* (Paris: Auber, 1947), pp. 184-208.

6.   Cf. Julius Guttmann, *Philosophies of Judaism*, pp. 67-69, 102, 106, 132-33, 162, 164-65.

7.   Sifre D., 329, p. 139b; Hullin 7b. On God's relation to the world in rabbinic thought, cf. Moore, *Judaism*, Vol. I, 263-280. For a discussion of God's providence, cf. A. Marmorstein, *The Old Rabbinic Doctrine of God: I. The Names and Attributes of God* (London: 1927), p. 21.

8.   Aboth 3.16.

9.   BR 1.1. ". . . . . No man sins unless he has denied Him who commanded him not to commit that sin." T. Shebu'oth 3.6. Cf. J. Peah 16a, "No man speaks slanderously of another until he denies the Root (i.e. God)." Cf. Moore, *op. cit.*, Vol. I, 467. On the Torah as the repository of all wisdom, cf. Aboth 5.22.

10. DR 8.6; Shabbat 104a; Megillah 2b; Tan. Yithro 11; Tan. B. V, 20; Tehillim 78, 192 b.

11. B'midbar R. 19.10 on which cf. James Parkes, *The Conflict of the Church and Synagogue* (London: Soncino Press, 1934), p. 105; Tan. B. II, 116; Moore, Vol. I, *op. cit.*, pp. 251-262; Lauterbach, *Midrash and Mishnah*, pp. 2 ff.

12. Søren Kierkegaard, *Fear and Trembling*, trans. Walter Lowrie (Princeton: Princeton University Press, 1941).

13. Cf. *supra*, pp. 58 ff.

14. Cf. *supra*, pp. 117 ff.

15. Cf. *supra*, p. 66.

16. Norman O. Brown, *Love's Body* (New York: Random House, 1966), pp. 7 ff.

17. Mt. 10:35-37.

18. Mt. 10:36.

19. Cf. Otto Rank, *The Myth of the Birth of the Hero*, trans. F. Robbins and Smith Ely Jeliffe (New York: Vintage Books, 1959), pp. 66-72.

20. Cf. Richard L. Rubenstein, *After Auschwitz*, pp. 209 ff.

21. R. Judah bar Ilai depicts God as looking to the Torah as the pattern and then creating the world. This is vaguely reminiscent of Plato's *Timaeus*. Tan. B. I, p. 4; cf. BR 1.1, and 1.4 where R. Benayah says, "The world and its fullness was created only for the sake of the Torah." Even the miracles did not happen gratuitously, but were stipulated in the pre-existent Torah. Cf. BR 5.5.

22. BR 5.5.

23. Solomon Schechter, *Some Aspects of Rabbinic Theology*, pp. 219-241.

24. Cf. *supra*, pp. 101 ff.

25. Tillich, *op. cit.*, pp. 184 ff. Erich Fromm, *Escape From Freedom*, pp. 168 ff.

26. Friedrich Nietzsche, *The Gay Science*, trans. Walter Kaufmann, in *The Portable Nietzsche* (New York: Viking Press, 1954), pp. 451 ff. Nietzsche, *The Antichrist*, in *op. cit.*, pp. 585 ff. Cf. Walter Kaufmann, Nietzsche: *Philosopher, Psychologist, Antichrist* (New York: Meridian Books, 1956), pp. 319 ff.

27. G. W. F. Hegel, *Phänomenologie des Geistes* (Hamburg: Felix Meiner, 1952), pp. 158-171, trans. J. B. Baillie, *The Phenomenology of the Mind* (London: George Allen and Unwin, Ltd., 1931), pp. 251-267 Cf. Hyppolite, *op. cit.*, pp. 185 ff.

28. Hegel, "The Spirit of Christianity and Its Fate" in *Hegel: Early Theological Writings*, pp. 185-205.

29. This is implicit in the conception that the world was created for the sake of the Torah. Cf. BR 12.2; Tan. B., V, 112. "When the Torah came into the world freedom came into the world." BR 53.7. Nevertheless, a few rabbis do see service of God in

terms of the master-slave relationship. Cf. R. Jeremiah's remarks in BM 85b.

30. Cf. Joseph Sandler, "On the Concept of the Superego" in *The Psychoanalytic Study of the Child* (New York: International Universities Press, 1960), Vol. XV, 128-162; Roy Schafer, "The Loving and Beloved Superego in Freud's Structural Theory" in *The Psychoanalytic Study of the Child*, Vol. XV, 163-190.

31. Cf. Tan. B., I, 97 and II, 8. R. Akiba asserts that though God is omnipotent, he is never arbitrary.

32. Cf. *supra*, pp. 106 ff.

33. *Loc. cit.*

34. Thomas J. J. Altizer, *The Gospel of Christian Freedom*, pp. 102 ff.

35. Aboth 6.2.

Chapter 9

1.   "Outwardly, but not inwardly religious . . . hypocritical . . ." *Webster's New International Dictionary*, 1939.

2.   Mt. 23:5, 6.

3.   Mt. 23:26-28.

4.   Mt. 23:33, 34.

5.   Moore, *Judaism*, Vol. II, 192. R. Travers Herford, *The Pharisees* (London: Macmillan, 1924).

6.   Their attitudes are summarized by Moore, *op. cit.*, pp. 193 ff.

7.   BR 9.7.

8.   Sukkah 52a.

9.   *Loc. cit.*

10. M. Sanhedrin 10.1.

11. Sukkah 52a.

12. Balaam's story is to be found in Num. 22:1-25:9.

13. R. Travers Herford, *Christianity in Talmud and Midrash* (London: Williams and Norgate, 1903), pp. 63-77, but cf. L. Ginz-

berg, "review of R. Travers Herford," in JQR (OS), Vol. XV, 1905, 177.

14. B'midbar R. 14:20; Cf. WR 1.13 and 14 which contains a number of opinions concerning the difference between Jewish and Gentile prophets; Sifre D., pp. 150 a, b; Tan. Balaak which asserts that Balaam was only fit to receive prophecy at night; Midrash Tannaim (Ed. Hoffmann), pp. 227 ff.

15. Sanhedrin 103b.

16. BR 35.2; PK 10, 88a.

17. Tehillim, 5, 55.

18. Sanhedrin 101b-102a; J. AZ 1, 39b.

19. The *ha-motzi* is the traditional benediction recited before partaking of bread.

20. Sanhedrin 102b.

21. For the sources which deal with the repentance of Manasseh, cf. Ginzberg, VI, 375, n. 108.

22. Ex. 33:20.

23. Isaiah 6:1.

24. Deut. 4:7.

25. Isaiah 55:6.

26. Ex. 23:26.

27. II Kings 20:6. The rabbinic source is Yebamoth 49b; cf. PR 4.14.

28. I Kings 21:25.

29. *Ibid.*

30. J. Sanhedrin 10, 28b.

31. I Kings 21:29.

32. Sanhedrin 102b.

33. *Ibid.*

34. *Ibid.*

35. I Kings 20:3-9.

36. Sanhedrin 102b; cf. Tan B. II, 16.

37. PK 25, 160b; J. Sanhedrin 10, 28b; Ta'anit 25b; PRE 43; Shir haShirim R. 1.5 where R. Joshua b. Levi is the authority.

38. Sanhedrin 102b.

39. Cf. *supra*, p. 154.

40. I Samuel 21:7, 22:9-22.

41. Tehillim, 52, 184.

42. *Loc. cit.*

43. Cf. W. Bacher, *Die Agada der Babylonischen Amoraer* (Budapest: 1878), p. 51. Bacher maintains that R. Judah was given the epithet because of his iron perseverance in matters of study.

44. Hagigah 15b; Sanhedrin 106b.

45. Cf. *supra*, pp. 30-31, 122.

46. Ruth 4:17.

47. Deut. 23:3 ff.

48. Yebamoth 76b.

49. Cf. *supra*, pp. 43 ff.

50. WR 13.1: Sifre on Numbers, ed. Friedmann, 167, p. 60a; Pesahim 66a; ARN 1, 3.

51. BR 30.9; Sanhedrin 108a; MHG on Gen., ed. Margulies, Vol. I, 151.

52. BR, ed. Theodor-Albeck, 80.4. This tradition is partly absent from the current edition.

53. Kiddushin 81a-81b; cf. Bacher, IIa, p. 3.

54. Avodah Zarah 18a.

55. Typical of the rabbinic attitude was R. Simeon b. Yohai's comment that Israel's exile would end were the community to keep two Sabbaths in full accordance with their traditions. Shabbat 118b. It is also implicit in the pervasive theme that Exile was God's punishment for Israel's infidelity. Cf. Ekah R., Proem 6, 8, 9, 12 etc.; Yoma 9b; Sanhedrin 63b; Shabbat 119b.

56. The examples of rabbinic appreciation of the power of repentance are too numerous to list. For a representative sample, cf. Montefiore and Loewe, *A Rabbinic Anthology*, pp. 315-333; cf. Moore, *Judaism*, Vol. I, 507-519.

57. Romans 3:20, 23.

58. Romans 6:3-4; 7:1-4.

59. Romans 7:12.

60. Romans 7:6.

61. Erik Erikson, *Young Man Luther*, pp. 162 ff.

62. Schechter, *Studies in Judaism*, First Series, p. 244.

63. Cf. Gershom Scholem, *Major Trends in Jewish Mysticism*, pp. 287 ff.

64. Cf. *supra*, pp. 20 ff.

Chapter 10

1. Sartre, *Being and Nothingness*, pp. 556 ff.

2. Sartre, *The Words*, trans. Bernard Fechtman (New York: Braziller, 1964).

3. Sartre, *Being and Nothingness*, pp. 557 ff.

4. Sartre, *The Words*, pp. 193 ff.

5. Nietzsche, *The Gay Science*, trans. Walter Kaufmann in *The Portable Nietzsche* (New York: Viking Press, 1954), pp. 95, 96.

6. BR 54.6; cf. ARN 7, 33-34. The tradition in ARN specifies Job rather than Abraham as embodying this measure of hospitality.

7. ARN 12, 48-49.

8. "R. Tarphon said . . . It is not thy part to finish the task, yet thou art not free to desist from it." Aboth 2.16.

9. Cf. *supra*, pp. 126 ff.

10. Isaiah 53:1-11. Cf. Moore, *Judaism*, Vol. I, 546 ff.

11. Elie A. Cohen, *Human Behavior in the Concentration Camp*, trans. M. A. Braaksma (New York: W. W. Norton and Co., 1953), p. 148.

12. *Op. cit.*, p. 149.

13. This was related to me personally by Prof. Viktor Frankl at Duquesne University in Pittsburgh, Pa., in February 1960.

14. Viktor Frankl, *From Death Camp to Existentialism* (Boston: Beacon Press, 1959), p. 74.

15. Cf. Edmund Bergler, *The Battle of the Conscience: A Psychiatric Study of the Inner Working of the Conscience* (Washington: Institute of Medicine, 1948), pp. 261-293. Theodore Reik, *The*

Compulsion to Confess (New York: Farrar, Straus and Cudahy, 1959), pp. 469-474.

16. Anna Freud, *The Ego and the Mechanisms of Defense,* trans. Cecil Baines (London: The Hogarth Press and the Institute of Psycho-Analysis), pp. 64 ff.

17. Cf. Robert W. White, *The Abnormal Personality* (New York: The Ronald Press, 1948), pp. 544-586. White quotes Bleuler to the effect that the central disorder in schizophrenia is a fragmentation of integrated behavior, p. 548.

18. Whether we take the early or the late Freud, his picture of human existence has a fulcrum character to it. In the early Freud, the individual seeks to balance the demands of instinct and the necessary constraints of the social order; in the later Freud the balance is between the forces of life and death, primordial *eros* and *thanatos*. Cf. especially the oft-quoted concluding paragraphs of *Civilization and Its Discontents,* pp. 142-146, and the almost pre-Socratic tone of his last sentence: "And now it may be expected that the other of the two 'heavenly forces,' eternal Eros, will put forth his strength so as to maintain himself alongside of his equally immortal adversary." With regard to Kierkegaard, cf. *The Concept of Dread,* pp. 38 and 55. Kierkegaard sees anxiety as a "sympathetic-antipathy." It pulls and pushes at the same time. In this double action, we have an analogue of the *coincidenta oppositorum* view.

19. I have in mind the biological reflex of autotomy in which some animals such as the lizard dispense with an organ which causes excessive pain and grows it again. In the act of sexual intercourse, the goal of a lessening of the tension felt by the penis contains some elements of autotomy in the phenomenon of detumescence. Cf. Fenichel, *The Psychoanalytic Theory of Neuroses,* pp. 56, 77, 144. Cf. his comments on anticipatory autocastration, *op. cit.,* p. 364.

Index